T0288245

Civil War

CAMPAIGNS
in the
HEARTLAND

STEVEN E. WOODWORTH
AND CHARLES D. GREAR
SERIES EDITORS

The Confederate Heartland

Charles D. Grear

The
CHATTANOOGA
Campaign

Edited by Steven E. Woodworth
and Charles D. Grear

Southern Illinois University Press
Carbondale and Edwardsville

Library of Congress Cataloging-in-Publication Data
The Chattanooga Campaign / edited by Steven E. Woodworth
and Charles D. Grear.
    p. cm. — (Civil War campaigns in the heartland)
Includes bibliographical references and index.
ISBN-13: 978-0-8093-3119-2 (cloth : alk. paper)
ISBN-10: 0-8093-3119-5 (cloth : alk. paper)
ISBN-13: 978-0-8093-3120-8 (ebook)
ISBN-10: 0-8093-3120-9 (ebook)
1. Chattanooga, Battle of, Chattanooga, Tenn., 1863.
I. Woodworth, Steven E. II. Grear, Charles D., [date]
E475.97.C53 2012
973.7'359—dc23   2011045002

John Y. Simon, 1933–2008
Scholar, Mentor, Friend

CONTENTS

ILLUSTRATIONS

ACKNOWLEDGMENTS

The editors would like to express their sincere gratitude for the consistent helpfulness and extraordinary patience of Southern University Press editor Sylvia Frank Rodrigue, as well as to the rest of the SIU Press staff for their help during the development of this project. The contributors deserve special recognition for their diligence and cooperation with this volume. They made this book a labor of joy—more important, the book would not exist without them. Lastly, the editors would like to thank their families for all the constant support in all their endeavors.

Steven Woodworth wants to take this opportunity to welcome to the project his new coeditor, Charles D. Grear. Since the idea for the series was partly his, it is especially appropriate that he should now join me in its production. This volume has already profited immensely from his historical insights as well as his diligence, organizational skills, and attention to detail—and he's also a fine mapmaker. I look forward to a long and happy collaboration.

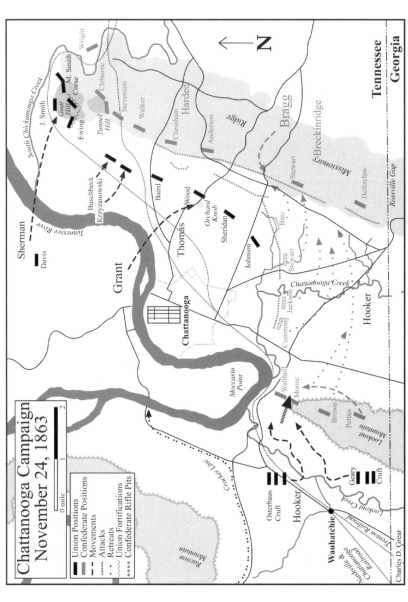

On November 24, 1863, while Sherman moved to take up a position astride the northern end of Missionary Ridge, Hooker pushed around the point of Lookout Mountain, sending the Confederates there retreating across Chattanooga Valley to join the rest of their army on Missionary Ridge.

Charles D. Grear

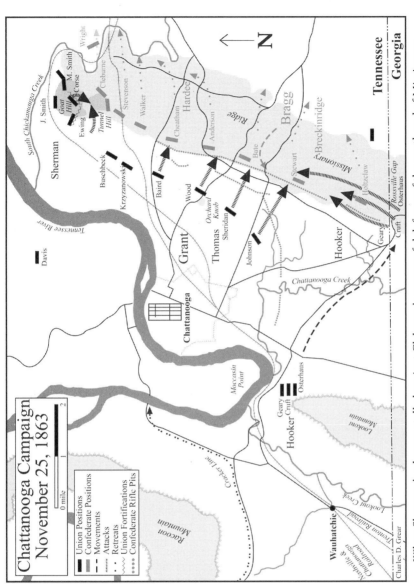

Chattanooga Campaign November 25, 1863

Legend:
- ▬ Union Positions
- ▬ Confederate Positions
- ▬ Movements
- ···· Attacks
- ···· Retreats
- ···· Union Fortifications
- ···· Confederate Rifle Pits

0 mile   1   2

N ←

Tennessee
Georgia

Labels on map:

Sherman
J. Smith
Goat Hill
M. Smith
Corse
Ewing
Tunnel Hill
Wright
Cleburne
Stevenson
Walker
Cheatham
Hardee
Buschbeck
Krzyzanowski
Anderson
Bate
Missionary Ridge
Bragg
Breckinridge
Stewart
Holtzclaw
Rossville Gap
Osterhaus
Baird
Wood
Orchard Knob
Sheridan
Johnson
Grant
Thomas
Hooker
Geary
Cruft
Davis
Tennessee River
Maccasin Point
Chattanooga
Chattanooga Creek
Geary
Cruft
Osterhaus
Hooker
Lookout Mountain
Cracker Line
Raccoon Mountain
Wauhatchie
Lookout Creek
Nashville & Chattanooga Railroad
Trenton Railroad
Charles D. Grear
South Chickamauga Creek

When Sherman's advance stalled against Cleburne's resourceful defense of the north end of Missionary Ridge, Grant sent Thomas's four divisions forward in a grand frontal assault against the west face of the ridge, and Hooker's belated arrival at Rossville Gap, on the Confederate left flank, sealed the Union victory.

The Chattanooga Campaign

INTRODUCTION

The Campaign for Chattanooga in the fall of 1863 was important in several respects. The city was a key strategic location, the gateway both to East Tennessee and to the Deep South. The campaign would determine whether the Confederacy would reap the fruits of its hard-fought victory at Chickamauga or the Union would wrest back the initiative in the heartland of the continent, setting the stage for an 1864 campaign that would drive even deeper into the vitals of the Confederacy.

After the September 18–20 Battle of Chickamauga, Rosecrans ordered his army to withdraw into Chattanooga. Because of the way the battle had ended, Bragg would not have been able to pursue the Federals without launching a frontal assault against solid Union lines at Rossville Gap. Wisely, he chose not to do so, though some of his subordinates at the time and many historians since have not been able to understand the situation or give Bragg credit for the wisdom he showed. The Battle of Chickamauga had simply offered its nominal victor no opportunity for decisive results.

Thus matters stood for several days until Rosecrans, still smarting from the sudden turn the battle had taken on the afternoon of the last day at Chickamauga, withdrew his troops from the high ground overlooking Chattanooga and controlling all of its practical routes of supply. This opened up the possibility of decisive victory for Bragg, and he moved promptly to take advantage of it, establishing a virtual siege of the Army of the Cumberland in Chattanooga. Only via a difficult and circuitous wagon track across Walden's Ridge north of Chattanooga could the Federals in the town receive a scant minimum of food during the weeks that followed.

In the face of this crisis, President Abraham Lincoln and Secretary of War Edwin Stanton acted decisively. They ordered two corps of the Army of the Potomac under the command of Joseph Hooker to travel rapidly by rail to reinforce their comrades at Chattanooga. More important, they created the Military Division of the Mississippi, encompassing all of the departments west of the Appalachians, and elevated Ulysses S. Grant, fresh from his conquest of Vicksburg, to command the new division with orders to remedy the situation around Chattanooga. Grant set out at once for the beleaguered city, and while he was still underway he availed himself of specific authority in his orders to relieve Rosecrans of command of the Army of the Cumberland and replace him with George H. Thomas.

The most important task awaiting Grant on his arrival in Chattanooga was opening and securing a viable supply line for the troops there. He lost no time implementing a plan that Rosecrans's staff had been working on, starting with a river-borne coup de main that seized Brown's Ferry on the Tennessee River in the predawn hours of October 27 and opened the possibility of moving supplies through the Tennessee River Gorge below Chattanooga. For Bragg it was equally important to close that supply line. Forty-eight hours after the Brown's Ferry operation, James Longstreet, acting half-heartedly on Bragg's repeated and insistent orders, made a lame attempt to regain control of Lookout Valley and the Tennessee River Gorge, leading to the nighttime Battle of Wauhatchie. In an essay that examines the Confederate side of these operations, Alex Mendoza shows how a combination of factors made the First Corps of the Army of Northern Virginia an ineffective force for countering Grant's bold move. Mendoza advances the thesis that, in losing Lookout Valley, First Corps commander James Longstreet had plenty of help from his subordinates. Meanwhile, the Union side of the Battle of Wauhatchie is the subject of Stewart Bennett's carefully detailed study.

Grant's next task was to defeat the Confederate Army of Tennessee, which held the high ground ringing Chattanooga from Lookout Mountain on the southwest to Missionary Ridge on the south and southeast. By late November his plans were complete, and on November 24 he put them in motion. While Joseph Hooker led a force of three divisions, one from each of the three Union armies near Chattanooga, in driving the Rebels from the slopes of Lookout Mountain, William T. Sherman led three divisions of the Army of the Tennessee in crossing its namesake river above the town and before nightfall reaching a point that would allow it to strike the Confederate right flank on Missionary Ridge the following morning.

Grant's plan for November 25 foresaw Sherman making the main attack. Once he and his Vicksburg veterans had started the discomfiture of Bragg's army by beginning to drive in its right flank, Thomas and the four divisions of his Army of the Cumberland would advance to join the assault on the ridge, first taking the rifle pits at the base of the ridge and then, after regrouping and catching their breath, plunging up the slope to storm the defenses from the front while Sherman continued to roll them up from the right. Hooker's three-division detachment was too large to leave idle, so it would advance to strike the Confederate left on Missionary Ridge after first checking to make sure that the Confederates had indeed abandoned Lookout Mountain.

Morning came, and Sherman and his troops attacked with their accustomed verve and élan. The situation they encountered proved vastly more difficult and complicated than Grant and Sherman had anticipated. At the heart of their problems was unusual terrain and an excellent Confederate division commanded by one of the most outstanding division commanders of the war in the person of Patrick R. Cleburne. Cleburne recognized the inherent strength of the defensive position available to him and made effective use of that position by skillfully placing his troops and then seizing the initiative at key moments in the ensuing battle. Steven E. Woodworth's essay analyzes the Union side of this operation while John R. Lundberg's chapter considers the Confederate side.

Observing the disappointing developments on his left, Grant in mid-afternoon proceeded to the next part of his plan and ordered Thomas to implement the first phase of his own attack by advancing his four divisions to seize the rifle pits at the base of Missionary Ridge. In a tour de force of historical investigation, Brooks D. Simpson looks at the varying accounts of what happened at Grant's headquarters on Orchard Knob when Grant decided to order the attack—who said what to whom and who made what decisions.

Thomas's troops carried the ridge at the same time that Hooker struck the Confederate left, anchored at Rossville Gap on Missionary Ridge, and began to roll it up. Sam Elliot analyzes Hooker's successful attack in his chapter of this volume.

Nightfall on November 24 found the Confederate Army of Tennessee in headlong retreat, covered by Cleburne's division acting as rear guard. The following day, Union pursuit closed in on the retreating Rebels as they reached Ringgold Gap in Taylor's Ridge. Justin Solonick's examination of the effective Confederate rearguard action at Ringgold Gap evaluates the engagement in the light of the difficulty any victorious Civil War army faced in trying to pursue and destroy a defeated foe. A number of factors made defeated Civil War armies all but indestructible, and in this case those factors were augmented by strong defensive terrain and a highly skillful stand by, once again, the redoubtable Cleburne.

The Union victory at Chattanooga had important effects on morale in both North and South. Ethan Rafuse explores the reactions of Northern newspapers, especially those in Cincinnati, Ohio, to the developments of the Chattanooga campaign. Charles Grear looks at the reactions of Confederate soldiers from the Trans-Mississippi states to yet another defeat.

In the final chapter in this volume, Timothy B. Smith looks at the efforts to preserve the Chattanooga battlefield for future commemoration and study. These efforts ultimately led to the incorporation of a series of small, widely separated parcels of land into the Chickamauga and Chattanooga National Military Park. Of wider significance, as Smith shows, preservation efforts at Chattanooga, by the end of the century already well on its way to being an urban environment, pioneered a different approach to battlefield preservation that was subsequently used at Antietam and other important battle sites.

1
—

A PERFECT STORM OF INEFFECTIVENESS:
THE FIRST CORPS AND THE LOSS
OF LOOKOUT MOUNTAIN

Alex Mendoza

At dawn on October 28, 1863, General Braxton Bragg, the commander of the Army of Tennessee, left his headquarters on Missionary Ridge to converse with one of his lieutenants, Lieutenant General James Longstreet, on the crest of Lookout Mountain. Longstreet's force, which had arrived from Virginia the previous month, was responsible for the left of the Confederate lines that laid siege to the Union army in city of Chattanooga. Just a day earlier, an early morning assault on Brown's Ferry, on the south bank of the Tennessee River, had allowed the Federals to gain a foothold on the landing that could open up a supply line toward the Nashville and Chattanooga Railroad and points north. As the two generals conferred about plans to regain Brown's Ferry and continue to harass the Federals, one of Longstreet's signal officers reported that the Yankees were advancing from the south and up Lookout Valley between Raccoon and Lookout Mountains. Longstreet's First Corps and his cavalry detachment from Bragg's army had failed to account for a seven-thousand-man force which had marched undetected toward Brown's Ferry. Clearly, this astonished both Bragg and Longstreet who stood helpless on the crest of Lookout Mountain, watching the Federal column under Major General Joseph E. Hooker advance with beating drums and flags waving.[1]

The mere fact that the First Corps, Army of Northern Virginia, was in the vicinity of the key sector that would ultimately lead to a break in Bragg's siege line was curious. After all, the corps' two divisions had come to Bragg's army on the eve of the Battle of Chickamauga, heralded upon their arrival. Longstreet's men, their success at Chickamauga now a distant memory, were stationed on the far left of Bragg's army. The events of the previous four weeks had diminished their battlefield accomplishments and extended rumors that their commander had conspired to oust the commanding general.

Longstreet, a renowned veteran of the war in the eastern theater and a trusted subordinate of General Robert E. Lee, weeks earlier had plotted with several generals in the Army of Tennessee to remove Bragg by signing their names to a petition urging the authorities in Richmond to consider changing commanders in the Confederacy's foremost western army. In addition, one of Longstreet's divisions served as the platform for two up-and-coming generals who aspired to gain the command of Hood's division. These two First Corps brigadiers, Micah Jenkins and Evander Law, were working at cross-purposes in Tennessee due to a bitter rivalry that stretched all the way back to antebellum South Carolina. The other division commander, Major General Lafayette McLaws, had his own argument with Longstreet and his transfer to the West. Accordingly, the First Corps, which had arrived to provide Bragg with the support needed to defeat the Federals, would later leave the Army of Tennessee under ignominious circumstances, a victim of its inner turmoil and infighting within the senior officers' ranks. The First Corps was so dysfunctional in the fall of 1863 that it became entangled in a perfect storm of recrimination and internal strife that contributed directly to the loss of Lookout Mountain, and by extension, Chattanooga.

Following the Rebel victory at Chickamauga, Bragg's army approached the retreating Federals at Chattanooga on September 23. Though the town's population was only about 2,500 in 1860, it remained a strategically important link to the Confederate heartland. The Union army had rallied to establish a semicircular three-mile line around the town. In fact, the Federals occupied many of the same fortifications built by Bragg's troops a month earlier when Chattanooga was still in Confederate hands. In their desperate state, the Yankees confiscated every major building and burned outlying homes as they prepared for the expected Rebel assault. Yet that attack never came. In the wake of victory, Bragg paused. Instead, the commanding general decided on a different course of action, laying siege to Chattanooga with hopes of starving the Federals into submission. By the end of September, the Army of Tennessee, along with Longstreet's First Corps, had established a siege line around the town.[2]

The Confederate siege line extended from the Tennessee River on the east to the base of Missionary Ridge, along the Western and Atlantic Railroad, on the west. By October 8, the First Corps held the Rebel army's left flank, snaking around the northern edge of Lookout Mountain, across Lookout Valley, to the foot of Raccoon Mountain. Law's brigade stood on the extreme left of the corps' line, extending as far as a five-mile picket line along the southern bank of the Tennessee from the western edge of Lookout Mountain. To Law's right and across the valley was Jenkins's brigade. Jenkins, who had recently arrived from Virginia after the Battle of Chickamauga, actually held command of Hood's division while Hood recuperated from wounds incurred during the battle. McLaws's division stood on Jenkins's right flank, in the Chattanooga Valley west of Chattanooga Creek. Longstreet's corps numbered approximately twelve thousand troops.[3]

The First Corps' officers and rank and file took their positions on the Confederate siege line with optimistic spirits and a renewed vigor that victory on the field of battle usually provides. Since a frontal assault was out of the question for the Rebel high command, Longstreet's troops resorted to harassing the enemy with artillery. While the Confederates continued to annoy the Federals with long-range shelling, the forty-five-thousand-man Union army in Chattanooga maintained its morale and probed for weaknesses. On October 19, the Union War Department ordered Major General Ulysses S. Grant to go to Chattanooga to relieve Major General William S. Rosecrans and break the Rebel stranglehold on the city while leading all Union forces west of the Appalachians. With the impending arrival of Grant, one of Longstreet's closest friends prior to the war, the Confederates would be on the verge of losing what they had gained.[4]

Yet Grant, who immediately ordered Major General George Thomas to assume command of the army at Chattanooga, would not have to struggle mightily to seize the initiative, particularly when facing the dysfunctional Army of Tennessee and the First Corps, Army of Northern Virginia. The trouble actually began with the First Corps' arrival in the West. Longstreet had, in fact, left Lee's army with a bias against Bragg. Not only did he desire to return to his old commander, General Joseph E. Johnston, who commanded the Department of the West, Longstreet also felt he could fare better than the commander of the Tennessee army. "I doubt if General Bragg has the confidence in his troops or himself either," Longstreet wrote Lee on September 5. "He is not likely to do a great deal for us."[5] Despite the fact that Longstreet claimed to have "no personal motive" in seeking to remove Bragg, his letter revealed a prejudice toward his new commander. Nevertheless, Longstreet arrived to Bragg's army on the eve of the second day of battle, leading his men ably and taking advantage of an inadvertent gap in the Union lines to provide the pivotal thrust that marked the Confederate victory over Rosecrans's army. In the wake of the Federal rout, Bragg moved to besiege the Federals at Chattanooga.[6]

It was in the environs around Chattanooga that Longstreet's First Corps joined the preexisting internal tensions within the Army of Tennessee's high command. For a variety of reasons having nothing to do with Longstreet's arrival, recriminations and internal conflict had plagued the army since the aftermath of the Kentucky Campaign in the fall of 1862. These tensions grew as the barren victory at Chickamauga influenced Bragg to take action against his subordinates, some of whom had failed to carry out his orders. Accordingly, in the week following the Rebel victory in northern Georgia, Bragg relieved Lieutenant General Leonidas Polk and Major General Thomas Hindman for failures during the Chickamauga campaign. Polk's removal was precarious, especially considering how popular he was in the Army of Tennessee. In fact, before Bragg had suspended Polk, the latter had met with Longstreet and Major Generals D. H. Hill and Simon B. Buckner on September 26 to discuss the "mismanagement manifested in the conduct of the operations in this army." The generals basically agreed that Bragg had mishandled the Battle of Chickamauga. At the meeting, the generals urged Longstreet to write Davis and suggest Bragg's removal. Polk and his associates probably figured that Longstreet's reputation in Virginia and his close ties to Lee would give him greater influence with the authorities in Richmond. The support Longstreet received from the army's senior officers did not appear to be motivated by their desire to see Longstreet supersede Bragg, but rather, to have Johnston—or anyone else—assume command.[7]

While awaiting further orders in Atlanta, Polk wrote his fellow dissident officers requesting that they write statements to exonerate him. On October 4, less than a week after Polk's removal, Longstreet, Hill, and Buckner met once more, this time adding Major General John C. Breckinridge to the group. Dissatisfied with the conditions in the army and the removal of their fellow commanders, they wrote a petition to be circulated among the ranking officers of the Army of Tennessee requesting Bragg's removal. The round-robin moved through the officers' ranks, through Buckner's, Hill's, and finally, Longstreet's corps, and collected twelve signatures of corps, division, and brigade commanders. The petition forced President Jefferson Davis to pay attention to the deteriorating conditions in the Tennessee army. Davis left for Missionary Ridge on October 6, but paused in Atlanta to confer with Polk about the conditions in the army. En route to Bragg, Davis conferred briefly with Longstreet and Buckner about the state of affairs in Tennessee. Then, on October 9, the president decided to take action, calling a meeting with Bragg and his disgruntled generals. Davis hoped that in his presence the men would demonstrate deference to the beleaguered Bragg. If Davis knew anything about the Army of Tennessee, he did not show it by calling on Bragg's lieutenants to demonstrate any semblance of faith in their commander. In fact, the Confederate president received the opposite.[8]

Assembling in Bragg's office, the four corps leaders, Longstreet, Buckner, Hill, and Benjamin F. Cheatham (Polk's replacement), sat nervously. Davis, with Bragg present, spoke first, addressing the issue at hand: the barren victory at Chickamauga. Davis asked Longstreet's opinion. The general hesitated. "I think that I understood the meaning of his question, but evaded it by a general answer," Longstreet later wrote. Likely recalling Davis's cold response to his opinion at a prior military conference, Longstreet responded that since he was a new addition to the Tennessee army, he "should not be called to an opinion." The Confederate president insisted, however, and Longstreet stated: "I said that my estimate of Gen. Bragg as a Field Marshall [is] not high, and . . . the little experience I had with him had not increased it." Buckner, Cheatham, and Hill spoke in turn concurring with Longstreet's assessment of Bragg and the campaign. Dissatisfied with the results of his military tribunal, Davis dismissed the generals and planned his next maneuver.[9]

If Bragg's generals thought their testimonies would influence the president to remove their commander, subsequent events demonstrated otherwise. Embarrassed with the outcome of the military conference, Bragg offered his resignation, but Davis refused it because he felt that "no change for the better could be made in the commander of the army." Not willing to concede failure to Bragg's critics, who had campaigned for the general's removal and the appointment of Johnston, the president "prevailed upon [Bragg] to stay where he was, assuring him of his support if it were needed in the future." Determined to support Bragg, Davis recognized that if he removed the beleaguered general, he would have to appoint Joseph E. Johnston, an enemy of the administration, to command the foremost western army. Moreover, if Davis removed Bragg, he would have to concede that he erred in appointing the North Carolinian to the helm of the Army of Tennessee. Thus the president resumed his inspection of the Tennessee army and met separately with Longstreet and Buckner on October 10. Both meetings proved equally disappointing. Davis refused to concede to his political foes by appointing Johnston. Yet the dissension in the army's high command remained so strong that action seemed necessary.[10]

The first step in the reorganization of the Army of Tennessee began on October 11, when the president authorized Bragg to relieve any officer who failed to cooperate with him. While Bragg maneuvered to eliminate his opposition, Davis embarked on a public relations campaign to sway troop sentiment toward their commanding general. On October 12 and 13, the president made several speeches complimenting Bragg and denouncing the "shafts of malice that have been hurled against him." By the time Davis left the Army of Tennessee on October 14, he issued a proclamation urging the southern soldiers to support their commanding general. Thriving on the president's steadfast support, Bragg reorganized his army, relieving D. H. Hill, reducing Buckner from corps to divisional command, and transferring troops to reduce the influence of his critics. Only Longstreet, based on his preceding reputation in Virginia and his performance at Chickamauga, seemed above reproach. Yet the authorities in Richmond remained suspicious that the First Corps commander conspired against the administration's goals.[11]

Longstreet's fractured relationship with his commander was just one of the problems facing the First Corps during the siege at Chattanooga. In the wake of the petition and the military conference with Davis, Longstreet left for his headquarters on the eastern edge of Lookout Mountain, having communicated little with Bragg. Longstreet was certain that Bragg would hold him in disdain. Yet the relationship with his commander paled in comparison to the growing rancor within his own corps.

To start with, Lafayette McLaws was bitter and angry, not only at Longstreet but in being transferred to Tennessee. In a private letter, McLaws confided to his wife that he despised his new assignment in the West. "This seems to be a most detestable climate and the men are suffering by the change from Virginia," McLaws wrote, "where there was order and system and satisfaction and a fine country with a fine climate." McLaws's anger was notable, especially in light of the fact that he and Longstreet were former friends and West Point classmates who had fought together from the Seven Days to Gettysburg before their journey to the Tennessee-Georgia border. McLaws had served admirably at Antietam and Fredericksburg but faltered under Lee's command at Chancellorsville. In the army's subsequent reorganization, McLaws had been passed over for promotion in favor of A. P. Hill and Richard S. Ewell. Citing favoritism toward the Virginians, McLaws sought a transfer from Lee's command. When McLaws fell ill the previous winter, Lee asked Longstreet to ascertain the ability of the Georgian to campaign actively in the summer of 1863. Receiving assurances from his division commander, Longstreet retained McLaws but promised Lee to keep an eye on his lieutenant. "I thus became responsible for anything that was not entirely satisfactory in your command from that day," Longstreet later told McLaws.[12]

At Gettysburg, Longstreet's reluctance to follow Lee's orders, as well as his command decisions on the battle's second day infuriated McLaws. In a letter to his wife, McLaws blamed Longstreet for the failure in Pennsylvania. He wrote, "I think the whole attack was unnecessary and the whole plan of battle a very bad one. General Longstreet is to be blamed for not reconnoitering the ground and for persisting in ordering the assault when his errors were discussed. During the engagement he was excited giving contradictory orders to every one, and was exceedingly [overbearing]. I consider him a humbug: a man of small capacity, very obstinate, not at all chivalrous, exceedingly conceited, and totally selfish. If I can it is my intention to get away from his command." McLaws's conduct in the West showed that the resentment had not abated. Upon his arrival in northern Georgia, McLaws received orders to pursue the Federals toward Chattanooga, but faltered, claiming that his command would suffer heavy losses and requesting more ambulances. For the next several weeks, McLaws remained uncooperative, thus prompting Longstreet to report his recalcitrance to Bragg in mid-October. Bragg apparently convinced Longstreet to give his division commander one more chance. Although Longstreet suggested to McLaws that "he should brush up and be more prompt and active," the relations between the two men portended trouble for the First Corps in the upcoming campaign.[13]

Adding to the corps' dysfunction was the growing bitter rivalry between the other division's senior brigadiers, Law and Jenkins. The problems worsened when Jenkins's brigade arrived shortly after the battle at Chickamauga. Longstreet placed Jenkins, whom he considered his protégé, in command of Hood's division. Jenkins would have commanded the unit when it journeyed to the Army of Tennessee in September if Hood had not been urged to return by his men. After Hood's wounding at Chickamauga temporarily incapacitated him, Longstreet sought to make Jenkins's command of the division permanent, revealing to McLaws that he had recommended Jenkins for the position.[14] Longstreet's choice of Jenkins seemed logical, considering the South Carolinian ranked Law, the division's temporary commander at Gettysburg and Chickamauga, by two and a half months. Thus, Longstreet likely thought that in addition to his view of Jenkins as "a bright, gallant, and efficient officer," military protocol necessitated that he recommend the senior officer present.[15]

However, Longstreet failed to consider how the men of Hood's division would react to their new commander or how Law would respond to being passed over. Even though Longstreet's decision to appoint a division commander should not have to depend on the approval of the units in question, the men of Hood's old unit held a certain loyalty to Law, who had a valid claim to command the division in that he had personally led Hood's troops on two occasions in the adoptive Texan's absence due to battlefield injuries. Longstreet was also probably unaware of a rivalry between the two South Carolinians that dated to their cadetship at the Citadel Academy and their tenure as faculty members of Kings Mountain Military Institute in Yorkville, South Carolina. After a brief period at the Kings Mountain academy, Law had helped found a military school in Tuskegee, Alabama, prior to the war. In his adopted home state, Law organized and served as colonel of the 4th Alabama, then rising to command an Alabama brigade, composed of the 4th,

15th, 44th, 47th, and 48th Regiments. After being wounded at First Manassas, Law had recovered and led his brigade from the Seven Days to Gettysburg. At Gettysburg, Law had assumed command of Hood's division after its commander was wounded during the second day of battle. Law led the division for two and a half months, until Hood returned to the First Corps before the transfer to Tennessee. When Hood was wounded again at Chickamauga, Law believed he would inherit permanent command of the division.[16]

Longstreet objected, however, to Law's assuming command of the division. In addition to favoring Jenkins, Longstreet disapproved of Law as a division commander for several reasons. First, Law had earned Longstreet's displeasure during the Siege of Suffolk in April 1863, when the Federals captured two of Law's companies. Although Longstreet did not file formal charges, he pointed out that "there seems to have been a general lack of vigilance and prompt attention to duties on the part of most of the parties connected with this affair." The relationship between Longstreet and Law worsened during the Gettysburg Campaign when, according to one of Law's military aides, the junior officer questioned Longstreet's orders to attack the Federal left flank on Little Round Top after arriving late to his designated position. After the battle, Longstreet failed to acknowledge the leadership and valor displayed by his brigade commander and mildly criticized him in his official report because his corps had to wait for Law's arrival on July 2, implying that it could have swept the Union left during the battle.[17]

The awkwardness of commanding Hood's unit was not lost on Jenkins or the men in the division. Upon Jenkins's arrival in northern Georgia, when Longstreet proposed to designate him as division commander, the veterans of Hood's division protested the appointment, stating it was "against the wishes of a large majority." The division's brigade commanders petitioned Longstreet to leave Law in command because Law had "the confidence of all the officers and men." Longstreet dismissed the officers' petition and proceeded to assign Jenkins the command of Hood's division. Longstreet had dealt with troops' animosity to officers who showed favoritism in promotion when he was stationed on the Texas frontier before the war, yet for some reason he failed to appraise the dynamics of the citizen-soldier in comparison to the army regular:. namely, the potential volatility of volunteers who might refuse to follow any officer appointed to command them that they disliked, for whatever reason.[18]

So, as the Confederates faced the portending reinforcement of the Federal force in Chattanooga, Longstreet was dealing with the animosity of his commanding general and the additional strain caused from the internal discontent brewing within his own corps. The animosity did not take long to fester and inflict damage on the First Corps' ability to engage the Union army. If the

Federals were to reopen their supply lines, the key point was Brown's Ferry. The responsibility for Brown's Ferry and Lookout Valley rested with Longstreet's corps. He had positioned two regiments of Law's Alabama brigade on the south bank of the Tennessee and instructed his brigade commander to reconnoiter the valley to ascertain how strong a force would be needed to protect the Confederate left. Law ordered his men along a five-mile picket line between the south bank of the river and the northern base of Raccoon Mountain, up to Little Suck Creek. The brigade commander deployed the 4th and 15th Alabama to picket the river while he kept the remaining three regiments in reserve, along with a section of artillery on the western face of Lookout Mountain. Law also positioned sharpshooters in the woods on the south bank to harass the Federals on the opposite shore. He recalled that his sharpshooters were so accurate that they succeeded in "killing many mules" and "blockading the road completely."[19]

Nevertheless, the Federals launched their plan to seize Brown's Ferry on October 27, when a flotilla of Union flatboats landed on the south bank of the Tennessee River and overwhelmed the remnants of Law's force holding the key landing. The Rebels held Brown's Ferry with an undermanned force because Law had left his post to visit Hood in hopes of seeing if the Kentuckian could help him secure the promotion to lead the division. Without Law's presence, Longstreet was deprived of his firsthand knowledge of the terrain and the Federal movements. To add to the Confederate miscues around Lookout Mountain, Law's rivalry with Jenkins escalated during the Federal movements in late October. Jenkins was still temporary commander of the division. As such, he ordered three of Law's regiments to his sector east of Lookout Mountain and away from Brown's Ferry. Law later said he believed there was no "rhyme or reason" in moving these troops from one side of the mountain to another, and Jenkins's order suggests he wanted to demonstrate to Law his authority as a division commander. After weeks of idleness, Jenkins and Law probably did not figure their rivalry would boil over during a Federal movement in late October.[20]

Thus on the morning of the twenty-seventh, Law's troops awoke to the lead elements of Federal soldiers landing near Brown's Ferry. The Confederates hastily organized themselves to defend their positions. Colonel William B. Oates of the 15th Alabama heard the firing and took 150 men to Brown's Ferry from his position on Raccoon Mountain. While the Federals quickly constructed fortifications near the shore, Oates instructed two of his companies to seize their position. Oates's Alabamians came upon the Yankees building abatis. The Confederates opened fire, startling the Federals and forcing them to order a retreat toward the river. As the two lead companies of the 15th Alabama plunged ahead, Oates led the remaining men toward the Federal right to cut off their retreat. The Rebels swept over a ridge near the shore, but they encountered the lead elements of the 6th Indiana Infantry, some of the first troops to be ferried across the Tennessee as support for the landing party at Brown's Ferry. In response to the threat, the Federals fired a volley into the advancing Confederate line, causing it to waver. Oates tried to rally his men, but to no avail. As he made his way toward the Federal breast-works, a bullet ripped through his right hip and thigh. After Oates fell, his men withdrew. The fight at Brown's Ferry had lasted about twenty minutes, and the Confederates had lost six men killed and fourteen wounded. By 7:00 A.M., the Confederates retreated toward Lookout Mountain, covering their retreat with artillery fire. Oates's Alabamians met with Law and the rest of his brigade up the valley, where Law positioned them near Lookout Creek to oppose a further Union advance. Yet the damage was done. The Federals had established a landing on the south side of the Tennessee. The First Corps had been caught ill-prepared for the assault.[21]

Longstreet, for his part, hardly paid attention to Brown's Ferry prior to the critical moments of the Federal advance because he regarded it as a diversion. There is no record explaining why the First Corps commander insisted that the Union army's real threat to the Confederate position on Lookout Mountain came from the south and not Brown's Ferry. Perhaps he remained miffed that during the president's visit Davis and Bragg had dis-counted his proposal to move against Bridgeport and "swing around towards the enemy's rear." Since Davis left Missionary Ridge, Longstreet and Bragg had failed to communicate about the army's intentions during the siege of Chattanooga. It is also probable that Longstreet simply made a mistake and gambled on predicting the enemy's intentions. With the awkwardness of the president's military conference still lingering on Longstreet's mind, the First Corps commander was guilty of not calculating all possible threats to his line. Although historians later argued that Longstreet's mistakes on Lookout Mountain resulted from his petulance in failing to obtain the command of the Army of Tennessee, the contemporary evidence does not provide definite support for this premise.[22]

The loss of Brown's Ferry forced Bragg and Longstreet to talk for the first time since the fateful military conference with Davis. After receiving Longstreet's report of the situation on the Confederate left, Bragg decided to meet with him to discuss strategy. As described in the opening paragraph of this essay, it was at dawn on the twenty-eighth that Bragg rode to the top of the mountain where he met with Longstreet. Years later, Longstreet recalled that the acrimony that characterized the October 9 meeting had not abated in the weeks since. The First Corps commander noted that Bragg complained of "false alarms" from Longstreet's sector and proceeded to outline his plans to retake Brown's Ferry. While the two men "engaged in an examination of the enemy's new position," one of Longstreet's signal officers reported that "the enemy was advancing in force from Bridgeport." A breakdown in communications between Longstreet's headquarters and the Confederate cavalry assigned to his sector had allowed a force of seven thousand Federals to march undetected down Lookout Valley toward Brown's Ferry.[23]

Bragg immediately ordered the Confederate artillery on Lookout Mountain to harass the Union column, but the distance proved too far for the Rebel guns. Bragg was infuriated. He had lost Brown's Ferry the previous day, and with the Union advance on Lookout Valley, it appeared that the Federals had succeeded in establishing a line of supply into the city. Bragg demanded that Longstreet do something to regain the initiative and returned to his headquarters on Missionary Ridge, complaining of Longstreet's "lack of ability." Bragg's outburst likely distressed Longstreet since he considered attacking Brown's Ferry as unreasonable because the Federals had entrenched and solidified their positions along the banks of the Tennessee. Longstreet was probably apprehensive about mounting a headlong attack against a fortified foe, something to avoid if possible. The solution to his dilemma appeared an hour after he witnessed Hooker's column combine with the Federals at Brown's Ferry. A second Union force, the rear guard for the main column, appeared in Lookout Valley and bivouacked at Wauhatchie, about three miles south of the Brown's Ferry landing. That unit of approximately fifteen hundred men, under the command of Brigadier General John Geary, would be the focus of the attack Longstreet intended.[24]

In the wake of the Brown's Ferry loss and his meeting with Bragg, Longstreet hastily devised a plan to strike at Geary's five regiments, ordering a night attack in order to avoid detection and to take advantage of the confusion it would likely bring. While a nighttime assault would likely catch the Federals off guard, it also depended on the timing and cooperation of the Confederate units, two characteristics conspicuously absent from the First Corps during the last month. After a last-minute midnight reconnaissance with Jenkins, Longstreet returned to his headquarters under the impression that since he and his lieutenant failed properly to reconnoiter the Federal position, the assault would be canceled. Whether Jenkins understood Longstreet's ambivalence remains unclear since the South Carolinian gave orders for the operation. Between 12:30 and 1:00 A.M. on October 29, the First Corps moved against the Federals near Wauhatchie. In less than three hours, the battle for the control of Lookout Valley had finished. The Confederates suffered 408 casualties to 416 for the Union forces and the Federals remained in control of the valley.[25]

The failure to retake Brown's Ferry and the resulting entanglement at Wauhatchie seriously damaged Bragg's siege, for now the Federals could receive food and supplies into the city. Clearly the First Corps' miscues were not lost on the commanding general. On November 3, Bragg held a conference with his leading lieutenants to discuss future strategy in the wake of the Federals' success.[26] Prior to meeting with his generals, Bragg had consulted with President Davis in regards to Longstreet's mismanagement at Lookout Mountain. While Davis was reluctant to relieve anyone from command—including Bragg—the president suggested transferring the First Corps to East Tennessee, and Bragg gladly acquiesced. To one of his subordinates, Bragg said he wanted to send Longstreet to Knoxville to "see what he could do on his own resources." Accordingly, on November 4, Bragg ordered Longstreet to move toward East Tennessee with the divisions of Hood and McLaws, two artillery battalions, and a cavalry detachment.[27]

Bragg's decision to detach Longstreet's corps in the face of a numerically superior enemy force remains one of the most controversial decisions of the Chattanooga Campaign. Yet it is understandable why Bragg gave up on Longstreet and the First Corps as his siege was effectively broken by the loss of Lookout Valley. After all, Longstreet—who had already demonstrated his displeasure at serving under Bragg—had failed to secure the pivotal left flank of the Confederate army. Furthermore, his corps had begun to exhibit a real affinity for infighting and recrimination. In the wake of the failed assault on Wauhatchie, Jenkins blamed Law for falling back prematurely and forcing his unit to retreat in the face of the enemy. Law, predictably, rejected Jenkins's claim, countering that since he believed that "the object for which my position was occupied had been accomplished, I withdrew." To no one's surprise, Longstreet sided with Jenkins's version of events, despite the fact that Colonel John Bratton, of Jenkins's brigade, confirmed Law's interpretation of the battle. Clearly, the First Corps' command structure was fractured with internal rivalries and bitterness.[28]

As Longstreet's men prepared to leave the environs of Chattanooga for Knoxville, it is important to note, the corps' performance had been much less effective than its reputation in Virginia had suggested it would be. One could say that in the wake of the Battle of Chickamauga the First Corps had been caught in a whirlwind of ineffectiveness that hampered its ability to function within the Army of Tennessee.

To start with, Longstreet's overconfidence served as the first element to hurt the First Corps' ability to function efficiently. Leaving Lee's army in September, Longstreet held a bias against the western theater in general and Bragg in particular. Longstreet was not alone in thinking this. Lee agreed, suggesting that the First Corps could have made quick work of the Federals in Tennessee-Georgia and returned to the Army of Northern Virginia before too long. Yet Longstreet's prejudice toward Bragg proved more problematic. Longstreet arrived to the Army of Tennessee believing he was a better commander than Bragg. Always confident in his own abilities, he quickly fell under the spell of the army's other disgruntled generals who also held Bragg in contempt. As a result, Longstreet soon assumed a leading role in the anti-Bragg faction that resulted in the transfer of several senior officers and set his signature to a petition demanding Bragg's removal from command. Clearly Longstreet's role in these efforts reflected poorly on him. Flirting with insubordination, the First Corps commander may have been correct in his assessment of Bragg, but his actions paralyzed further communication with the commanding general, obviously hampering interaction in the high command and limiting the effectiveness of the Confederate siege at Chattanooga.[29]

The friction stemming from Longstreet's conflict with Bragg carried over into late October and the losses at Brown's Ferry and Lookout Mountain. The First Corps commander had always been confident in his persona. In late October, Longstreet demonstrated that same degree of confidence in his hesitancy to attack the Federals from his position on Lookout Mountain. Longstreet was likely convinced that anything Bragg proposed was impractical. Thus Longstreet erred in determining that the true Federal threat stemmed from Brown's Ferry and not the Trenton area to the south. Convinced that Bragg would like to see him fail and skeptical that any offensive strategy could salvage the Confederate situation near Lookout Mountain, Longstreet led a half-hearted effort to regain the valley with his inefficient plan of assault on Wauhatchie.

The failure at Brown's Ferry and Wauhatchie highlighted a second element of controversy that ripped the First Corps: the rivalry between Jenkins and Law. Both men pursued the command of Hood's old division to the point it impacted the corps' harmony on the eve of the Federal assault on Brown's Ferry. Prior to October 27, Law had left his position on Lookout Mountain to lobby Hood—who was convalescing miles south in northern Georgia—for his support in gaining permanent command of the division. Even though Jenkins outranked Law, the latter believed that his familiarity with the men and long service within the division (unlike Jenkins, whose previous service had been in another unit) entitled him to its command. Jenkins, for his part, also contributed to the disorder by ordering Law's men to report to his side of Lookout Mountain. As Law's biographers have noted, there was a logical rationale for this action other than Jenkins's flexing his muscles of authority over Law. The disharmony only continued with the failed assault on Wau-hatchie and the recriminations that followed. The impact of the rivalry was reflected in Longstreet's official report, in which Longstreet complained of a lack of cooperation between the two men and citing the "jealousy between the two brigades" as the central reason for the loss of Lookout Valley.[30]

Finally, the First Corps also had the other division commander, McLaws, at odds with Longstreet. McLaws and Longstreet might have been longtime friends dating to their days at West Point, but by the time of the Gettysburg campaign McLaws was reluctant to follow his superior's orders. McLaws certainly blamed Longstreet for the army's failures in Pennsylvania, and his actions in Tennessee suggested that the resentment had not abated. And while Longstreet had reported this estrangement to Bragg in midst of the Confederate siege in Chattanooga, it was also a possible reason why the First Corps commander failed to include McLaws's force in the assault on Wauhatchie.

Clearly, the First Corps' internal problems would be exacerbated upon its transfer to East Tennessee. Yet the traditional view that Longstreet's brooding and sulking behavior directly led to the Confederate losses near Lookout Mountain is not supported by the evidence, which shows that it was a combination of factors that reduced the First Corps' abilities near Chattanooga. Certainly, it was the behavior of Longstreet and his senior officers, who allowed honor, bitterness, and personal ambitions to override their military bearing and professional duty to the Confederacy that led to the losses at Brown's Ferry and Wauhatchie. To be sure, the Civil War is replete with examples of officers who allowed personal ambition and their principles to influence their military bearing. Yet for the First Corps, it surfaced with most of the senior officers at approximately the same time. It thus became a perfect storm of ineffectiveness that contributed to the Confederate losses at Chattanooga.

Notes

1. James Longstreet, *From Manassas to Appomattox* (New York: Konecky and Konecky Press, 1974), 474–75; Brent Journal, October 28, 1863, Braxton Bragg Papers, Western Reserve Library, Cleveland, Ohio (hereafter cited as Bragg Papers); Alexander Mendoza, *Struggle for Command: General James Longstreet and the First Corps in the West* (College Station: Texas A&M University Press, 2008), 97–98.

2. Steven E. Woodworth, *Six Armies in Tennessee: The Chickamauga and Chattanooga Campaigns* (Lincoln: University of Nebraska Press, 1999), 144–45; Peter Cozzens, *The Shipwreck of Their Hopes: The Battle of Chickamauga* (Urbana: University of Illinois Press, 1995), 18–19; Thomas Lawrence Connelly, *Autumn of Glory: The Army of Tennessee, 1863–1865* (Baton Rouge: Louisiana State University Press, 1973), 232.

3. Cozzens, *Shipwreck of Their Hopes*, 19–20; James Lee McDonough, *Chattanooga: A Death Grip on the Confederacy* (Knoxville: University of Tennessee Press, 1984), 24–25; Connelly, *Autumn of Glory*, 255–57.

4. Woodworth, *Six Armies in Tennessee*, 129–49; Cozzens, *Shipwreck of Their Hopes*, 1–7; Wiley Sword, *Mountains Touched with Fire: Chattanooga Besieged, 1863* (New York: St. Martin's Press, 1995), 46–54.

5. U.S. War Department, *The War of the Rebellion: A Compilation of the Official Records of the Union and Confederate Armies*, 128 vols. (Washington, D.C., 1880–1901), series 1, vol. 29, pt. 2: 699 (hereafter cited as *OR*; all references are to Series 1 unless otherwise indicated).

6. *OR*, 30, pt. 2: 289; 30, pt. 4: 705; 30, pt. 2: 37. See also Connelly, *Autumn of Glory*, 230.

7. *OR*, 30, pt. 2: 67; Mendoza, *Struggle for Command*, chapter 3.

8. Diary entry, September 30, 1863, John Euclid Magee Diary, 1861–1863, Rare Book, Manuscript, and Special Collections Library, Duke University, Durham, North Carolina; Polk to My Dearest Wife, October 3, 1863, Polk to My Dearest Daughter, October 10, 1863, in William M. Polk, *Leonidas Polk: Bishop and General*, 2 vols. (New York: Longmans, Green, and Co., 1915), 2: 298–99; *OR*, 30, pt. 2: 47; Connelly, *Autumn of Glory*, 237–40; Longstreet to John C. Brown, April 14, 1888, James Longstreet Papers, Duke University; Peter Cozzens, *This Terrible Sound: The Battle of Chickamauga* (Chicago: University of Illinois Press, 1993), 529–32; Jeffry Wert, *General James Longstreet: The Confederacy's Most Controversial Soldier—A Biography* (New York: Simon and Schuster, 1993), 326–27; John C. Brown to James Longstreet, April 14, 1888, Longstreet Papers, Duke University; Archer Anderson Collection, Eleanor S. Brockenbrough Library, Museum of the Confederacy, Richmond, Virginia; Steven E. Woodworth, *Jefferson Davis and His Generals: The Failure of Confederate Command in the West* (Lawrence: University Press of Kansas, 1989), 241.

9. Longstreet to Frank A. Burr, 25 November 1883, James Longstreet Papers, Frederick M. Dearborn Collection, Houghton Library, Harvard University, Cambridge, Massachusetts (hereafter HL); Longstreet to E. P. Alexander, 26 August 1902, Alexander Papers, Southern Historical Collection, University of North Carolina at Chapel Hill (hereafter SHC); Longstreet, *Manassas to Appomattox*, 465. See also Cozzens, *This Terrible Sound*, 532–33; Connelly, *Autumn of Glory*, 245.

10. Mendoza, *Struggle for Command*, 66–67; M. B. Morton, "Last Surviving Confederate General," in *Confederate Veteran* 17 (February 1909): 83; W. C. Vann Woodward, ed., *Chesnut's Civil War* (New Haven: Yale University Press, 1981), 482.

11. G. Moxley Sorrel, *Recollections of a Confederate Staff Officer* (New York: Konecky & Konecky Press, 1994), 201; Brent Journal, 11 October 1863, Bragg Papers; Archer Anderson to My Dear Father, 13 October 1863, Archer Anderson Collection, Museum of the Confederacy; Mendoza, *Struggle for Command*, 69–70; William C. Davis, *Jefferson Davis: The Man and His Hour* (New York: Harper and Row, 1993), 550.

12. Lafayette McLaws to Dear Wife, October 14, 1863, McLaws Papers, SHC; James Longstreet to Lafayette McLaws, July 25, 1873, McLaws Papers, SHC; John C. Oeffinger, ed., *A Soldier's General: The Civil War Letters of Major General Lafayette McLaws* (Chapel Hill: University of North Carolina Press, 2002), 1–61; Robert K. Krick, "Longstreet versus McLaws—and Everyone Else—at Knoxville," in Robert K. Krick, *The Smoothbore Volley That Doomed the Confederacy: The Death of Stonewall Jackson and Other Chapters on the Army of Northern Virginia* (Baton Rouge: Louisiana State University Press, 2002), 85–98.

13. Frances Dawson, *Reminiscences of Confederate Service* (Charleston: News and Courier Book Press, 1882), 101; James Longstreet to Braxton Bragg, October 16, 1863, James Longstreet Papers, HL; Lafayette McLaws to Dear Wife, July 7, 1863, SHC.

14. James Longstreet to Lafayette McLaws, October 18, 1863, McLaws Papers, SHC. Richard McMurry argues that Hood returned to his division prior to Chickamauga to prevent an outsider (Jenkins) from assuming command. See Richard McMurry, *John Bell Hood and the War for Southern Independence* (Lincoln: University of Nebraska Press, 1982), 76.

15. Longstreet, *Manassas to Appomattox*, 467.

16. J. B. Polley, *Hood's Texas Brigade: Its Marches, Its Battles, Its Achievements* (Dayton: Morningside Press, 1976), 213; J. Gary Laine and Morris M. Penny, *Law's Alabama Brigade in the War between the Union and the Confederacy* (Shippensburg, Pa.: White Mane Publishing, 1996), xiv–xvii, 178–79, 186–202, 208–22; Guy R. Swanson and Timothy D. Johnson, "Conflict in East Tennessee: Generals Law, Jenkins, and Longstreet," *Civil War History* 31, no. 2 (June 1985): 101–4; James J. Baldwin, in *The Struck Eagle: A Biography of Brigadier General Micah Jenkins, and a History of the Fifth South Carolina Volunteers and the Palmetto Sharpshooters* (Shippensburg: Burd Street Press, 1996), 16, argues that Law resented Jenkins's authority as senior faculty member at Kings College and "relations between the two men eventually became quite bitter." Jenkins biographer, James K. Swisher, in *The Prince of Edisto: Brigadier General Micah Jenkins, C.S.A.* (Berryville, Va.: Rockbridge, 1996), 100, refutes the existence of a prewar rivalry.

17. *OR*, 18, 326–27, pt. 2, 358; Laine and Penny, *Law's Alabama Brigade*, xv, 57–59, 120–21.

18. Laine and Penny, *Law's Alabama Brigade*, 178; Harold B. Simpson, *Hood's Texas Brigade: Lee's Grenadier Guard* (Fort Worth: Texian Press, 1970), 331–32; Polley, *Hood's Texas Brigade*, 213–14; Charles E. Brooks, "The Social and Cultural Dynamics of Soldiering in Hood's Texas Brigade," *Journal of Southern History*, 67, no. 3 (August 2001), 535–72.

19. *OR*, 31, pt. 1, 224; M. Law, "Lookout Valley: Memoranda of Gen. E. M. Law," Ezra Ayers Carmen Papers, New York Public Library; Woodworth, *Six Armies in Tennessee*, 150–56.

20. Penny and Laine suggest that Jenkins's recall of three regiments of the Alabama Brigade was the "sort of irritant one might inflict upon a subordinate in the hope of driving him away." Penny and Laine, *Law's Alabama Brigade*, 182. See also James Lee McDonough, *Chattanooga: A Death Grip on the Confederacy* (Knoxville: University of Tennessee Press, 1983), 47; Woodworth, *Six Armies in Tennessee*, 129–49; Cozzens, *Shipwreck of Their Hopes*, 1–7; Sword, *Mountains Touched with Fire*, 46–54.

21. William C. Oates, *War between the Union and the Confederacy and Its Lost Opportunities, with a History of the Fifteenth Alabama and the Forty-Eight Battles in Which Was Engaged* (Dayton: Morningside Press, 1985), 275–77; Sword, *Mountains Touched with Fire*, 120–21; Cozzens, *Shipwreck of Their Hopes*, 63–65.

22. Longstreet, *Manassas to Appomattox*, 468; Wiley, *Mountains Touched with Fire*, 123–24. Historians taking this view are Cozzens, *Shipwreck of Their Hopes*, 57; Connelly, *Autumn of Glory*, 256–66; Woodworth, *Jefferson Davis and His Generals*, 248; Woodworth, *Six Armies in Tennessee*, 156–57; Judith Lee Hallock, *Braxton Bragg and Confederate Defeat* (Tuscaloosa: University of Alabama Press, 1989), 2: 121–26; Judith Lee Hallock, *A Monumental Failure: General James Longstreet in the West* (Fort Worth: Ryan's Place Press, 1997).

23. George W. Brent to James Longstreet, October 27, 1863 [11:00 P.M.], Bragg Papers; *OR*, 31, pt. 1: 217; Longstreet, *Manassas to Appomattox*, 474–75; Brent Journal, October 28, 1863, Bragg Papers; St. John Richardson Liddell, *Liddell's Record*, ed. Nathaniel Cheairs Hughes (Baton Rouge: Louisiana State University Press, 1997), 156–57; Wert, *General James Longstreet*, 335; Woodworth, *Six Armies in Tennessee*, 162–63.

24. George Brent to James Longstreet, October 28, 1863, Bragg Papers, Western Reserve; Liddell, *Liddell's Record*, 157; McDonough, *Chattanooga*, 88–89; Sword, *Mountains Touched with Fire*, 128–29; Connelly, *Autumn of Glory*, 259; Cozzens, *Shipwreck of Their Hopes*, 78–79.

25. Longstreet, *Manassas to Appomattox*, 476–77; *OR*, 31, pt. 1: 223; Micah Jenkins to G. M. Sorrel, November 2, 1863, Micah Jenkins Papers, South Caroliniana Library, University of South Carolina Library, Columbia, South Carolina; Woodworth, *Six Armies in Tennessee*, 164–67.

26. *OR*, 31, pt. 1, 455.

27. Braxton Bragg to Jefferson Davis, October 29, 1863, Dunbar Rowland, ed., *Jefferson Davis, Constitutionalist: His Letters, Papers, and Speeches*, 10 vols (Jackson: Mississippi Department of Archives and History, 1923), 6: 69–71; Woodworth, *Davis and His Generals*, 248; Connelly, *Autumn of Glory*, 262–66; Liddell, *Liddell's Record*, 157. Bragg's detachment of Longstreet is largely condemned by historians. Stanley Horn, in his study of the Army of Tennessee, declared that "Bragg fail[ed] to realize the folly of dividing his force in the face of an ever stronger enemy." Bragg's most recent biographer, Samuel J. Martin, *General Braxton Bragg, C.S.A.* (Jefferson, NC: McFarland, 2001), 348–49, argues that it was President Davis's idea to detach Longstreet to relieve the Army of Tennessee commander from further distruption in operating around Chattanooga. Stanley Horn, *The Army of Tennessee* (Norman: University of Oklahoma Press, 1993), 294. Connelly, in his study of the western army, argues that it was a "major command blunder" that "had given way to personal motives." Connelly, *Autumn of Glory*, 261–63. Wiley Sword maintains Bragg's decision to detach Longstreet was more "an emotional reflex than a considered strategy." Sword, *Mountains Touched with Fire*, 147. McDonough writes: "It made no military sense, of course, unless one was blind, as Davis and Bragg apparently were, to the Union concentration at Chattanooga." McDonough, *Chattanooga*, 98. Cozzens's *The Shipwreck of Their Hopes*, 105, states: "Bragg had committed his most egregious error of his checkered career." Bragg biographer Judith Lee Hallock takes the stance that in light of Longstreet's failures at Brown's Ferry and Wauhatchie, Bragg "probably did not injure his chances at Chattanooga any more by sending him than by keeping him." Hallock, *Braxton Bragg*, 126. Don Seitz, in his 1924 biography of the commander of the Army of Tennessee, *Braxton Bragg* (Columbia: University of South Carolina Press, 1924), 390, 406, suggests that the North Carolinian relented to Longstreet's constant pressure and detached him against his better judgment. More recently, Woodworth's *Six Armies in Tennessee*, 174–175, and Edward Carr Franks, "The Detachment of Longstreet Considered: Braxton Bragg, James Longstreet, and the Chattanooga Campaign," in *Leadership and Command in the American Civil War*, ed. Steven E. Woodworth (Campbell, CA: Savas Woodbury Press, 1995), 29–65, have provided alternate views of Bragg's decision to order Longstreet to East Tennessee.

28. Mendoza, *Struggle for Command*, 101.

29. Ibid., 71–73, 100–102.

30. *OR*, 31, pt. 2, 219; Mendoza, *Struggle for Command*, 98–103.

2

"LOOKOUT MOUNTAIN FROWNED DOWN UPON US":
THE UNION ARMY AND THE STRUGGLE
FOR LOOKOUT VALLEY

Stewart Bennett

I n the dark of night the men of the 73rd Ohio and 33rd Massachusetts Regiments struggled with the difficult terrain up the steep hill, as the bullets flew past. Holding their fire, they moved up through the dark shadows before them and in no time felt the hail of an enfilading volley that staggered the line, dropping men with each tortuous step. As they came closer to the crest of the hill, another volley spewed forth a sheet of leaden hail. This time, however, the Union troops answered with a volley of their own. Private William Fletcher Hughey of the 73rd Ohio recalled the nightmare upon that field of battle: "Men were falling in every direction, screaming and crying in pain. The Maj. gave the order to fix bayonet and charge . . . moving forward amid cheers and yells, firing and falling by scores. We were getting in very close quarters, almost within reach of the points of our bayonets, and feeling as though we were certain of victory and thinking nothing but victory. When alas my hopes were all blasted, and that very suddenly."[1]

For Hughey, the 73rd Ohio, and the rest of Major General Joseph Hooker's Eleventh and Twelfth Corps, it had only been a few days' march for the men to arrive on this moonlit evening in late October 1863 and to take part in one of the few nighttime battles of the Civil War. This fight on the evening of October 28 continued into the early morning hours of the twenty-ninth and would be remembered as the Battle of Wauhatchie. Even before this battle ensued, much was changing in the western theater of the war. Major General Ulysses S. Grant had just assumed command of the newly created Military Division of the Mississippi. Soon after, he replaced Major General William S. Rosecrans as commander of the Army of the Cumberland in Chattanooga with Major General George H. Thomas and approved a plan to rescue the Union army now trapped within Chattanooga. To attempt a breakthrough of the infamous "Cracker Line" would prove risky, but to do nothing about the present state of affairs would likely cause the loss of the great Army of the Cumberland.[2] President Abraham Lincoln expected results, and Grant

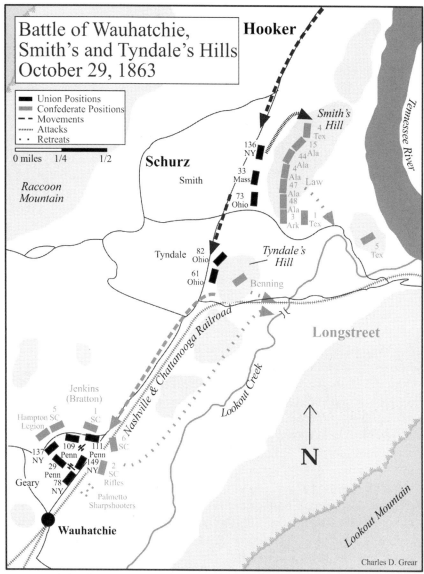

Battle of Wauhatchie, Smith's and Tyndale's Hills October 29, 1863

Amid the chaos typical of one of the war's rare night attacks, Longstreet's Confederates lunged into Lookout Valley in a muddled attempt to cut off the recently opened Union Cracker Line, only to be met by an equally confused but ultimately successful repost from Hooker's Federals.

had shown through his actions that he was the man to make the needed changes around Chattanooga. Grant took control of the situation and moved forward to break the stranglehold the Confederate Army of Tennessee held over the supply lines to Union forces in Chattanooga. Grant's plans included a forced Union crossing of the Tennessee River at Brown's Ferry on October 24 that would correct part of the supply problem. The other part of the plan was to have Hooker move his troops out of Bridgeport, Alabama, cross to the south side of the Tennessee River by way of Whitesides, then proceed to Wauhatchie, and finally up to Brown's Ferry. This would help to solidify the Union hold on the southern side of the Tennessee River and make Chattanooga more accessible for much-needed Union supplies. Major General John M. Palmer and a division of the Fourteenth Corps would move down the north side of the Tennessee River, cross at Whitesides, and take control of the road to the rear of Hooker's troops after they had passed.[3] The plan to break the cracker line was set. Hooker and his command were on the move.

On October 26, Hooker moved his troops out of Bridgeport toward their final destination at Brown's Ferry. These troops included much of the Eleventh Corps commanded by Major General Oliver O. Howard, consisting of two divisions: the Third Division under Major General Carl Schurz and the Second Division commanded by Brigadier General Adolph von Steinwehr. In addition there was a company of the 5th Tennessee Cavalry and only a part of a company belonging to the 1st Alabama Cavalry. These troops were to act as advance guards. Also included was a small part of the Second Division of the Twelfth Corps, under the command of Brigadier General John W. Geary, amounting to a paltry four regiments along with two sections of Knapp's Pennsylvania battery. It was, as Geary stated, merely a "fraction of my command."[4]

Hooker and his force moved along the railroad from Bridgeport working to open and secure that line until reaching their final destination at Brown's Ferry. However, along the way, regiments were left to defend important strategic areas such as the bridgehead at the Tennessee River crossing and to take and hold passes in the vicinity of Raccoon Mountain.[5] At one point along the Raccoon Mountain line, Confederate forces of the 4th and 15th Alabama Regiments found themselves surprised and almost trapped by the advancing Union army. Realizing their own forces were too small to contend with this new threat, these Alabamians "hurried out of the valley with all speed." One Alabamian of the 4th Infantry observed that this was a strategically important move for the Union forces because it gave possession of the wagon road back to them.[6] Even though Hooker and his soldiers were making progress through the valley, his troop numbers were dwindling due to leaving soldiers as pickets along the route. Although Confederate resistance had been slight to none during the first phase of the journey, Lookout Mountain and its valley would be the true test of the small army's nerve.

On October 28, Hooker's forces moved into and through Lookout Valley. Various Union soldiers along the march observed that Confederate resistance seemed minimal, while others found the opposite to be true. Much of the discrepancy in their reports may have been because the soldiers were struggling down a long, winding road in a narrow column, and while some may have encountered enemy fire along the way, they had no effective means of communicating with their comrades ahead or behind them. Howard recalled such problems and admitted, "My column at that time, with the best closing up which could be effected in that rocky country, must have been at least six miles in extent. This included my usual ammunition and baggage train. The Confederate gunners, therefore, had a lengthy artillery practice."[7] For many soldiers, Lookout Mountain had a mystique all its own. For some, it took on human traits, as one soldier recalled: "Old Lookout got his eye upon the column looking down from his couple of thousand feet of crag, where he lay stretched out, lazily, miles on the other border of the valley." Others saw a more foreboding mountain, believing that "the bold promontory of Lookout Mountain frowned down upon us and its rebel cannon welcomed us with a demonstrative salute." Even Schurz believed, no doubt due to the Confederates' occupation, that "the commanding form of Lookout Mountain frowned down upon us with a rebel battery on top. We presumed that there must be a rebel force at its foot, but it was hidden from us by dense woods."[8] He was right.

As Confederates from high upon Lookout Mountain signaled the situation in the valley below, Confederates could be seen in the near distance. This required the Union movement to pause. The 73rd Pennsylvania and 154th New York deployed as skirmishers in order to clear the road for the army to proceed. This was a first for the New Yorkers, who had never deployed in this way before, but they made the most of it by rushing toward the enemy. The Confederates' strength was unknown due to the dense growth along the hillside in which the southerners had been waiting. One of the 154th New Yorkers, Major L. D. Warner, recalled, "But our boys did not stop to count noses. With such cheers as would have done credit to the lungs of three times their numbers, they charged boldly into the wood and up the hill. . . . [T]he enemy . . . fled after firing a few shots, and our boys soon rested on the crest of the hill without any greater casualty than the loss of the little finger of one man. . . . [N]o further resistance was offered by the rebel infantry, and we proceeded on our way down the valley."[9]

While much of the Confederate skirmishing ceased along the road, Hooker's troops were by no means out of harm's way. Moving north into

Lookout Valley, the soldiers found the area to be around two miles in width and anchored to the west by Raccoon Mountain with the ominous Lookout Mountain to the east. There was also a range of undulating hills running north and south with wooded crests rising two or three hundred feet, dividing the small valley for approximately three miles. To the north, between these two giant mountains, was the Tennessee River and Brown's Ferry, where part of the Army of the Cumberland was to meet them.[10] That is, if the Confederates had not already pushed these soldiers back into the river and into Chattanooga. The trick, however, was getting to Brown's Ferry.

The road on which Hooker's forces traveled took them uncomfortably close to the foot of Lookout Mountain. Now Confederate lead began to rain down from the north point of Lookout Mountain and to fall within the valley. and, according to Corporal Andrew J. Boies of the 33rd Massachusetts, "we were welcomed by solid shot and shells that came over our heads from the top of Lookout Mountain, and am glad to say that no harm was done us during the day with the exception of Sergeant Adams of Co. F, 33d regiment, who was killed by a bursting shell."[11] Another soldier recalled, "owing, however, to the great height of the mountain or the imperfection of rebel gunnery and projectiles, or both, no harm was done. They wasted their ammunition, frightened a few timid ones, and hurt nobody. It was, however, a grand review and salute."[12] Hooker could also be found taking in the moment and making himself conspicuous to the Confederate cannon fire. Some found him quietly sitting upon his horse as an assuring act to show that there was no danger to the troops as the Confederates "vigorously shelled the column." One New Yorker of the 136th recalled, "While we were in this dangerous place Hooker rode right out, in plain sight of the rebels. He seemed to [show] but little [concern] for the shells."[13]

The column continued its forward movement closer to Brown's Ferry and deeper into Confederate territory. Suddenly, upon the road ahead could be seen bright flags and, more importantly, the gleam of bayonets and gun barrels. Some might have thought this to be the Confederate stand against this small Union army now that it was cut off from all known help or rescue. At any moment, Confederates could have been expected to pour forth from Lookout Mountain and cover the Union hosts in a gray tide. Howard and others peered through field glasses and instead saw the Union troops of Brigadier General William B. Hazen just ahead. These Union men had come out of camp, due to the Confederate cannonading, to meet Hooker's federals who had served in the Army of the Potomac. Howard would later recall of the meeting, "we took in the memorable words: 'Hurrah! hurrah! you have opened up our bread line!' It was a glad meeting; glad for us, who felt that we had accomplished the difficult march; glad for them, who had for some time been growing thin on supplies."[14] With the long journey behind them, Hooker looked to place his forces around a mile south of Brown's Ferry. Geary's forces, however, were at the rear of the march and were given the responsibility of holding the two roads leading to Kelley's Ferry. Therefore, Geary was ordered to camp near the small hamlet of Wauhatchie, which was three miles south of Howard's forces.[15]

While they were in their new camp, Hooker, Howard, and many of their soldiers enjoyed a band as it played during the evening. Others such as Colonel Adin Underwood of the 33rd Massachusetts examined the situation around them. As Underwood considered the state of affairs before the Eleventh Corps, the scene reminded him of the Battle of Chancellorsville and how the Eleventh had been surprised, routed, and shamed.[16] Regardless of how weak the Confederate defense of the valley may have appeared or how impotent most of the cannonading from Lookout Mountain may have been, Confederates still roamed the area and peered down from Lookout Mountain's heights. Schurz was another apprehensive officer who, writing after the war, recalled that "from the same height the enemy could easily observe every one of our movements, and it occurred to some of us that the separation by nearly three miles of bad road of Geary's small force from ours was really an invitation to attack under circumstances very favorable to the enemy." Schurz added the sobering reminder, "Such was the disposition made by General Hooker, and all we could do was to surround ourselves by strong picket lines, well thrown out, to guard against a surprise. So we went into bivouac." Back toward Wauhatchie, in Geary's camp, Private James T. Miller of the 111th Pennsylvania was restless, for he also realized the precarious situation. In writing to his father, he stated, "we had reached a point some six miles from Chattano[o]ga and went into camp and lay down to sleep in plain sight of the rebs on lookout mountain and within range of their guns."[17] While the Union slept, Confederates moved within the valley.

The day's events did not go unnoticed by the Confederate troops or their commanders. Colonel Edward P. Alexander understood the situation in Lookout Valley as Hooker's Eleventh and Twelfth Corps marched within his view. Using the signal station on Lookout Mountain, Alexander was able to communicate with other stations and particularly with the overall commander of the Confederate forces, General Braxton Bragg. It was also Alexander who ordered the Confederate rain of cannon fire upon the Union troops, thus recalling, "the range was too great to do them any very serious harm, but just far enough to give my gunners an excellent chance & excuse for an afternoon of target practice during which we put in a few very pretty shots, & had all the fun to ourselves, for they did not attempt to reply."[18] Bragg had no time for target practice or what Alexander would call fun. The Confederate left appeared to be collapsing right before his eyes, and the man he believed was at fault for this debacle was Lieutenant General James Longstreet. Longstreet was responsible for the eastern portion of the Confederate line, and that included the important area comprising Lookout Valley. Longstreet had recently lost Brown's Ferry to Union forces. This had happened right under his nose, and now he and Bragg watched as Hooker and his men moved through the valley and joined forces with the Army of the Cumberland at this strategic ferry. Something had to be done, and Longstreet asked permission to move upon Hooker's troops in a night attack. There was a good reason that night attacks during this nation's great struggle were rare: they usually did not turn out as well as hoped. Nevertheless, Bragg realized that if the Union army were not pushed north across the Tennessee River, the siege would most definitely end in Confederate disaster. It was a time for drastic measures.[19]

Longstreet decided on using Hood's division, now led by Brigadier General Micah Jenkins. This division included Brigadier General Evander M. Law's Alabama Brigade, Colonel John Bratton's South Carolina Brigade, Jerome Robertson's Brigade of Texans and Men of Arkansas, and Henry Benning's Georgia Brigade. Longstreet expected these troops to attack and destroy or capture Hooker's Eleventh and Twelfth Corps, believing these Union troops to have "more notoriety for their want of steadiness under fire than for anything else." This characterization of the Union troops was most likely attributable to the fact that some of them had been part of the Union army that was surprised and routed at Chancellorsville. However, that was in the past. Jenkins's assault would prove whether the Union corps had changed or were to still be found wanting.[20] The plan for the night attack, according to Longstreet, included Jenkins's assembling his three brigades and moving along the base of Lookout Mountain once it was dark. Law was also ordered to advance his brigade at nightfall and to take possession of the heights in his front, which would give him command of the road between the Union forces in the valley. Longstreet reminded Jenkins to hold the area of Law's troops with "a sufficient force, while a portion of his command moved up the road and captured or dispersed the rear guard." Jenkins was also directed that if time allowed and the situation was conducive, to move upon the main force and if possible, force the Union army across the river. However, there was a caveat. If daylight was quickly approaching, he should move the Confederate forces back across the bridge and to Lookout Mountain as quickly as possible.[21]

Later that evening, Longstreet found that Jenkins's division "was so much delayed that I fear nothing was accomplished . . ." and concluded that "it was too late to make any move against the main camp." Instead Longstreet sent word to Jenkins to "see if he could find any wagons behind, and stragglers, and return to his camp." He further added, "When I left the railroad, there seemed to be no prospect of doing anything. . . . I presume that little or nothing was accomplished."[22] Presuming, ignoring, and the lack of planning brought on by the Confederate leadership on Lookout Mountain had gotten the Confederates where they were the night of October 28, 1863. Longstreet had presumed wrong. Jenkins and his division were already on the move, and they would find more than a few loose wagons and stragglers.

Law's brigade moved forward, crossing the "lower bridge over Lookout Creek, near its mouth," taking position on a wooded hill overlooking the Brown's Ferry Road after driving off the Union pickets in the area.[23] For the next hour, Law's men would strengthen the position by adding rail and log breastworks, at least before hearing the gunfire from the Confederate left. Bratton's brigade also crossed the bridge and moved toward Wauhatchie for the planned attack. Robertson's brigade was placed in line with Law's troops. However, one regiment was placed in reserve on a road to Law's left while another guarded the bridge over Lookout Creek to the rear of Law's position as well as Law's right flank, which was unprotected for about a half mile to the Tennessee River. Commanding the Lookout Creek bridge was also of great strategic importance. This was not some shallow and easily manageable body of water. Colonel William C. Oates of the 15th Alabama Regiment knew it well from guarding that part of the Confederate line before his wounding at Brown's Ferry and described it as being "of horse-shoe shape . . . the banks, except at the crossing, were precipitous, the water deep, with difficult jungles of vine and undergrowth on each side." Benning's brigade took up the Confederate line to the left of Law's position thus controlling the Brown's Ferry Road to the south. In case Bratton found the force too large to manage at Wauhatchie, he would be able to fall back behind Benning and move across the creek bridge to safety with the other brigades following suit.[24] The plan had its good and bad points. However, too much reliance had been placed on the cover of darkness and an escape route consisting of one bridge, which was dangerously close to the main body of enemy troops. Also, the other unknown variables were the fighting spirit of Geary's Twelfth Corps and the rest of the Union forces camped back by Brown's Ferry. These variables would be realized later that evening.

It was around 4:30 P.M. when Geary's Twelfth Corps reached Wauhatchie. It had been a grueling march over rough roads. Now the corps would make camp at this juncture where the Brown's Ferry Road intersected with Kelley's Ferry Road, which made its way west toward Raccoon Mountain and the Tennessee River. Although little could be said of Confederate aggression, while moving through Lookout Valley, Geary could feel the cold stare from on top of Lookout Mountain, where "active signaling was plainly discernible to the naked eye." Wauhatchie offered a spectacular view of the mountains and valley. However, more importantly, Geary spied a knoll that commanded the area. Upon this knoll he stationed Knapp's Battery, or at least the four guns that had accompanied the march from Bridgeport. At the bottom of this knoll to the north sat the simple log structure of an area farmer and local magistrate by the name of Rowden. Just east of the knoll and Rowden's cabin lay the route to Chattanooga. Paralleling this road and just east of it also ran what was known as the Nashville and Chattanooga Railroad. This railroad had about a three foot embankment that could prove useful in battle or fatal depending on who controlled it. Still north of Rowden's homestead, "was a recently harvested cornfield of approximately 1,000 feet square, still studded with the remnants of cornstalks and referred to by a number of Geary's men as the stubble cornfield." Just north of this field, was a branch of Lookout Creek. To the west of the knoll in the distance, mud could be expected due to the swampy nature of the terrain and the recent heavy rains in the area. Woods comprised the majority of the area from the southern part of the knoll as well as the south end of the stubble cornfield.[25]

Geary ordered his men to "bivouac upon their arms, with cartridge boxes on, and placed my guns on a knob about 30 yards to the left of the railroad and immediately to the left of Rowden's house, so that they could command either of the cardinal points."[26] Geary further ordered that his commanding officers have their men ready for battle in case any alarm was sounded. Not only were the Confederates watching, but Hooker had made a costly mistake. While gathering the Eleventh Corps together closely around Brown's Ferry, Geary and Wauhatchie were a good three miles south of Hooker's and Howard's position. Although pickets had been posted from both camps and were covering all the approaches, Hooker later admitted that "no attempt was made to establish and preserve a communication between them." Geary had every reason to be cautious. Hooker dismissed the situation by admitting that substantial communications were difficult due to the smallness of the commands and the large distance between the two camps. Besides, Hooker wanted to make sure that he retained control of both avenues to Kelley's Ferry before the Confederate forces moved upon it. He had also sent a regiment toward the Lookout Creek bridge only to have around midnight "a little skirmishing with the enemy." The situation was about to change. Meanwhile at Wauhatchie, Geary had expected that if an attack did fall upon his men, it would most likely come from the south. There was no serious concern about

the northern area of Wauhatchie, according to Geary, for the Eleventh Corps
had marched in and through that location, giving reasonable assurance that
the enemy was not in possession of this vicinity. Relying on this logic, Geary
later wrote, "I had not anticipated an attack from the direction it came,
although I had provided for all contingencies." With evening preparations
made, the 29th Pennsylvania was placed as the grand guard for the evening
and, finally, the corps settled in under a moonlit night.[27]

Before midnight or shortly thereafter, Geary's camp received its first
wake-up call. Picket-firing could be heard from the area east of the railroad
and north of Geary's camp. The Twelfth Corps moved into action with the
111th Pennsylvania taking a position along the Kelley's Ferry Road in order
to control the railroad and all approaches from the left and right. An hour
after the firing ceased, Geary allowed the men to return to their quarters
for sleep but reminded them to keep vigilant and, if called back into action,
to take the same ground. Soon after midnight the alarm was sounded again
as the Union pickets struggled to hold back the oncoming Confederates.[28]

Now Geary could tell the direction of the blow by the sounds of the
picket fire. As Geary and his men strained to see the oncoming tide of men,
he recalled, "the moon was fitful and did not afford light sufficient to see a
body of men only 100 yards distant, and during the fight their whereabouts
was mostly revealed by the flashes of the fire-arms."[29] Now, with no question
of there being an attack, Geary formed his lines for battle. The 137th New
York moved to around fifty yards west of the Kelley's Ferry Road, forming
the left of Geary's line. To the right of these New Yorkers was the 109th
Pennsylvania. To this regiment's right was the 111th Pennsylvania but facing toward the railroad with their left flank to the north. As the fighting
increased, the enemy fire caught the 111th Pennsylvania regiment on this
left flank. Lieutenant Colonel Thomas M. Walker of the 111th acted quickly:
"I immediately changed front to the rear on the first company, facing nearly
north, the right resting near the railroad and the line running nearly parallel with the road to Kelley's Ferry." All moved as best as could be expected
through the darkness. The movement was handled quickly and successfully
connected the regiment's left flank with the 109th. These two regiments were
also able to throw together what few fence posts they could find for protection. The southerners continued to move forward also maneuvering around
to the left and right. Now Geary's line was perpendicular to the railroad with
the right of the 111th angling back its right flank to face the railroad.[30] For
Private James T. Miller, "the greybacks came on quite thick and the battle
began in earnest and raged along the whole line . . . the rebles were from
5[ooo]to 8000 and we had about 1000 and four pieces of cannon." While the

Confederates did not have the numbers in this attack that Miller believed they had, his confusion can be attributed to the darkness, which could also give the attacking army a psychological edge.[31]

The Confederates were on the move. Jenkins's brigade, also referred to as the Palmetto Brigade and led by Colonel John Bratton, had crossed Lookout Creek and moved south near the creek with the Palmetto Sharpshooters, 2nd South Carolina Rifles, 1st South Carolina, and the 5th South Carolina Regiment. The 6th South Carolina was in the advance with pickets thrown out along the front, including the Brown's Ferry Road. Hampton's Legion followed to the rear of Bratton's force and was held in reserve.[32] Private Frank M. Mixson of the 1st South Carolina recalled the movement toward Geary's line: "We commenced the advance through these woods—underbrush, hills, hollows and holes—and kept as quiet as we could." Upon reaching the Eleventh Corps, Mixson found, like Miller of the 111th Pennsylvania, that the darkness cloaked the reality of the situation: "We had struck them but a few moments when they were ready to receive us, and lo and behold, we were in front of Hooker's army corps—one of the best corps of fighters in the entire Yankee army." Numbers were deceiving. Geary's Eleventh Corps numbered only around 1,500 men at the time.[33]

By the time the South Carolinians crossed the branch just north of Geary's position, the Eleventh Corps could be seen "hurrying hither and thither" and extinguishing their campfires. Bratton's men had crossed the "Rubicon" and immediately pushed forward en echelon: the 2nd South Carolina Rifles to the front of the Confederate left; the 1st South Carolina on their right flank, advancing with the 5th South Carolina on *their* right flank. The Palmetto Sharpshooters advanced upon the railroad, hoping this would be Geary's flank. As the 2nd South Carolina Rifles, 1st South Carolina, and 5th South Carolina Regiments moved to and through the stubble cornfield, the Union line erupted in a blaze of rifle fire lighting up the night and clearly delineating Geary's line.[34] Lieutenant Albert R. Greene of the 78th New York listened: "We could distinctly hear the tramp of men at the double quick across the open field in front of us. It was so dark that they could not be seen, but they seemed to know our position perfectly." It was at this point, according to Greene, that "We distinctly heard the command to those men, 'By the left flank!' But before the command of execution was uttered, on our lines, 'Battery! Fire!' and the flash of the four guns lighted up our whole front, showing for an instant the line coming toward us. Then in the darkness the flash of the rebel muskets marked their line and the bullets began to come." The 2nd South Carolina Rifles took the brunt of this deadly fire, staggering the men at first and then causing those left in the ranks to fall back.[35]

As the firing continued thick and fast, Colonel A. Coward of the 5th South Carolina commanded his men to lie down. Coward recalled the order was too late for one soldier: "A man at my side . . . Smith from Yorkville, was in the act of obeying the order, when I heard a thud and a sob. I put my hand on his shoulder and said: 'Smith, were you hit?' 'In the neck, Colonel, and it's gone plumb through me.' I knelt beside him and took his hand as he gaspingly said: 'Colonel, if you ever get back home, tell my old mammy I died doing my duty for South Carolina.' These last words came between the ejections of gulps of blood from his mouth." Smith would die and be left on the battlefield.[36]

The path of the 1st South Carolina was hazardous as well, recalled Lieutenant L. J. Perry: "Here we met face to face, seventy-five yards apart, the blazing line of the enemy. We could see before us a long line of people, a great, dark multitude, standing as firm as the stately oaks behind them. The battle raged furiously. It looked as if all the artillery of the heavens were pounding us with bullets of iron."[37] The 1st South Carolina made it into the stubble cornfield but the firing continued thick and fast causing the regiment to lie upon the dirt as the fighting continued.[38] One South Carolinian recalled, "After being here under one of the heaviest firing I ever saw for perhaps an hour, men being killed and wounded every second, I was lying down alongside Col. [F. Whitner] Kilpatrick, who was on his knees making observations—a minnie ball struck the colonel, killing him instantly, passing through his heart."[39]

The 5th South Carolina continued its forward progress moving toward Geary's line at a southwest angle on its way to flanking the 137th New York. Coming on the heels of this Union regiment was the 149th New York to continue the left flank. It would have been in a good position to meet the oncoming 5th South Carolina if it had not been for the Union army's own mules and horses. As the left of the Union line continued west, it also encompassed the corps' wagon train and teams. Also, roughly twenty Union horsemen, including generals and their staff, were upon this increasing line to the west when the Confederate volley, coupled with a Union response and the confusion of darkness caused these horses to scatter and break toward the rear of the line. In doing so, two or three ambulances and wagon teams belonging to Union headquarters joined in on the confusion and headed straight through the 149th New York, "in a dozen different places." According to Lieutenant Colonel Charles B. Randall of the 149th, "The regiment was thus entirely broken to pieces and disorganized, with no company formations whatever, and all exposed to a terrific fire." Acting quickly, Randall began re-forming his lines and was soon after ordered to have the regiment "by the side of the wagon road, perpendicular to the line of battle, to guard against an attack upon our right flank."[40]

In the meantime, the 5th South Carolina Regiment was jubilant. The Union wagons were close and in their sights as they rushed in from the far left flank of the Union line. One soldier recalled, "We raised the 'rebel yell' and charged forward in the face of a galling fire, passed the wagon train, which was parked in an open field and moved forward, without halting, for three hundred yards." Getting the wagons and supplies were part of the overall plan but keeping them proved to be harder than they thought. Bratton would later mention that although they had taken the wagons, they were unable to keep possession. This was due to the quick thinking of Lieutenant Colonel Samuel M. Zulich of the 29th Pennsylvania. Although the Union left had been turned and the wagons captured, Zulich would not give them up without a fight. According to Colonel William Rickards Jr. of the 29th Pennsylvania Infantry, Zulich, "having collected and organized a number of loose men, drove off the enemy and brought it [the wagons and supplies] safely to the rear."[41]

It was also during these early moments on the far left flank in front of the Union line that Brigadier General George Greene of the Third Brigade, Second Division, was urging the men and some stragglers to stand firm until the moment he received a ghastly wound. The general "was struck in the face by a rifle ball, which entered at the lower left corner of his nose and passed diagonally across his mouth, badly breaking his upper jaw and tearing out through his right cheek." With the great loss of blood and the loss of his voice, Greene could do nothing but move to the rear and to the hospital. Command of the brigade thus fell upon Colonel David Ireland.[42]

Although deadly, the flashes of fire from both rivals did not escape the notice of Confederate General Bratton, "the sparkling fire making a splendid pyrotechnic display."[43] Surely, the flow of the battle was not meeting the expectations of Micah Jenkins. Every minute lost trying to break the federal line meant less time collecting the spoils of war and getting back across Lookout Creek safely. It would only be a matter of time before Union troops at Brown's Ferry would be mobilizing and marching to Geary's aid. Although the rest of the division was in position, he must have wondered how long Law would be able to hold back a Union onslaught. The battle continued. Seeing the broken ranks of the 2nd South Carolina Rifles, Bratton threw in his reserve, the 6th South Carolina, in place of the 2nd South Carolina Rifles' decimated ranks and sent Hampton's Legion into the battle on the right flank of the 5th South Carolina.[44]

As the South Carolinians continued across the field, Geary cautioned his blue line to make every shot count and to fire low—a demanding order to carry out during a night battle. Geary later recalled that this first action began at 12:30 A.M.[45] The guns of the 137th New York and the 109th and 111th Pennsylvania roared and produced a sheet of fire and lead that decimated the attacking forces and lit up the night, causing the 2nd South Carolina Rifles to stop dead in their tracks. As the two sides slugged it out, the 1st Pennsylvania Light Artillery, Knapp's Battery of four Parrott guns command by Captain Charles A. Atwell continued to join in on the destruction. Atwell directed the four cannon on the knoll back and to the left of the Rowden residence. Later on in the fight, Lieutenant Edward R. Geary, the son of Brigadier General John W. Geary, and one of these guns would move to the rear and right of the residence. Colonel Rickards of the 29th Pennsylvania Infantry had sent most of his companies on picket duty before the fight ensued and was left with Companies C and G who had retreated from the Brown's Ferry Road back to the Union line as the Confederates pressed forward. Now they were posted to support Atwell's guns and would later move to the right along the railroad embankment when needed.[46]

There were no safe positions for man or cannon this night. Grape or canister shot would have been ideal against the wave of Confederate guns but the battery was comprised of four Parrott guns and could only fire spherical case. Realizing this, the fuses were cut close allowing them to burst early for a close killing, and that they did, but at great sacrifice to the Union army. Of the Union troops, mostly of the 111th Pennsylvania, many were accidently hit by these shells, "Lieutenant Marvin D. Petit . . . struck in the head by a shell . . . Pvt. John M. Barr . . . a mortal wound when his left thigh was shattered . . . Lt. Albert E. Black . . . vicious wound to both legs . . . Pvt. George H. Moore . . . killed instantly by one of the shell bursts and Myron E. Smith has a severe wound on the right arm." "Some of the shells exploded in our midst" recalled First Lieutenant John Richards Boyle, of the 111th Pennsylvania. "One of these took off the head of the intrepid Lieutenant Pettit, of Company B, and another tore the muscles from both legs of Lieutenant Black . . . inflicting ghastly wounds . . . which maimed him for life." Knapp's Battery made some quick adjustments, and soon the Confederates began to feel the Union's wrath.[47] A private in the 29th Pennsylvania saw the harrowing effects, "a few shells exploded over the 111th killing and wounding several. The rebs suffered terribly, some of them being almost cut in half where the shells had gone through them."[48]

The battle continued to gain momentum. The 2nd South Carolina Rifles moved along the Confederate left toward the railroad.[49] At this point, Bratton's Confederates were overlapping Geary's line. To the Confederate far left were the Palmetto Sharpshooters, with the 2nd South Carolina Rifles to their right, the 6th South Carolina to their right followed by the 1st South

Carolina who covered the front of the line. To the 1st South Carolina's right was the 5th South Carolina and finally the Hampton Legion anchored the far Confederate right with its left to the 5th South Carolina.[50]

Hampton's Legion had been lying in the road behind the line of battle being before ordered to move out. One of the members of the Hampton Legion remembered, "Yankees began shelling and musket were being shot. I believe if my hat had been iron I could have caught it full of bullets. Col. Gary ordered us to fall in, but all men refused to obey on account of danger, and he finally ordered us to crawl out on all fours to the woods where we formed."[51] Once the Hampton Legion had entered the woods all entered a gully and soon after orders were given to move forward. However, "Everyone was afraid so each one told the other to move forward. I became disgusted with the cowardice shown by our men, so two other men and myself were the first to leave the gully." The Hampton Legion made its way around the 5th South Carolina and made its attack on the Union left. The Hampton Legion was finally on the move and found themselves, like the 5th South Carolina before them, in the area of the wagon park.[52] However, the 139th New York was as ready as they could make themselves under the harsh circumstances. Companies B and G turned back at right angles as the Hampton Legion marched by the left flank hitting these Carolinians with a sheet of fire, again blazing through the darkness of night. This helped to bring on confusion in the southern ranks causing the men to fall back. Geary's left had held, barely. Now, the fighting once again moved back to the right of the Union line.[53]

While the firing continued along the left, front, and right of the battlefield, Confederate movements began to favor the Union right and center. Since the Union right was only refused by a couple of companies of the 111th Pennsylvania, it left much of the Union right open on its right flank. It also left Lieutenant Geary, his men, and the lone cannon under his guidance open to enemy fire. "We accordingly advanced beyond the skirt of woods we were in, out into open field," recalled a lieutenant of the Palmetto Sharpshooters, "and there halted in front of a battery which was belching forth its iron hail of destruction into the regiments on our right. Here the Colonel commanded us to concentrate our fire on it; and with some murderous volley the sheet of flame and smoke was no longer to be seen gushing forth."[54]

Over on the Union line, Private David Monat of the 29th Pennsylvania could see the southerners moving out in the field before him, "I heard their commander give the order 'Halt! Front, ready, fire!' and then they dashed down to the Rail road bank and halted. If they had come on it would have been all up with us as we had no troops on our side of the track, only the 1 gun of the battery." This was the gun commanded by Lieutenant Geary.[55]

Confederate forces concentrated on the four Union guns, especially since every cannon blast they produced lit up the knoll and the Union position. This gave a tell-all glimpse of where Southern guns should aim and of the crowded conditions of the Union line at that point. Lieutenant Geary and his men understood the peril before them, and along with the other three cannons, continued to blast away at whatever moved in the darkness before them. The hail of southern lead was too much for many on the knoll as the men began to fall fast around the battery. Thirty-five out of forty-eight horses of the artillery also fell among the dead and dying soldiers as the battle whirled around them. Shouts from the South Carolinians could be heard crying out, "Pick off the artillerist!" Captain C. A. Atwell commanding the section of three artillery guns fell with mortal wounds to the hip and spine. Lieutenant Geary and his men continued to fire away at the oncoming Carolinians. Finally, as young Geary finished sighting a shot and thundered the command "Fire!" a Confederate bullet struck him in the forehead killing him instantly.[56]

The onslaught of lead was so destructive around the cannons at this time that only two guns could be manned after the attack subsided. Still, the Union line held. Captain Moses Veale of the 109th Pennsylvania fought near one of the guns of the battery during the battle. While commanding his men, he was hit four times with one of these bullets smashing into his right shoulder. He continued with the regiment until the end of the battle and later received the Medal of Honor for his service that day.[57] Two hundred twenty-four spherical shells had been fired from the four guns by the time the battle waned. However, Major John A. Reynolds lamented, "With regard to the effectiveness of the fire of the battery, the same defect that usually occurs with the paper fuses was very apparent on this occasion, not more than one in four of the projectiles exploding."[58]

Rickards of the 29th Pennsylvania moved what troops he had over toward the railroad embankment to help stop the Confederates from pushing through. Around this time, the 149th New York reorganized after the stampede near the wagon trains and moved to fill the gap near the railroad. This regiment held its left flank with the 111th Pennsylvania's refused right facing the railroad.[59] The 2nd South Carolina Rifles and the Palmetto Sharpshooters continued their movement respectively along the Union right and across the railroad. The firing continued to erupt all along the Union line. Geary's left flank still consisted of the 137th New York with Companies B and G anchoring the far left flank in a refused position. On the right of this regiment was the 109th Pennsylvania. This regiment's right flank was covered by the 111th Pennsylvania while part of this regiment's right flank was in a refused position across the wagon road facing east. At this point the line continued toward the east with the refused right flank of the 111th Pennsylvania near the 149th New York. Upon and around the knoll were placed the four cannon, again with one piece having been recently handled by Lieutenant Geary behind the Rowden dwelling and firing toward the northeast. Companies C and G of the 29th Pennsylvania, which had supported the four-gun battery, were now along the line facing the railroad embankment. Interestingly, the 78th New York took a position facing along the embankment of the railroad in a position to cover the far right flank of the line with the regiment's left near the 149th New York. However, the 78th New York was still being held in reserve.[60]

The Union men had procured sixty rounds of ammunition per person before the battle began. Around 3:00 A.M., the supply of ammunition had become critical, forcing some to scavenge what they could from the hospital, the wounded, and even cutting the cartridge boxes from the dead. One veteran of Pennsylvania recalled later, "officer after officer fell in the line, men were mangled and killed—some of them by our own cannon—mules broke from their tethers in the rear, and, with clanking chains, plunged madly about. Ammunition was nearly exhausted and recourse was about to be had to the bayonet and the spike." It was true: In the end, General Geary was ready to hold the line at the point of the bayonet if needed until relief arrived.[61] They would need every cartridge they could find, for more Confederate soldiers were moving to the Union right. If this Confederate attack should come to fruition, it just might become one of the strongest assaults of the battle.[62]

The South Carolina brigade continued its pounding of the Union line from the front, left, and right. The situation became grave for Geary's right flank when troops of the 2nd South Carolina Rifles and the Palmetto Sharpshooters made their way deep along the right and gained possession of the opposite side of the railroad embankment. The severe fighting was at close range as the 149th New York and 29th Pennsylvania stubbornly held their ground. The fighters of the Confederacy were dug in close, and the Union fire failed to dislodge them until Rickards took a great risk.[63] Thinking quickly, he ordered one of the cannons moved outside of the railroad embankment, to the other side, at a point approximately 150 yards south of the line. At this distance, the cannon could command an enfilading fire on the Southerners along the embankment and sweep them back toward the woods to the north. Major John A. Reynolds of the 1st New York Light Artillery, being the chief of artillery, refused on the grounds that the Confederates would take the gun. Besides, he remonstrated, there were no horses to pull the gun. Rickards acted quickly, taking the responsibility for the decision and his actions. He volunteered men from the 29th Pennsylvania for the task, and soon the gun once used by Lieutenant Geary was pulled over to the other side of the railroad by Companies C and G. Rickards recalled, "After two or three shots we got the range, and swept the enemy from the bank. This seemed to have a depressing effect upon the enemy, for their fire now ceased, and we remained masters of our position."[64]

Bratton's Confederates had been fighting for well over two hours. The sounds of battle filled the air while sheets of flame from rifles and cannons lit the battlefield to reveal the destruction and horrors of war. Men were cut down, while others were cut in half. The Union soldiers struggled to keep their battered line together while the Confederates attempted to complete that one final effort that would break the fragile Union line. This elusive victory, however, was taking an unexpected toll on the South Carolinians. That final thrust was soon to come from Bratton and his men. He confidently believed, "The position of things at this time was entirely favorable to a grand charge. . . . [T]he enemy, with his left driven, crowded and huddled upon his center, occupied the base. His line of fire at this time certainly was not more than 300 or 400 yards in length, and but from 50 to 150 yards in breadth." Bratton added, "the sparkling fire making a splendid pyrotechnic display and encouraging the hope that the balls intended for us were lodging on themselves."[65] As Bratton contemplated the grand assault and what could possibly have been the final stroke for victory, orders arrived for him from Jenkins to withdraw and move his men in good order back across Lookout Creek. Time had run out for the South Carolinians, for within these orders was the ominous warning that "the enemy were pressing in the rear." Bratton confirmed the information and began to extricate his brigade from the battle. However, his final act would be to send the 6th South Carolina to a position behind the railroad where it was ordered to fire into the mass of Union soldiers. This was probably done to insure that his troops were able to safely disengage from the enemy, or it could have been out of frustration, or perhaps it was a little of both. With this last act completed, the South Carolina brigade disengaged and made its way to and across Lookout Creek. The Confederate plan at Wauhatchie had failed. Bratton would write correctly, "Our loss, I regret to say, is most serious."[66]

For Geary and his men, the battle was finally over. Around 3:00 A.M., stillness fell across the battlefield and not a moment too soon. It was said that within the 137th New York, not two hundred cartridges could be found in the regiment. Lieutenant Colonel H. Hammerstein and his 78th New York had been held in reserve throughout the battle. Although his men never fired a shot, the regiment had two men wounded. The 78th New York now moved through the darkness and took its place, single file, along the Union line. As they moved out, others continued their search for ammunition among the dead. Skirmishers were also ordered out while all other able-bodied men dug entrenchments. All were busy with the tasks at hand until a noise was heard again from the north. Geary's battle-scarred men readied themselves for the worst.[67]

It was after midnight when, throughout Hooker's camp, the rattle of musketry and the roar of cannons could be heard coming from the south. Howard, hearing the sounds resonating throughout Lookout Valley, quickly alerted his men of the Eleventh Corps. He would recall later, "Everybody who was fully awake said at once: 'Our men at Wauhatchie are attacked.'"[68] Hooker sent a desperate message to Howard to rush his nearest division double quick to Geary's aid in order to prevent what might be developing into a disaster. Howard had already called for his two division commanders, Schurz and Steinwehr when Hooker's message overtook him exclaiming, "Hurry or you cannot save Geary. He has been attacked!" Schurz's men were the first to be ready and on the move.[69] Hooker had every reason to be frantic, having left Geary and his men three miles south of the rest of the army and an easy target for Confederate attack. Now, with the sounds of battle and the grave possibility of losing Geary and his division, Hooker needed to right his mistake as rapidly as possible.

In the confusion, it seemed Hooker could not get out of his own way. Not only did he send orders to Howard to move quickly to Geary's aid, he also sent orders to one of Howard's division commanders, Schurz, to also move quickly. Conflicting orders of Hooker's staff also went to Schurz's Second Brigade under Colonel Wladimir Krzyzanowski early during the commotion in camp. This order required the colonel and his brigade to escort Confederate prisoners to Chattanooga. Apparently Hooker forgot or did not realize that Krzyzanowski's Second Brigade was part of Schurz's division. Although these orders were countermanded soon after, it still muddied the effort to provide quick relief to Geary's troops.[70] While order was being restored to Schurz's division, Steinwehr's small division, of two brigades moved past Schurz and down the road toward the sounds of fighting at Wauhatchie. Howard's Eleventh Corps was finally moving through the darkness toward Geary's beleaguered position. The route to Geary's command was not easy. The three miles between the two camps was interspersed with open and heavily wooded terrain. For a while, the full moon helped many a soldier moving along the path. However, as the scattered clouds obscured the moonlight, the woods and thickets were transformed into utter darkness. The road and the territory around it were muddy and marshy, which only hampered the soldiers hurrying to their comrades still further south.[71] The greater problem, however, was what could not be seen lurking in the shadows and hills just east of the road.

In the gap of a mile and a half or so between the Union pickets of the Eleventh Corps and those belonging to Geary's Twelfth Corps were the hills left unoccupied by Union forces. It was among these hills that Law's Confederate troops readied themselves for any Union reinforcements that might head down the Brown's Ferry Road. The 73rd Ohio was the first to move down this road leading Steinwehr's division when Law's Alabamians fired from the dark hillside into the unsuspecting division. Watching the situation develop, Hooker now ordered Steinwehr to attack and capture the hill.[72] The objective of relieving the Union troops at Wauhatchie had now changed. Not only was the struggle raging to the south but the sporadic gunfire from the hills to the northeast toward Lookout Mountain continued to become more serious and deadly. Hooker could no longer focus all of his attention on the battle to the south. Instead, he needed to contemplate the true intentions of the Confederates. The question was whether Wauhatchie was a diversion for the real prize of taking Brown's Ferry and forcing the Union army back across the Tennessee River. With the situation developing rapidly, Hooker decided to remain within the vicinity of Smith's and Tyndale's Hills, mainly Smith's Hill. As Schurz's division broke into brigades and moved toward the hills, Howard requested and received clearance from Hooker to continue on toward Wauhatchie along with two companies of cavalry. Hooker agreed, stating, "I shall be here to attend to this part of the field." With this, Howard began his move south.[73]

Bullets continued to fly from the hill nearest Hooker. The assignment to take this hill fell upon Colonel Orland Smith commanding the Second Brigade. Smith advanced his men on the left of the road, to the foot of the hills, and placed the 73rd Ohio to the right facing the hill with its left flank to meet with the 33rd Massachusetts. Skirmishers of the 73rd Ohio under Captain Luther M. Buchwalter, moved into position and readied themselves for the task at hand. The Ohioans moved as quickly as possible under the circumstances. There were precarious obstacles to overcome such as the difficult undulations of the land, the steep slope of the hill, fallen timber throughout the wooded hillside, and dense underbrush. The men advanced a few hundred yards when Law's skirmishers made themselves known with a fire from the hill tops. Now the Union battalion was ordered to wheel to the left and charge the hill with the assurance that the 33rd Massachusetts would be on their left flank. This time during the redeployment of his skirmishers, Buchwalter fell mortally wounded when the Confederates let loose a fire from the right of his line.[74] Even on a moonlit night, the shadows of the forest made a perfect cover of darkness for the Confederate defenders and kept the Union soldiers stumbling around, blindly looking for the enemy and for the 33rd Massachusetts.

The 33rd Massachusetts would also be looking for the 73rd Ohio, but for the time being, it was at the base of the hill advancing forward. The New Englanders' line extended from the road, moving gradually up the hill to the left until its skirmishers were almost at the crest on the far left. The men of Massachusetts also had difficulties with the terrain. Lieutenant Colonel Godfrey Ryder Jr. recalled reaching "a crooked ravine some 20 feet deep running parallel with the hill-side, the sides of which were almost perpendicular, slippery with leaves and clay, and covered with brush, and its appearance rendered still more formidable by the deceptive moonlight. . . . the regiment gallantly plunged into it ––the dead and living rolling down together—[we] climbed the opposite side, and halted in some disorder."[75] The Confederates lit up the hillside with a deadly fire running the length of their line tearing through the New Englanders front, flank, and rear. Many were killed or wounded from this exchange. Still, the New Englanders were not sure of their enemy's exact position or the position of the Ohioans for that matter. Thus many believed they might have been fired into by their comrades, so the 33rd Massachusetts fell back to the road. This time it moved forward with the bayonet.[76]

The 73rd Ohio was still receiving intermittent fire from the hilltop. After a short rest, the Ohioans charged forward with a cheer. Confederate skirmishers were driven before them. Onward they climbed moving closer to the enemy lines, which finally revealed formidable breastworks along the crest of the hill. Suddenly, the hillside erupted in continuous Confederate gunfire. Men in blue fell rapidly, including William Fletcher Hughey. Hughey later recalled, "I was struck in the face, as I thought by a cannonball, and for a moment thought my whole head was shot away, but my presence of mind did not desert me. . . . I found that my jaw was broken and my mouth cut about 4 inches longer than its usual length. . . . I felt a sharp pain run through my right wrist and hand . . . [which] had also been pierced by a minni ball. . . . I also had a slight wound in my left shoulder." Hughey would find his way back down the hill only to faint from the loss of blood. He would live to fight another day, but many would breathe their last breath on the side of what would soon come to be known as Smith's Hill, named after Colonel Orland Smith for the attack he led up this hill, which would also be the position he and his troops would occupy after the battle.[77] The Ohioans continued forward and were near the top of the hill when suddenly they were hit by gunfire coming from their right flank that enfiladed their line. From the left also came cries of, "Don't fire upon your own men." Still it was not ascertained just where the 33rd Massachusetts was on the right flank—if there at all. Due to these problems, Major Samuel H. Hurst had his men fall back a short distance until he felt certain at least one flank was protected.[78]

While these Union regiments continued to regroup, the 136th New York was ordered to move to the far left of the line and to the left flank of the 33rd Massachusetts. The New Yorkers withheld their fire so that they could not be found and moved forward with the bayonet. This seemed to work, for one New Yorker later wrote, "the rebels thus failed to get a range upon the men, and their bullets harmed only the trees and branches above the heads of the steadily advancing line."[79] The men pushed forward against the constant fire from the front and finally took the hill, only firing upon the Confederates one volley as they retreated down the other side and toward Lookout Creek. Around this same time, the New Englanders also fixed bayonets, held their fire, and moved once again up the towering hill. This time they made it to within a few yards of the breastworks, received fire but, "with a cheer, it turned by the right flank, gained the crest, crossed the rifle-pits, and charged upon the enemy's flank with the bayonet, at the same time pouring a volley into his retreating ranks." The 33rd had control of the hill, posted pickets, and readied itself for any Confederate counterattack that might come their way. The 73rd Ohio was preparing to advance upon the hill once again when news of the New Englanders' success reached them. Now they moved forward with alacrity. This time they took the hill and watched as Law's troops beat a hasty retreat.[80]

The ease with which some of the Union soldiers broke the Confederate line was partly due to their tenacity and also, according to Confederate General E. McIver Law, due to a vacant area of space, "caused by detaching a company for service as vedettes between my right and the river." Although Law believed the line had been reestablished, he also found that the noise of battle toward and around Wauhatchie had subsided. Law soon after received a message from Jenkins stating that the troops around Wauhatchie were withdrawing and to hold the line until the troops to the south had retired. Soon after receiving this information, Law received word from General Jerome Robertson, who reported "a strong force of the enemy was moving over the adjoining hill on our right," which was toward the Confederate rear and Lookout Creek. The only escape route for the Confederate army that morning. Although no federal troops moved further than the crest of the hills, it was enough to alarm Law as to what could be, and later of what could have been but never came to Union fruition.[81]

To Law's left, the federals were moving forward against Benning's Georgia Brigade. Brigadier General Hector Tyndale led the First Brigade of the Eleventh Corps past Smith's Hill on his way to relieve Geary's men at Wauhatchie. Suddenly, his troops were hit with gunfire from the hillside on the left of the road and just south of Smith's Hill. Tyndale recalled the fighting started about the same time as that on Smith's Hill. Like Smith's brigade, Tyndale filed his men off the road and faced the hill, which later became known as Tyndale's Hill. Now the 61st and 82nd Ohio Regiments pushed forward into the darkness over the steep, rugged hillside making it to the top and driving the Confederates before them. The Confederates would make a final stand on the crest of the hill but Tyndale's Ohioans forced the Southerners down the hill's back slope. Tyndale would later realize the lost opportunity in not cutting the Confederates off: "The enemy fell back through the dark woods, as their line of retreat was imperiled, and, had we known the country and our position, it was possible that it would have been lost to them." Fighting along Tyndale's Hill ended before that on Smith's Hill.[82]

According to Law, before the second attack on Smith's Hill but during the attack on Tyndale's Hill, he received a message from one of Jenkins's staff, Captain John W. Jamison, that Bratton had met with a large Union force and that Jenkins decided to withdraw from the fighting at Wauhatchie. He also added that it was Law's duty to make sure to hold his position until Bratton's men had withdrawn. Just before receiving this information, Law had sent a message to Jenkins explaining that his forces were being attacked and that it was quite possible for the Union army to turn Law's right flank thus putting Bratton's forces in peril. Soon after, Law received word that Bratton's troops were near the Lookout Creek crossing. At this point, the second assault upon Smith's Hill took place, but as the firing ceased, "I gave orders for the whole line to retire to the hill on which it had first formed; thence into the hollow behind it, and thence by flanking to the left into the road and across the bridge." Law believed the Confederate force's "movement was executed in a quiet and leisurely manner, the enemy in front making no effort to follow." However, this was not completely true. One soldier of the 4th Texas admitted, "There, the regiment not only showed its back, but stampeded like a herd of frightened cattle, it being one of those cases when 'discretion is the better part of valor'; and, instead of being ashamed of the performance, we are merry over it."[83] Whether the Federal troops ran the Confederates off the hills or the Southerners retreated in good order, the fact remained: the Confederate army lost the fight for Lookout Valley that moonlit night in October.

Meanwhile, back at Wauhatchie, the men steadied themselves for what they heard coming down the road from the north. Soon they found that it was two companies of cavalry with General Howard. Geary recalled that it was around 3:30 A.M. when the battle came to an end. The sounds of musket fire faded into the night and the wounded of both sides could be heard. Later, as the sun rose, the dead of both armies were revealed along with the intensity of the night's battle. The Union line held but at a great price. Howard first came upon Greene, who was frightfully wounded but not mortally. Soon after, Howard appeared to Geary. Remembering the somber moment, Howard recalled that Geary "was astonished to see me suddenly appear at his side in the smoke of battle, and I was surprised to find that as he grasped my hand he trembled with emotion. Without a word he pointed down and I saw that Geary's son lay dead at his feet, killed by his father's side while commanding his battery in this action." Many soldiers this night gave all and many fathers, mothers, brothers, and sisters felt the cruel realities of sacrifice and war. For Geary, and many others, it would be a wound felt well beyond the war. Geary would live on, but looking back he realized, "I have gained a great victory and there is none to share the laurels with me. But oh! How dear it has cost me. My dear beloved boy is the sacrifice [and] could I but recall him to life, the bubble of military fame might be absorbed by those who wish it."[84]

Near sunrise, Colonel Friedrich Hecker's brigade of Schurz's division reported to General Geary at Wauhatchie. After a most strenuous evening, the beleaguered Twelfth Corps finally received relief.[85] The sacrifice was great for both armies. In the end, Geary's men at Wauhatchie suffered 216 total casualties while Bratton's South Carolina Brigade suffered 356 total casualties.[86] Law's casualties in the defense of Smith's Hill and Tyndale's Hill were far less than that of the South Carolina Brigade with around 43 in total casualties not including the low casualty figure of 9 from Robertson's brigade. Law would later admit that the total casualties were "slight." This total would be held against Law later by Longstreet and Jenkins in their attempts to try to prove Law's lack of aggressiveness in that sector during the battle. Furthermore, they believed the battle was lost because Law retreated early, thus causing Bratton's men to be recalled before a final assault could be made. However, in the fight for Smith's Hill, the 33rd Massachusetts incurred 86 total casualties, or one-third of the number taken into the engagement while Hurst of the 73rd Ohio reported that "One-half of my line officers and one-third of my men were either killed or wounded in this brief but desperate struggle." Together the two regiments were believed to have had about 500 soldiers, with the Ohio casualties being 65 men out of less than 200 men in the regiment.[87]

The Battle of Wauhatchie and its environs could also be considered the Battle of Lookout Valley, for this was truly what was at stake for both sides of the conflict. Jenkins had about 5,000 effective soldiers at his command but only released about 1,500 into the fight at Wauhatchie. Jenkins's nemesis, Geary, also brought to battle remnants of the Twelfth Corps numbering around 1,500 troops. Geary also had the advantage of a section of four guns and a defensive position that included high ground. Although the Confederate leadership believed the night attack would give them the element of surprise, this was all but erased since Geary's men had been alarmed before the attack and were prepared for a possible Confederate advance. Also to be considered was the fact that Geary had held the 78th New York in reserve until the end of the fighting. Bratton's South Carolinians may have had a final charge left in them but Geary had the 78th New York to position at any critical section that might need held. Had the final attack come to fruition and the Confederates taken possession of the field, it is highly doubtful that many, if any, Union prisoners, could have been successfully marched north so near the Union line, crossed the creek, and entered Confederate lines without some form of Union aggression from Hooker's men stopping them. Nor is likely that much war material could have been retained. Time was of the essence and too much was lost trying to overwhelm Geary's men. This was especially true since the sounds of battle had alarmed Hooker's army and that soon after, fighting could be heard coming from the hills to the north. The plan for capturing the Union supply at Wauhatchie had its difficulties. Had these wagons and supplies been captured, it would have been extremely difficult and time consuming to gather them together, drive them north dangerously close to the main Union camp, and cross at the only bridge over Lookout Creek. Also, had Jenkins tried to physically control the junction at Wauhatchie, his whole division would more than likely have been captured, especially with daylight breaking. Besides, there were no Confederate reinforcements moving to their aid nor were they expected to, but what could be expected was a Union onslaught advancing from Brown's Ferry.

While controversy swirled around as to which Confederate officer caused the retreat of Bratton's South Carolinians, Jenkins or Law, the Union leadership also looked for scapegoats. Hooker's belief that Wauhatchie needed to be protected because of the Kelley's Ferry Road and Brown's Ferry Road junction was understandable. However, depending on Geary's small division along with its wagons and little to no reserve ammunition was a mistake. The three-mile area of Lookout Valley was known to be swarming with Confederate soldiers, and all Union movements were visible to Confederate leadership on top of Lookout Mountain. Moreover, in the event of an attack by Confederate forces, Union communications between the two camps was nearly nonexistent and sending reinforcements to Wauhatchie from Brown's Ferry meant a forced march of about three miles and maneuvering for battle in the dark of night—all of which should have alarmed Hooker, and it did that and more: It made him panic. For example, Hooker sent Schurz conflicting orders as to how to use his brigades. Other examples included his orders to attack Smith's and Tyndale's Hills, moving on the Brown's Ferry Road to relieve Geary at Wauhatchie, and even his headquarters staff almost sending off one brigade to Chattanooga with Confederate prisoners. Hooker would blame Schurz in his after-action report for the delay in relieving Geary's forces. However, in the end, Schurz would be exonerated from the statements brought forward by Hooker.[88]

Hooker also lost a chance for glory along Smith's and Tyndale's Hills. Union troops lost many good men in storming and taking these hills. However, once taken, the men did little more than fire a volley into the retreating Confederates and dig trenches. Union leadership failed to take an aggressive stance by continuing a vigorous attack on the Southerners. By not doing so, all four brigades of Jenkins division were able to recross Lookout Creek at the only bridge of escape, and many at their own leisure. While it is true the Union army command would be acting aggressively across unknown terrain and in darkness, they knew how near they were to Lookout Creek, and if the Confederate army had their backs to the creek with little space between them and the Union army and only one bridge in which to reach safety, it is highly probable that Jenkins division could have been utterly defeated.

When examining the larger picture, Bragg and his Army of Tennessee were handed a serious defeat in the battle for Lookout Valley. The defeat played out as the catalyst for Bragg to free himself of Longstreet and his corps, which included Hood's old division led by Jenkins. It also weakened Bragg's own forces in front of an ever growing Union army in and around Chattanooga. In just days, the Confederates would leave all of Lookout Valley to the Union and move further upon Lookout Mountain.[89] By holding on to Lookout Valley, the Union army grew more confident. Those of Hooker's army who had been pushed around earlier in the east at Chancellorsville by Lee's army had now moved west only to battle old enemies from the eastern theater, namely Longstreet and the First Corps. This time it was the men from the eastern Army of the Potomac that would taste the fruits of victory and feel the satisfaction of redemption.

One soldier of the 111th Pennsylvania Regiment recalled how the Tennessee River was finally opened from Bridgeport to Chattanooga in only five days after General Grant had taken command of the situation around Chattanooga. The soldier recalled, "the suffering Army of the Cumberland was amply furnished with all needed supplies, and the spirit of the troops was fully restored. . . . [I]t convinced us all that in him [Grant] the nation had found an extraordinary military chief."[90] Union victory in Lookout Valley established communications to Chattanooga, an uninterrupted supply line along the Tennessee River, and an ever growing Union army in and around Chattanooga. Soon after the Confederate loss of Lookout Valley, Longstreet and his troops were released and sent to the northeast. It was only a matter of time before the Confederate forces, still in Bragg's command, would be sent streaming down Lookout Mountain and Missionary Ridge in defeat toward Ringgold.

As the campaign for Chattanooga progressed, important events such as the "Battle above the Clouds" on Lookout Mountain and the intense fighting on Missionary Ridge took place. However, it was the small yet intense fights within Lookout Valley at places such as Wauhatchie, Smith's Hill, and Tyndale's Hill that, although almost forgotten, set the stage and prepared the way for the final outcome of the campaign. After the battle for Lookout Valley, one Union soldier found what he called "a tribute to the victorious valor of Hooker's men, not to be overlooked, recorded in chalk on a house near the fight, by some plain spoken, much whipped rebel . . . 'In the year of our Lord A.D. 1863, the Yanks drove the rebs out of this valley. Bully for them!'"[91] The battle for Lookout Valley was over for many a soldier, blue and gray. For the rest of the Chattanooga Campaign, like the message left in chalk, the answer was already written on the wall.

Notes

1. William Fletcher Hughey Diary, 1864, Private collection of Steve Braun, Canton, Michigan. Also available at http://www.civilwardads.com/CivilWarArchives/WilliamHughey.htm (accessed December 29, 2010).

2. Ulysses S. Grant, *Personal Memoirs of U. S. Grant*, 2vols. (New York: Charles L. Webster & Co., 1892), 2:26.

3. Ibid., 35–36.

4. Hartwell Osborn, *Trials and Triumphs: The Record of the Fifty-Fifth Ohio Volunteer Infantry* (Chicago: A. C. McClurg & Co., 1904), 120; U.S. War Department, *The War of the Rebellion: A Compilation of the Official Records of the Union and Confederate Armies*, 128 vols. (Washington, D.C., 1880–1901), ser. 1, vol. 31, pt. 1: 92, 112 (hereafter cited as *OR*; all references are to Series 1 unless otherwise indicated).

5. *OR*, vol. 31, pt. 1: 92.

6. Turner Vaughan, "Diary of Turner Vaughan, Co. C, 4th Alabama," *Alabama Historical Quarterly* 18 (Winter 1956): 599.

7. Oliver Otis Howard, *Autobiography of Oliver Otis Howard: Major General, United States Army* (New York: Baker and Taylor Co., 1908), 1: 464.

8. Adin Ballou Underwood, *The Three Years' Service of the Thirty-Third Massachusetts Infantry Regiment 1862–1865* (Boston: A. Williams & Co., 1881), 154; Patricia Fife Medert, ed., *The Civil War Letters of Captain B. F. Stone Jr., 73rd Regiment O.V.I.* (Chillicothe, Ohio: Ross County Historical Society, n.d.), 201; Frederic Bancroft and William A. Dunning, eds., *The Reminiscences of Carl Schurz*, vol. 3, 1863–69 (Garden City, N.Y.: Doubleday, Page & Co., 1917), 59.

9. Major L. D. Warner to Fay, November 5, 1863, Major L. D. Warner, New York State Bureau of Military Statistics, Civil War Newspaper Clipping Collection, 154th, New York State Military Museum., http://dmna.state.ny.us/historic/reghist/civil/infantry/154thInf/154thInfCWN.htm (Accessed July 1, 2011).

10. Hartwell Osborn, "The Eleventh Corps in East Tennessee," *Military Essays and Recollections Read before the Commandery of the State of Illinois, Military Order of the Loyal Legion of the United States* (Chicago: Cozzens and Beaton, 1907), 4:357.

11. Andrew J. Boies, *Record of the Thirty-Third Massachusetts Volunteer Infantry, from Aug. 1862 to Aug. 1865* (Fitchburg, Mass.: Sentinel Printing Co., 1880), 46–47.

12. Warner to Fay, November 5, 1863.

13. Osborn, "Eleventh Corps in East Tennessee," 358; John Michael Priest, ed., *John T. McMahon's Diary of the 136th New York, 1861–1864* (Shippensburg, Pa.: White Mane Publishing Co., 1993), 67.

14. Howard, *Autobiography of Oliver Otis Howard*, 464–65.

15. *OR*, vol. 31, pt. 1: 94, 57.

16. Underwood, *Three Years' Service*, 156–57; Christian B. Keller, *Chancellorsville and the Germans: Nativism, Ethnicity, and Civil War Memory* (Bronx, N.Y.: Fordham University Press, 2007), 80–81.

17. Bancroft and Dunning, *Reminiscences of Carl Schurz*, 3:60; Jedediah Mannis and Galen R. Wilson, eds., *Bound to Be a Soldier: The Letters of Private James T. Miller, 111th Pennsylvania Infantry, 1861–1864* (Knoxville: University of Tennessee Press, 2001), 123.

18. Gary W. Gallagher, ed., *Fighting for the Confederacy: The Personal Recollections of General Edward Porter Alexander* (Chapel Hill: University of North Carolina Press, 1989), 310–11.

19. Nathaniel Cheairs Hughes Jr., ed., *Liddell's Record: St. John Richardson Liddell* (Baton Rouge: Louisiana State University Press, 1985), 156–57. Controversy surrounds the Confederate plan of attack for the battle of Wauhatchie. This includes Longstreet's actual intentions, Bragg's expectations, Jenkins's final attack plan, and the relationship between Jenkins and Law and the part it may have played in the actual outcome of the night assault. For a through overview of these issues, see Alexander Mendoza's chapter in this book.

20. *OR*, vol. 31, pt. 1: 219, 223.

21. Ibid., 217.

22. Ibid., 223.

23. Ibid., 225–26. It should also be noted that there is some disagreement in the accounts as to whether more than one bridge was used in the attack upon Geary's troops the night of October 28, 1863. Brigadier General Henry L. Benning wrote shortly after the fighting had ended at Wauhatchie that Law's brigade had, indeed, crossed Lookout Creek over the lower bridge and that Robertson's brigade was doing the same. He then mentioned that Jenkins's brigade, being led by Bratton, "was already across the creek, having crossed it at the upper bridge." However, the Confederate leadership only mention one bridge. Law refers to the lower bridge near the mouth of Lookout Creek, and Robertson confirms Law's crossing the lower bridge but makes no mention of doing the same himself and refers to "bridge" in the singular throughout his report. Bratton, who was leading Jenkins's brigade, mentions crossing Lookout Creek "near the railroad bridge," which would be the same bridge that Laws and Robertson refer to since the railroad crosses the creek at its mouth. Moreover, given that Bratton's troops were engaged in the southernmost sector of the fighting and that he stated, "I then moved on to the bridge over Lookout Creek, . . . [where] we formed line of battle to cover the retreat and passage of General Benning's brigade, and were last to recross the creek,"

it is safe to say that only the one bridge was used. Frank Mixon, a private in the 1st South Carolina Regiment of Jenkins's brigade, also recalled, "crossing Chattanooga Creek on a bridge, the only way this creek could be crossed." After the battle, Mixon recalled that the Confederates "had cut the bridge away from the bank and had it on fire; this to prevent the Yankees from following us, as the creek was impassable except at the bridge." It would appear that all of the Confederate troops on this night did cross near the mouth of Lookout Creek along what was usually considered the lower bridge. If indeed, two bridges were used, one was the railroad bridge near the mouth of Lookout Creek and the other was possibly farther west, where the creek bends near Tyndale's Hill, on the Confederates' left. Either way, Confederates under Jenkins and Law would find getting back across these bridges to the safety of the Confederate line, while under heavy attack, quite precarious. *OR*, vol. 52, pt. 1: 89; *OR*, vol. 31, pt. 1: 225–26, 231–4, Frank M. Mixson, *Reminiscences of a Private* (Columbia, S.C.: Street Co., 1910), 45, 48–49. *OR*, vol. 31, pt. 1: 212, appendix E.

24. *OR*, vol. 31, pt. 1: 225–27; William C. Oates, *The War between the Union and the Confederacy and Its Lost Opportunities* (Dayton, Ohio: Press of Morningside Bookshop, 1974), 270.

25. Albert R. Greene, "From Bridgeport to Ringgold by Way of Lookout Mountain," in *Personal Narratives* (Providence, R.I.: Soldiers and Sailors Historical Society of Rhode Island, 1889), 4:20–21; Douglas R. Cubbison, "Midnight Engagement: Geary's White Star Division at Wauhatchie, Tennessee, October 28–29, 1863," *Civil War Regiments: A Journal of the American Civil War* 3, no. 2 (1993): 80–81; *OR*, vol. 31, pt. 1: 123.

26. *OR*, vol. 31, pt. 1: 113.

27. Ibid., 113, 94.

28. Ibid., 113, 121, 126.

29. Ibid., 113.

30. Ibid., 113, 121, 126, 121, 125.

31. Jedediah Mannis and Galen R. Wilson, eds., *Bound to Be a Soldier: The Letters of Private James T. Miller, 111th Pennsylvania Infantry, 1861–1864* (Knoxville: University of Tennessee Press, 2001), 123.

32. *OR*, vol. 31, pt. 1: 231.

33. Mixson, *Reminiscences of a Private*, 45; *OR*, vol. 31, pt. 1: 116–17.

34. *OR*, vol. 31, pt. 1: 231.

35. Richard A. Baumgartner and Larry M. Strayer, eds. *Echoes of Battle: The Struggle for Chattanooga* (Huntington, W.Va.: Blue Acorn, 1996), 215; *OR*, vol. 31, pt. 1: 231.

36. Natalie Jenkins Bond and Osmun Latrobe Coward, eds., *The South Carolinians: Colonel Asbury Coward's Memoirs* (New York: Vantage Press, 1968), 88–89.

37. L. J. Perry, "Battle of 'Wills Valley,' Tennessee," *Confederate Veteran* 23 (1915): 163.

38. *OR*, vol. 31, pt. 1: 231.39. Mixson, *Reminiscences of a Private*, 46.

40. *OR*, vol. 31, pt. 1: 128, 133; John K. Stevens, "Of Mules and Men: The Night Fight at Wauhatchie Station," *South Carolina Historical Magazine* 90, no. 4 (October 1989): 294–97.

41. Stevens, "Of Mules and Men," 294–95; *OR*, vol. 31, pt. 1: 124.

42. Greene, "From Bridgeport to Ringgold," 23–24; *OR*, vol. 31, pt. 1: 127, 129.

43. *OR*, vol. 31, pt. 1: 232.

44. Ibid., 231.

45. Ibid., 114.

46. Ibid., 122–23.

47. Ibid., 114, 135; Cubbison, "Midnight Engagement," 90; Mannis and Wilson, *Bound to Be a Soldier*, 124; John Richards Boyle, *Soldiers True: The Story of the One-Hundred-Eleventh Pennsylvania Veteran Volunteers, and of Its Campaigns in the War for the Union, 1861–1865* (New York: Eaton, 1903), 163.

48. Baumgartner and Strayer, *Echoes of Battle*, 210–11.

49. *OR*, vol. 31, pt. 1: 231–32.

50. Ibid., 232.

51. Cubbison, "Midnight Engagement," 88.

52. Ibid., 88–89.

53. *OR*, vol. 31, pt. 1: 128.

54. Baumgartner and Strayer, *Echoes of Battle*, 209.

55. Ibid., 211.

56. George W. Skinner, ed., *Pennsylvania at Chickamauga and Chattanooga: Ceremonies at the Dedication of the Monuments Erected by the Commonwealth of Pennsylvania to Mark the Positions of the Pennsylvania Commands Engaged in the Battles* (Harrisburg, Pa.: William Stanley Ray, 1897), 133; W. F. Beyer and O. F. Keydel, *Deeds of Valor: How America's Civil War Heroes Won the Congressional Medal of Honor* (Detroit: Perrien-Keydel Co., 1907), 273; *OR*, vol. 31, pt. 1: 124, 135; Baumgartner and Strayer, *Echoes of Battle*, 211.

57. Beyer and Keydel, *Deeds of Valor*, 273.

58. Skinner, *Pennsylvania at Chickamauga and Chattanooga*, 268; *OR*, vol. 31, pt. 1: 135.

59. *OR*, vol. 31, pt. 1: 123.

60. Ibid., 128, 131–35, 125–26, 123.

61. Ibid., 115, 129; Skinner, *Pennsylvania at Chickamauga and Chattanooga*, 268.

62. *OR*, vol. 31, pt. 1: 124.

63. Ibid.

64. Ibid., 124, 135. Skinner, *Pennsylvania at Chickamauga and Chattanooga*, 133.

65. *OR*, vol. 31, pt. 1: 232.

66. Ibid., 232–33.

67. Ibid., 129, 131; Greene, *From Bridgeport to Ringgold*, 26.

68. Howard, *Autobiography*, 1: 466–67.

69. *OR*, vol. 31, pt. 1: 94; Howard, *Autobiography*, 1: 467.

70. Steven E. Woodworth, *Six Armies in Tennessee: The Chickamauga and Chattanooga Campaign* (Lincoln: University of Nebraska Press, 1998), 166–67; *OR*, vol. 31, pt. 1: 206–8.

71. Samuel H. Hurst, *Journal-History of the Seventy-Third Ohio Volunteer Infantry* (Chillicothe, Ohio, 1866), 86–87; *OR*, vol. 31, pt. 1: 185.

72. Hurst, *Journal-History of the Seventy-Third Ohio*, 87; Howard, *Autobiography*, 1: 467.

73. *OR*, vol. 31, pt. 1: 137–211; Peter Cozzens, *The Shipwreck of Their Hopes: The Battles for Chattanooga* (Urbana: University of Illinois Press, 1994), 97; Howard, *Autobiography*, 1:467–68.

74. *OR*, vol. 31, pt. 1: 108.

75. Ibid., 104.

76. Ibid.

77. William Fletcher Hughey Diary, n.d., Steve Braun Collection, Canton, Michigan. *OR*, vol. 31, pt. 1: 103.

78. *OR*, vol. 31, pt. 1: 109.

79. Ibid., 105–6; "Letter from the 136th Regiment, Lookout Valley, Tenn., November 4, 1863," *Geneseo (N.Y.) Livingston Republican*, November 26, 1863," New York State Bureau of Military Statistics, Civil War Newspaper Clipping Collection, 136th, New York State Military Museum, http://dmna.state.ny.us/historic/reghist/civil/infantry/136thInf/154thInfCWN.htm (Accessed on July 1, 2011).

80. *OR*, vol. 31, pt. 1: 106, 104, 109.

81. Ibid., 227–28, 230, 234; James J. Baldwin III, *The Struck Eagle: A Biography of Brigadier General Micah Jenkins, and a History of the Fifth South Carolina Volunteers and the Palmetto Sharpshooters* (Shippensburg, Pa.: Burd Street Press, 1996), 233; J. Gary Laine and Morris M. Penny, *Law's Alabama Brigade in the War between the Union and the Confederacy* (Shippensburg, Pa.: White Mane Publishing Co., 1996), 197. Law's decisions, subsequent movements of his command, and relationship with then-commander Micah Jenkins during the time of the Battle of Wauhatchie and whether it was Jenkins or Law who decided first to fall back from the engagement in Lookout Valley have been matters of great controversy since the battle was fought.

82. John McLaughlin, *A Memoir of Hector Tyndale* (Philadelphia: Collins, 1882), 78; *OR*, vol. 31, pt. 1: 111; Laine and Penny, *Law's Alabama Brigade*, 199. Hector Tyndale barely mentions the part he and his brigade played in the night engagement in the itinerary of the First Brigade found in the *Official Records*. Tyndale merely mentions that he and his men "joined the troops of the corps in successfully repulsing a night attack of the enemy on the 29th, at 1:30 A.M. Commenced building rifle-pits, &c., continuing the works without cessation during October 30 and 31." *OR*, vol. 31, pt. 1:111.

83. *OR*, vol. 31, pt. 1: 227–28; J. B. Polly, *Hood's Texas Brigade: Its Marches, Its Battles, Its Achievements* (reprinted, Dayton, Ohio: Morningside Bookshop, 1988), 215.

84. *OR*, vol. 31, pt. 1: 115–16; Howard, *Autobiography*, 1:469; William Alan Blair, *A Politician Goes to War: The Civil War Letters of John White Geary* (University Park: Pennsylvania State University Press, 1995), 132.

85. *OR*, vol. 31, pt. 1: 98, 110–11.

86. Ibid., 219, 116–17, 120, 232–33; J. L. Coker, "Battle of Lookout Valley or Wauhatchie," *Confederate Veteran Magazine* 28, no. 10 (October 1910): 473.

87. James Longstreet, *From Manassas to Appomattox: Memoirs of the Civil War in America* (Secaucus, N.J.: Blue and Grey Press, 1988), 477; *OR*, vol. 31, pt. 1: 228, 104, 109; Hurst, *Journal-History of the Seventy-Third Ohio*, 89.

88. *OR*, vol. 31, pt. 1: 92–95, 137–215.

89. Polly, *Hood's Texas Brigade*, 220–21.

90. Boyle, *Soldiers True*, 168.

91. Underwood, *Three Years' Service*, 173–74.

3

"THE VERY GROUND SEEMED ALIVE":
SHERMAN'S ASSAULT ON THE NORTH
END OF MISSIONARY RIDGE

Steven E. Woodworth

Grant planned to strike his main blow at the Confederate right and entrusted the job to William T. Sherman and his contingent of the Army of the Tennessee. Though Grant and Sherman both had high hopes for the attack, it failed to produce the results they expected. A careful study of the operation reveals why.

There were several reasons why Grant planned his main effort against the Confederate right on the northern end of Missionary Ridge. The primary Confederate line of supply and retreat lay closer to the northern end of the ridge, so that a Union success there would at least have made Bragg's retreat more difficult than would have been the case had Grant broken the Rebel lines farther south on the ridge. Another reason was that an attack on the northern end of Missionary Ridge offered the opportunity of striking the Confederate right flank. Finally, all previous experience in the Civil War indicated that a ridge would lose most of its strength as a defensive position if attacked end-on rather than frontally.

Grant also had several reasons for selecting William T. Sherman's corps-sized detachment of the Army of the Tennessee to make the assault on the northern end of Missionary Ridge. Since before the Battle of Shiloh, nineteenth months earlier, Sherman had been his most trusted subordinate, and Sherman's troops were from Grant's own Army of the Tennessee. Grant and the Army of the Tennessee had grown up together in this war. At its head he had won every one of his successes thus far in the conflict—Fort Donelson, Shiloh, and the long campaign to take Vicksburg.

Along the way, Grant had shaped and forged the Army of the Tennessee, building on his own personality and the regional character of its men, most of whom came from what was then called the Northwest but is now called the

Midwest. The region had been frontier little more than a generation earlier, and the men who served in the ranks of Grant's army had either helped farm land that their fathers had carved out of the wilderness or else had done the carving themselves only a few years before enlisting. They were capable and resourceful and tended to assume that they could handle anything the war brought their way. Grant knew them and knew their senior officers, whose promotions he had approved. Like him, the Army of the Tennessee was little inclined to stand on ceremony but was prepared to get at the enemy as quickly as possible, hit him as hard as possible, and keep moving on. This was just the force Grant wanted for his attack against Bragg's right flank on Missionary Ridge.

Sherman and his troops had arrived in the Chattanooga area scarcely ten days before the battle. On October 27 they had been in the vicinity of Tuscumbia, Alabama, working on repairing the Memphis and Charleston Railroad there and trying to protect it from guerrillas on orders from general-in-chief Henry W. Halleck in Washington. On that day, Sherman received new orders from Grant. Sherman's old boss was the newly appointed commander of the newly created Military Division of the Mississippi, encompassing all Union forces between the Appalachians and the Mississippi. Ordered to Chattanooga after a personal conference with Secretary of War Edwin M. Stanton in Louisville, Kentucky, Grant had arrived on October 23 to find the Army of the Cumberland virtually besieged there by Bragg's forces, which controlled the Tennessee River Gorge downstream from the city. With the troops in Chattanooga in a state of semi-starvation, Grant had taken immediate steps to open the route through the gorge, what the soldier's dubbed the "Cracker Line." He had also lost no time in sending orders to Sherman directing him to drop work on the railroads and march at once to Chattanooga with four divisions.[1]

Among the reasons Sherman was Grant's favorite subordinate was the fact that Grant could count on him to respond loyally and to march quickly when quick marching was needed. After receiving Grant's order, Sherman immediately got his army in motion, and over the next seventeen days his men covered well over one hundred fifty miles of bad road, mostly in bad weather. To crown their accomplishment, they dragged their wagons and artillery up the steep and rocky roads over the Cumberland Plateau. Sometimes the men had to line both sides of a wagon and literally lift it several feet up over a rock ledge in the road. On November 13 they reached Bridgeport, Alabama, on the Tennessee River, thirty-five miles downstream from Chattanooga.[2]

At Bridgeport, Sherman found a dispatch from Grant, who wanted him to hurry to Chattanooga ahead of his troops to discuss what should be done once they arrived. Small steamboats were by that time making regular runs on the Tennessee River between Bridgeport and Brown's Ferry, a few miles from Chattanooga, so Sherman took one of them on November 14 and at the ferry found an orderly waiting with one of Grant's own horses for him to ride the rest of the way. Sherman arrived at Grant's headquarters on the fifteenth, and the two old friends greeted each other heartily. Grant took Sherman for a tour of the Union earthworks defending Chattanooga, and they observed the Confederate positions on the slopes of Lookout Mountain and Missionary Ridge.

While they surveyed the terrain, Grant explained his plan. Most of the Army of the Cumberland's horses had starved during the siege, and those left were too weak to work. The lack of usable horses immobilized the Army of the Cumberland. It could attack straight ahead against targets immediately adjacent to Chattanooga, but that was all. Any flanking of the enemy would have to be done by another force, and that, as Grant explained, was where Sherman's Army of the Tennessee detachment came in. Sherman's troops were not to enter Chattanooga yet, Grant explained. Instead they were to make a roundabout march through the hills north of the town, keeping carefully out of sight of the Rebels, and reach the Tennessee River several miles upstream from, and thus northeast of, Chattanooga.

Grant invited Sherman to join him on a four-mile ride back into the hills to a vantage point from which they could survey the northern end of Missionary Ridge. "From the hills we looked down on the amphitheater of Chattanooga as on a map," Sherman later recalled. A good map, in fact, was exactly what Grant and Sherman did not have and could have used. Making do with what they had, as both men's custom was, they surveyed the terrain from their hilltop. The Confederate right lay on or just in front of Missionary Ridge, Grant explained, but its right flank stopped well short of the north end of the ridge. Grant wanted Sherman's troops to cross the river as stealthily as possible and then march south to seize the north end of Missionary Ridge. Once astride the ridge, Sherman's troops would, in theory, be able to sweep southward along its length, rolling up the Confederate line as they went. The concept seemed straightforward enough as the two generals peered at Missionary Ridge through the haze of the intervening three miles and studied its form, covered as it was with leafless trees.[3]

"Nothing remained but for me to put my troops in the desired position," Sherman later recalled. He was eager to get back to Bridgeport and get his divisions moving. By the time he got back to Brown's Ferry, however, it was evening and the last steamboat of the day had already left. Sherman would not be delayed by trifles. Very well then, he informed the commander of the detachment holding the ferry, he would take a rowboat, with four soldiers detailed to pull the oars. Down the river they went. Sherman took an occasional turn at an oar to keep warm and spell one of his borrowed rowers. Reaching the Union outpost at Shellmound, Sherman traded his four soldiers for four new men and kept going. They reached Bridgeport about dawn.[4]

Back at his camps, Sherman lost no time in putting his four divisions in motion. They had forty miles to go in bad roads and bad weather. The skies were gray and lowering, and cold rain fell most of the time. Nonetheless, morale was high among Sherman's troops. When they halted for the night after a day of slogging through deep mud, an officer in an Iowa regiment wrote, "Our army never was in better spirits or more enthusiastic for the cause than at present. We all expect a hot fight before long, but we expect nothing but victory."[5]

Despite the eagerness of the troops, the march was frustratingly slow. Horses and mules could move wagons only so fast along the muddy roads. During the march from Tuscumbia, the troops had sometimes outrun their slow-moving supply wagons and experienced hunger. For this stage of the journey, Sherman directed that each division's wagons follow immediately behind it, rather than form part of one big wagon train at the end of the column. In theory, this would keep the troops better fed on the eve of battle and would provide more hands readily available to help manhandle the wagons through or over obstructions. In practice, the experiment proved unsuccessful, at least as pertained to speed of movement, which was greatly reduced.

Further delaying the march was the Tennessee River itself. Swollen after days of rain, the river was high, and its strong current threatened to break the pontoon bridge at Brown's Ferry. Two of Sherman's division got across the bridge on November 20 and 21 under a steady rain, but then the current broke the span. Engineers struggled to repair it, and then the river broke it again. The process was repeated throughout November 22, and on the next day the bridge was steady enough to bear the crossing of another division. Then it broke again, and the engineers once more struggled against a Tennessee River that was higher and more powerful than ever.

Grant was impatient, in part at least because President Lincoln and Secretary Stanton were impatient, bombarding him with daily dispatches asking about the progress around Chattanooga and when Grant was going to finish with the Rebels there and send help to Ambrose Burnside, who was in turn complaining to Washington about how the Confederates were bothering him at Knoxville. Rather than accept an indefinite delay while the engineers battled the river, Grant ordered Sherman to leave his fourth division with Joseph Hooker's Army of the Potomac detachment in Lookout Valley and proceed with his other three. Grant would loan Sherman a division of the Army of the Cumberland for the operation against Missionary Ridge.[6]

Even as the third of the Army of the Tennessee divisions, Hugh Ewing's, was crossing the Tennessee at Brown's Ferry, Sherman began the movement that would take his command across the river. After crossing the river in the preceding days, the divisions of Morgan L. Smith and John E. Smith had encamped in the hills behind Chattanooga, out of sight of the Rebels. On November 23 Sherman ordered Morgan Smith to dispatch the brigade of his brother, Giles Smith, to march north five miles to the point selected for the crossing of the Tennessee. There Union engineers had constructed 116 pontoon boats. That would be enough to support a bridge all the way across the river, but before the boats were used for bridging, they were earmarked to serve another purpose. Sherman's orders directed Smith to load his brigade into the boats and set out down the river at midnight. His mission was to land on the Confederate side of the Tennessee (here the east bank) just below the mouth of Chickamauga Creek. Confederate picket posts guarded the riverbank here, and Smith's men were to surprise them and, if possible, take them before they could raise the alarm in the Confederate camps.

Major Charles Hipp of the 37th Ohio Regiment commanded a picked group of oarsmen, many of them boatmen in civilian life, and assigned four men to handle each of the big boats. In addition to its crew, each boat would carry twenty-five of Giles Smith's infantrymen. The operation was carefully planned, with each boat crew and landing party receiving detailed instructions on its mission. The boats were to hug the western (Union) bank of the river until they neared their target, so as to minimize the risk of accidental discovery from the Confederate eastern shore. The boats' oars were muffled with rags, to avoid every telltale sound. The first several boats targeted a series of Confederate picket posts along the river, each manned by a squad of Rebels and visible from a distance because of its campfire.

The men in the landing parties had strict orders to load but not to cap their rifles, except on the direct order of one of their officers. There was to be no accidental or undisciplined shooting. A fusillade of Union firing at one of the Confederate picket posts would fulfill the outpost's function as well as fire from the Confederates' own rifles. Instead Smith's men were to storm ashore quickly and quietly as possible and rush on the Confederates out of the darkness. If they encountered initial resistance, they would have to settle it with their bayonets.

Behind these first few boats came the main body of the flotilla carrying the rest of Giles Smith's brigade. They would stick to the west bank a little longer, passing the picket posts that their comrades in the lead boats would hopefully by then have secured. When they came even with a single campfire on the Union side, apparently a picket post but actually a signal, they would veer east and pull across the current to land their troops. Behind the lone Union campfire waited more of Sherman's troops, and after discharging their loads on the east bank, the boat crews would pull back across the river to toward the light of the campfire and begin embarking reinforcements.

The plan worked to perfection. The startled Confederate pickets surrendered without a shot except for one man had his finger on the trigger of his rifle and in his startled reaction to the sudden appearance of the Federals loosed an unaimed shot into the air. Tense minutes followed for Smith's men, but the main Confederate line was a considerable distance away, and no one seemed to have heard. At least, there was no reaction.[7]

The boatmen continued to ply their oars, and by daylight two entire divisions were on the east bank and had started to dig in. As the light rose, Union engineers moved on to the next phase of the operations. One by one they took boats out of service ferrying troops and incorporated the craft into their rapidly growing pontoon bridge. The speed of the ferrying operation was kept up by the arrival in mid-morning of the small steamboat *Dunbar*, which Grant had sent up the river from Chattanooga. With the *Dunbar* and a steadily dwindling number of pontoon boats continuing to shuttle back and forth across the river, a third division, Ewing's, was completely across by noon. At that point, the engineers declared the bridge open for business, and the fourth division, Jefferson C. Davis's borrowed Army of the Cumberland division, crossed the 1,350-foot span.[8]

Assigning Davis's division to hold an entrenched perimeter around the bridgehead, Sherman moved out with his other three divisions at 1:00 P.M. under low-hanging clouds in a light drizzle. The tops of the surrounding heights were sheathed in cloud, and the movement went unobserved by the Confederates. Sherman's men had expected to encounter resistance as they crossed the more or less level ground between the river and the northern end of Missionary Ridge, but to their surprise they found none, though the advancing line did flush out a few Confederate pickets who scampered off toward the ridge.[9]

The terrain was unknown and the advance was cautious, so that it was about 3:00 or 3:30 P.M. when skirmishers of the 47th Ohio of Joseph A. J. Lightburn's brigade, reached the foot of the northernmost extension of high ground, a little less than two miles from the river, and started up the slope. Sherman's three divisions were converging toward the northern end of Missionary Ridge, and so skirmishers of the 30th Ohio were already ascending the north slope on a slightly different axis of advance. The 47th's skirmish line joined the advance probably somewhat behind and to the left of the 30th's, though due to undulations in the slope and the curvature of the hillside, men of the two regiment's may not have been able to see each other.[10]

The 30th's skirmishers reached the summit and encountered a line of Confederate skirmishers coming the other way. These were Texans of James Smith's brigade, Cleburne's division. Finally learning of a Union movement against his right flank, Bragg had dispatched Cleburne to hold the northern end of Missionary Ridge. Cleburne was moving north at the same time that Sherman was moving south, and their skirmishers had met head-on. The Ohioans of the 30th, quickly joined by their fellow Buckeyes of the 47th, drove the Texans back. With no orders to do more than take the high ground, the 30th Ohio skirmishers halted, but the 47th's pursued the Rebels down another slope and across a saddle that was one hundred fifty feet deep and had a rough wagon road running through its bottom. On the far side of this deep saddle, the retreating Confederates started up yet another wooded slope. Still in pursuit, the Ohioans had reached the base of that slope when orders from Sherman caught up with them calling a halt for the night. Daylight had never been very bright on this cloudy, rainy day, and now with the sun going down, darkness closed in quickly.[11]

In many respects the entire operation, starting with the midnight crossing of the Tennessee, had been a complete success, and yet it had not quite accomplished its purpose. Sherman's divisions had crossed the river quickly, undetected, and had reached the position that Grant and Sherman had seen from the heights on the far side of the river and had selected as their target. Yet that achievement had failed to set up the situation the Union generals had envisioned, and the reason was the complicated geography at the north end of Missionary Ridge.

One aspect of that complication was the deep saddle between the hill Sherman's men held and the one to the south that the Confederates held. When viewed from a distance, Missionary Ridge appeared to be a straight, regular crease in the terrain but in reality was much different. Along its face, the ridge comprised a series of ravines and spurs that corresponded to alternating saddles and humps on its crest. At its north end, the saddles and humps were more pronounced. The final saddle was roughly three hundred yards wide and more than one hundred fifty feet deep. The bottom of the saddle was only about one hundred feet higher than the plain on which the town of Chattanooga sat. The depth and width of the saddle make the northernmost hump of the ridge more of a freestanding hill about half a mile long from north to south and perhaps three hundred yards wide, east to west. It is now known as Lightburn Hill, after one of the Union officers.

The gap separating this hill from the rest of Missionary Ridge angles through the ridge in such a way as to be practically imperceptible from Sherman's vantage point before he began the movement across the river.

It was quite perceptible to him on the morning of November 25 when shortly after dawn he surveyed it from the top of Lightburn Hill. Around midnight the night before, he had sent a dispatch to Grant reporting that his troops had gained a position astride Missionary Ridge almost to the railroad tunnel. That was true. Sherman's lines were only about three-quarters of a mile via the crest of the ridge from the point where the Chattanooga and Cleveland Railroad passed through the ridge via a tunnel. The tunnel ran underneath the next saddle south of the one where Sherman had halted his advance for the night. The saddle above the tunnel was almost as big as the one Sherman was confronting. Between the two saddles lay a piece of ridge about six hundred yards long, roughly comparable to Lightburn Hill. The more southerly of the two hills was known as Tunnel Hill. During the night, Smith's Confederates, on Cleburne's orders, had established their position and built log breastworks around the highest point on Tunnel Hill, near the southern end of its crest.[12]

Grant's orders to Sherman during the night had been unsurprising. He was to continue the previous day's advance, moving south along Missionary Ridge and rolling up the Confederate line. In theory, that should have been easy. The problem with such theory was geographic, but it was not the deep saddle that Sherman surveyed by first light. As was soon to appear, crossing the saddle would be the last easy thing Sherman's troops would encounter on this day.[13]

A few minutes after his presunrise hilltop survey of the saddle and the north slope of Tunnel Hill beyond, Sherman ordered skirmishers to advance across the saddle again, climb Tunnel Hill, and find out where the Confederates seemed prepared to make a stand. The assignment went to companies E and I of the 30th Ohio. The two companies charged downhill at a run, crossed the saddle, and ran up the far side, overwhelming a thin line of Confederate skirmishers occupying a trench, or "rifle pit" in the parlance of the day, located at the top of the slope. According to the captain of one of the companies, the entire operation had taken less than five minutes. From the Confederate skirmishers' trench, the Ohioans advanced along the ridge another hundred yards or so. From there they could look farther along the crest of the ridge through "thin and scattering" timber, to see the main Confederate line. The top of the ridge was about fifty yards wide, with steep slopes on either side. The ridgetop itself sloped gently upward toward the Confederate position, where a stout log breastwork stood on ground about thirty feet higher than that on which the Ohio skirmishers crouched. The ridgetop widened distinctly a short distance north of the Confederate breastwork, which occupied the highest and widest part of Tunnel Hill.[14]

With the enemy position located, Sherman gave his orders for the attack. The narrow confines of the position precluded the use of all his troops, so he assigned the assault to the division of his brother-in-law, Hugh Ewing. Ewing was to send Brigadier General John M. Corse's brigade directly along the ridgetop, following the route the 30th Ohio's skirmishers had taken, and then beyond them to attack the Confederate breastworks. Another of Ewing's brigades, that of Colonel John M. Loomis, was to march south on the west side of the ridge until it was even with the tunnel and then turn and charge the ridge. Ideally, a third brigade should have struck the east face of the ridge at the same time, but this was not feasible. Cleburne had cleverly arrayed several additional Confederate brigades on an irregular spur of the ridge that jutted east from its main spine south of Tunnel Hill almost to the meandering bends of Chickamauga Creek. These positions made an attack down the east side of the ridge impossible. Therefore, Ewing was to hold his third brigade, that of Colonel Joseph R. Cockerill, in reserve.[15]

However, since Corse's brigade was small, numbering only about 920 men, Sherman rode over to the part of the hill held by Lightburn's brigade and ordered Lightburn to support Corse with the rest of the 30th Ohio and two companies of the 4th West Virginia, another 200 men. Because Lightburn's position was closer to the saddle than Corse's, his troops were first to cross the saddle, climb the steep slope at the north end of Missionary Ridge, and arrive in front of the Confederate position. Rather than wait, the 30th's Colonel Theodore Jones led his twelve companies forward to attack the Confederate breastwork without Corse. Driven back, and with Corse's regiments still not yet having arrived on the ridgetop, Jones sent back to his own brigade commander for reinforcements, and Lightburn dispatched Lieutenant Colonel Louis von Blessingh with the 37th Ohio. By the time von Blessingh and his men arrived, the sun was rising, and Corse's brigade was also emerging onto the now somewhat crowded northern end of the ridgetop.[16]

Sizing up the narrow ridge top rising gradually in front of him almost like a gangplank, Corse immediately recognized that it did not offer enough width for him to deploy his entire brigade. So he ordered his skirmishers—five companies of the 40th Illinois and three of the 103rd Illinois under the command of Major Hiram Hall—to advance and renew the attack alongside Jones's and von Blessingh's men. This second assault consisted of about 600 men in thirty companies, Hall's eight companies on the right of the ridge top, Jones's twelve companies on the left, and to their left the ten companies of von Blessingh's regiment, finding no room on the ridgetop, had to advance along the eastern slope of Missionary Ridge.[17]

Von Blessingh ran into trouble immediately. On the eastern slope his regiment was a target for the crossfire of two Confederate brigades posted on the irregularly shaped spur to the east of the ridge. Though some of the fire was long-range, the number of bullets falling around the 37th Ohio "fairly plowed up the leaves and made the very ground seem alive," as one soldier recalled. With casualties mounting rapidly, von Blessingh had to fall back.[18]

Meanwhile, up on the ridgetop, Jones and Hall were faring little better. In this constricted space, defenders behind breastworks held all of the advantages. Some of the attackers pressed forward all the way to the breastworks and fought hand-to-hand across the log parapet. One member of the 40th Illinois even got over the parapet but was killed immediately. After several minutes of close fighting, the line had to fall back. The Confederates were encouraged by their success and launched a charge aimed at sweeping the Federals completely off the north end of Missionary Ridge. Hall's and Jones's men fell back to the trench line the skirmishers had taken earlier that morning and beat off the attack. It was not so much the ups and downs of the ridgetop but rather its narrowness that proved the decisive factor in these encounters. In constricted space, the attacker could use no more men than the defender, and man-for-man defenders always had the advantage, especially behind breastworks or entrenchments.[19]

Coming up in support of Hall with another regiment of his brigade, the 46th Ohio, Corse decided to lead the next attack in person. This time he chose five companies of the 46th, five of the 40th Illinois, and five of the 103rd Illinois. The rest of the brigade waited in reserve farther to the rear. Corse's attack closed in on the Confederate position, and again hand-to-hand fighting raged across the breastworks. For about an hour, the combat surged back and forth around the position. Occasional small Confederate counter-charges pushed the Federals back, but the blue-coats refused to be driven off and pressed back up to the works each time the Rebels drew back into them. The situation was already deadlocked when Corse suffered a severe wound in the leg and was carried to the rear. Without his fiery leadership, the attack lagged. Colonel Charles C. Walcutt of the 46th Ohio took over command of the brigade and recognized that it was going nowhere. Keeping a dense swarm of skirmishers up close to the Rebel works to snipe at the occupants, Walcutt pulled the rest of the brigade back to the captured entrenchments two hundred yards to the north.[20]

While Corse led his final effort against the northern end of the Confederate position on Tunnel Hill, Loomis advanced toward the tunnel itself from the west, drawing artillery fire from Confederate guns above the mouth of the tunnel and heavy small arms fire from Confederate infantry holding the buildings of a farm belonging to a man named Glass, located at the foot of the ridge just north of the railroad. Loomis reached a position about three hundred yards from the mouth of the tunnel and, for the moment, could go no farther. He was especially concerned about the vulnerable situation of his brigade's left flank, which was not in contact with Corse's brigade or any other Union troops. Seeking assets with which to shore up the dangling flank, Loomis called Colonel Adolphus Buschbeck, who commanded a small brigade of the Eleventh Corps, which Grant had sent to Sherman from Chattanooga as reinforcement. Buschbeck promptly sent two regiments to Loomis's support, the 27th and 73rd Pennsylvania. The Pennsylvania regiments moved up on Loomis's left and drove back the Confederate skirmishers that had been worrying his flank. Then, without orders, both regiments pressed after the retreating skirmishers up the slope of Tunnel Hill to the brow of the ridge, within a few dozen yards of Cleburne's breastworks.[21]

Now Loomis found himself with a different kind of left-flank problem, since the position of the Pennsylvanians as they lay prone or crouched behind trees and carried on a close-range fire-fight with Cleburne's Rebels was unstable and more severely threatened than Loomis's own left flank had been before the eastern troops' arrival. So Loomis called on his division commander, Ewing, for reinforcements. Sherman had about an hour earlier given Ewing control of Brigadier General Charles E. Matthies's brigade of John E. Smith's division, and Ewing now committed Matthies in support of Loomis and asked Smith for additional reinforcements. Smith had only one brigade left by this time, that of Colonel Green Berry Raum, and after sending it to support Loomis, he decided he might as well follow it.[22]

Meanwhile Loomis had ordered Matthies to advance and drive the annoying Rebels out of the Glass farm buildings. Matthies's troops charged under heavy fire from the farm and the ridge. The Confederates retreated, setting fire to the farm buildings as they left. Up the slope, the Pennsylvanians noted appreciatively the removal of the Confederates from the Glass farm enclave on their right rear, but they wanted more. Seeing Matthies's Federals in control of the blazing Glass farm site, the colonel of the 27th sent down a message that he needed support to hold his position. Matthies responded by leaving the 5th Iowa to hold the Glass farm, still under artillery fire from the battery above the tunnel, and led the rest of his brigade up the slope of Tunnel Hill north of the tunnel.

When Smith arrived and saw Matthies's troops scrambling up the slope, he became concerned that their position was precarious. Elements of three brigades, those of Corse, Matthies, and Buschbeck, were now engaging the Rebels at ranges of as little as one hundred feet, but the Confederates were protected by a log breastwork. The defenders also had the advantage of a central position from which they could concentrate their force quickly against any element of the attacking Union force. Returning to Sherman's command post on the detached hill, Smith conferred with Sherman and Ewing, and Sherman ordered him to send Raum's brigade to support Matthies. Raum placed two of his regiments in reserve in a somewhat sheltered sunken road at the base of the ridge and led the other two up the slope to relieve Matthies. As they were going up, Raum met Matthies himself coming back down with a painful though not incapacitating head wound. Matthies told Raum that his brigade was in bad shape. The men were nearly out of ammunition and had suffered heavy losses, including Colonel Holden Putnam of the 93rd Illinois.

Raum ordered his right regiment, the 17th Iowa, to move forward and pass over Matthies's troops, allowing them to withdraw and refill their cartridge boxes. His left regiment, the 8th Ohio, extended beyond Matthies's flank but kept even with the 17th Iowa. They were just approaching the rear of Matthies's line when the Confederates launched another of the countercharges they had mounted from time to time throughout the day. As in the other charges, the Confederates' goal was to push the Federals off the slope and far enough back to prevent their picking off Confederates inside the breastworks, as they had been doing for several hours. The Rebels leaped over their breastworks and charged down the hill into the teeth of heavy fire from Buschbeck's and Matthies's men. They had stopped previous charges and would probably have stopped this one save that at that moment another large force of Confederates charged around the curve of the hillside to the south and crashed into the Union right flank.

Having a wave of Rebel soldiers sweep down on their flank, seemingly out of nowhere, was so startling that many of the Federals believed the Confederates had issued from the mouth of the tunnel itself, having used the path through the ridge to infiltrate the Union flank. In fact, that had not been necessary. Instead, the wily Cleburne had moved some of his troops into the saddle south of Tunnel Hill and directly above the tunnel until they were even with the Union troops fighting on the slope of Tunnel Hill. The curve of the hillside hid them from the Federals until they charged around its shoulder and launched their surprise attack, striking the Union line squarely in flank.

In quick succession Buschbeck's two regiments crumbled, then the 5th Iowa and 93rd Illinois of Matthies's brigade, and finally the 17th Iowa of Raum's. Colonel Jabez Banbury of the 5th Iowa wrote in his diary that night that he and his men had had to "use our legs" to avoid being captured. Over on the line of the 17th Iowa, Colonel Raum was in a similar predicament. "I ran down Missionary Ridge as fast as my legs would carry me," he later wrote. Twice he tripped or slipped on the rough, rocky terrain and went tumbling head over heels. Each time he was able to scramble to his feet and keep ahead of the pursuing Confederates, who captured several hundred men of Buschbeck's and Matthies's brigades.

The winded and battered colonel reached the sunken road at the base of the slope and found his two reserve regiments, the 56th Illinois and the 10th Missouri, ready and waiting. They gave the Confederates a volley at thirty yards' range that halted the pursuit. After an exchange of several more volleys, the Confederates began to retreat up the hill. Raum's 80th Ohio had withdrawn northward along the slope when the rest of the line gave way and now turned its fire on the Confederates who had charged downhill from the breastworks, helping to speed their uphill retreat. Nevertheless, Cleburne had finally achieved his purpose in sweeping at least the western slope of Tunnel Hill clear of attacking Federals.[23]

Loomis's and Corses's brigades held their positions, and Matthies's and Raum's troops rallied at the base of Tunnel Hill, ready for further action. Raum was especially proud to see that when the 17th Iowa regrouped, every man was still carrying his rifle.[24] By this time, however, the short autumn afternoon was nearly over. Watching grimly from his hilltop command post to the north, Sherman realized that his attack had failed and that he would not have time to rearrange his troops and make another major effort before nightfall. Also watching from his command post atop Orchard Knob, two and three-quarters miles to the southwest, Grant had already set in motion the next phase of his attack plan, ordering Thomas to advance on the rifle pits at the foot of the west face of Missionary Ridge with the four Army of the Cumberland divisions that were already in position in front of the ridge as a first step toward assaulting the ridge itself.

In the analysis of Sherman's unsuccessful assault on the north end of Missionary Ridge, several factors emerge. First, Cleburne deserves credit for a very well managed defense. He seemed to have understood the tactical significance of the terrain around Missionary Ridge better than any other general involved in the battle, and he selected his positions very wisely indeed. He recognized the importance of the irregular spur of the ridge reaching out toward Chickamauga Creek on the east and posted strong formations on it. This gave him a crossfire on the northeastern approaches to the ridge that made Union operations there impossible.

Cleburne also recognized that the narrow northern nose of the ridge, overlooking the saddle opposite Sherman's detached hill, was indefensible precisely because it was so narrow and its slopes were so steep. Though some of his troops had begun to entrench there on the evening of the twenty-fourth after being driven off of the detached hill, Cleburne had pulled them back some three hundred yards to the broader and slightly higher knoll at the southern end of that section of ridge known as Tunnel Hill. There they had a splendid field of fire down the narrow, gently sloping corridor of ridgetop to the north, up which Corse's men had attacked the next morning.

It appears that Cleburne recognized that breastworks directly overlooking steep, irregular slopes like those on the side and nose of Missionary Ridge were actually very weak positions of defense because attackers could approach practically to the very logs of such breastworks under shelter of the steep slope itself, while defenders attempting to fire on them would have to rise up well above the top of the parapet, making themselves easy targets. Cleburne avoided this weakness by positioning his breastworks somewhat behind the brow of the hill. Military men had long known that defilade positions could be very strong, and the Duke of Wellington had made much use of them during the Napoleonic Wars. Union accounts of the fight for Tunnel Hill speak of the troops reaching the brow of the ridge and finding themselves still twenty-five or thirty yards from the Confederate parapet. That was enough space for alert defenders to deliver a volley that would drive the attackers to ground, and the effect was no doubt heightened by the fact that on reaching the brow of the ridge the attackers were probably winded and in somewhat loose formation due to the climb. Union accounts do not speak of any particular difficulty or danger in getting up the steep slopes themselves, except when they were exposed to a crossfire from another part of the ridge, such as the spur on the east side. This strengthens the supposition that Cleburne accepted the tendency of such slopes to be in defilade regardless of a defender's efforts to cover them and chose instead to make the terrain work for him rather than for his attackers.

The disadvantage Cleburne accepted in exchange for adopting this plan of defense was that it allowed skillful and determined troops such as those of Sherman's Army of the Tennessee to approach to within twenty-five or thirty yards of his breastworks and then to remain there for hours, crouching in the shelter of the brow of the ridge and keeping up a steady fire on his positions, inflicting casualties and at times driving the gunners away from his artillery. He countered this disadvantage by launching repeated short charges aimed at driving the attackers off the slope or at least under the brow of the ridge. The Federals' stubborn resistance to these local attacks for much of the day created the only real threat to Cleburne's position, and his situation never became desperate. His final counterattack, late in the afternoon, using the defilade approach via the saddle above the tunnel, succeeded at last in fully accomplishing the purpose at which his other charges had been aimed. This last attack was so effective that, coupled with the lateness of the hour, it persuaded Sherman to call off his offensive.

A second factor that emerges from an analysis of the failed attack on the north end of Missionary Ridge is that the peculiar nature of the terrain itself gave Cleburne the raw material for his superbly skillful defense. In contrast to the much lower terrain on which most of the Civil War's battles were fought and with which most of the troops at Chattanooga were familiar, Missionary Ridge was more readily defensible against attacks along its narrow crest than against its steep slope. This is true for two reasons. First, a gentle slope enhanced the field of fire of Civil War weapons, whereas a steep slope degraded their effectiveness. Second, the ridge's slopes were precipitate enough that an attacking line that straddled and overlapped the ridge top as it tried to advance lengthwise along the ridge would find that its overlapping portions on the steep slopes below were in defilade and unable to add their fire against the defenders. If the overlapping units wheeled and moved up the ridge until they could fire, their flanking attack would have transformed itself into a frontal assault, with the troops emerging from defilade into the teeth of a point-blank volley from the breastworks. The narrow ridgetop was like a gradually sloping gangplank, allowing only a few attackers to advance at a time and giving all the advantages to the defender.

On the other hand, the steep and irregular slopes that made up the ridge's western face offered the attacker substantial opportunity to advance under the cover of defilade. If defending commanders were not as astute as Cleburne in the placement of their works, or if the ridge in their localities did not offer sufficient width, as it did in the knoll at the south end of Tunnel Hill but often did not in other places, then the ridge's steep face became an advantage to the attackers. The assaulting infantry would emerge from the defilade of the ridge's steep and irregular slopes virtually directly onto the breastworks, making defense almost impossible. This proved to be the case along the length of Missionary Ridge south of the tunnel when the Army of the Cumberland made its attack in the late afternoon.

Sherman and Grant's mistaken belief that Missionary Ridge was a continuous crest throughout its length was irrelevant to the failure of the attack on Tunnel Hill. So too was Sherman's decision to halt for the night with his forces still on the north side of the saddle between the detached hill (called Lightburn Hill today) and Tunnel Hill itself. The presence of the 150-foot-deep saddle between the two had no bearing at all on the course of the battle.

Cleburne would have defended Tunnel Hill in the same place and with the same degree of success if the geography of Missionary Ridge had been exactly as it appeared from the far bank of the Tennessee and the saddle did not exist at all. The myth of Sherman blundering about on November 24, unable to find the true northern end of Missionary Ridge and thereby dooming Grant's battle plan, has been popular among historians and buffs eager for one reason or another to find fault with Grant's most trusted lieutenant, but it has no basis in reality.

Insofar as the geography of Missionary Ridge concealed potentially decisive factors, they lay not in such mundane questions as where the ridge began and ended but rather in the effect that the ridge's unusual topography would have on Civil War combat. The fact that Sherman halted on the twenty-fourth without making a point of securing the far side of the saddle indicates that he may have realized this. Grant, who did not have Sherman's vantage point on Lightburn Hill and had to watch the action from distant Orchard Knob, did not understand it. Neither did Bragg, who considered his line along the crest of Missionary Ridge south of the tunnel to be impregnable, not recognizing the fatal weakness of a position fronting such a steep, narrow ridge. Other than Sherman, the only senior officer at Chattanooga who recognized the significance of the terrain was the one in position to do the most about the defense of Tunnel Hill, and that was Patrick R. Cleburne.

Notes

1. William Tecumseh Sherman, *Memoirs of General W. T. Sherman* (New York: Library of America, 1990), 383; Ulysses S. Grant, *Personal Memoirs of U. S. Grant*, 2 vols. (New York: Charles L. Webster & Co., 1885), 2:45.

2. Sherman, *Memoirs*, 385–89; Grant, *Personal Memoirs*, 2:47, 59; Jabez Banbury Diary, November 4–10, 1863, W. G. McElrea Diary, November 13, 1863, and Enoch Weiss Reminiscences, all in Civil War Miscellaneous Collection, U.S. Army Military History Institute, Carlisle Barracks, Carlisle, Pennsylvania (hereinafter cited as USAMHI); Lucien B. Crooker, Henry S. Nourse, and John G. Brown, *The 55th Illinois, 1861–1865* (Huntington, W.Va.: Blue Acorn Press, 1993), 277; John Quincy Adams Campbell, *The Union Must Stand: The Diary of John Quincy Adams Campbell, Fifth Iowa Volunteer Infantry*, ed. Mark Grimsley and Todd D. Miller (Knoxville: University of Tennessee Press, 2000), 129–31; Thomas W. Connelly, *History of the Seventieth Ohio Regiment* (Cincinnati: Peak Bros., n.d.), 56.

3. Sherman, *Memoirs*, 388; Grant, *Personal Memoirs*, 2:58.

4. Sherman, *Memoirs*, 388–89.

5. Jacob Ritner and Emeline Ritner, *Love and Valor: The Intimate Civil War Letters between Captain Jacob and Emeline Ritner*, ed. Charles F. Larimer (Western Springs, Ill.: Sigourney Press, 2000), 238–39.

6. Campbell, *Union Must Stand*, 133–34; Crooker, Nourse, and Brown, *The 55th Illinois*, 278; Sherman, *Memoirs*, 281, 389; Grant, *Personal Memoirs*, 2:65–66.

7. Crooker, Nourse, and Brown, *The 55th Illinois*, 282–84; John S. Kountz et al., *History of the 37th Regiment O.V.V.I* (Toledo, Ohio: Montgomery and Vrooman, 1889), 31; U.S. War Department, *The War of the Rebellion: A Compilation of the Official Records of the Union and Confederate Armies*, 128 vols. (Washington, DC, 1880–1901), ser. 1, vol. 31, pt. 2:572 (hereafter cited as *OR*; all references are to Series 1 unless otherwise indicated); E. W. Muenscher, "Missionary Ridge: A Vivid Story of the Opening of the Battle on the North End," *National Tribune*, April 8, 1909, 2.

8. Crooker, Nourse, and Brown, *The 55th Illinois*, 282–84; *OR*, vol. 31, pt. 2: 572–73; Jabez Banbury Diary, November 24, 1863, Civil War Miscellaneous Collection, USAMHI; Campbell, *Union Must Stand*, 134–36.

9. Muenscher, "Missionary Ridge," 2; *OR*, vol. 31, pt. 2: 573; Campbell, *Union Must Stand*, 34–36, 224–27; Connelly, *History of the Seventieth Ohio Regiment*, 60–61; Thomas Taylor, *Tom Taylor's Civil War*, ed. Albert Castel (Lawrence: University Press of Kansas, 2000), 85.

10. Muenscher, "Missionary Ridge," 2; Crooker, Nourse, and Brown, *The 55th Illinois*, 282–84; *OR*, vol. 31, pt. 2: 573, 629.

11. Muenscher, "Missionary Ridge," 2; *OR*, vol. 31, pt. 2: 646; Campbell, *Union Must Stand*, 224–27; Taylor, *Tom Taylor's Civil War*, 84–87; Crooker, Nourse, and Brown, *The 55th Illinois*, 285.

12. *OR*, vol. 31, pt. 2: 43–44; Muenscher, "Missionary Ridge," 2.

13. *OR*, vol. 31, pt. 2: 43–44.

14. Muenscher, "Missionary Ridge," 2.

15. *OR*, vol. 31, pt. 2: 574.

16. Ibid., 629; Taylor, *Tom Taylor's Civil War*, 87–90.

17. Taylor, *Tom Taylor's Civil War*, 87–90.

18. Kountz et al., *History of the 37th Regiment*, 28.

19. Taylor, *Tom Taylor's Civil War*, 87–90.

20. Green B. Raum, "With the Western Army: The Battle of Missionary Ridge," *National Tribune*, April 24, 1902, p. 2; *OR*, vol. 31, pt. 2: 636.

21. *OR*, vol. 31, pt. 2: 634.

22. Ibid., 634, 643–44.

23. Raum, "With the Western Army," 2; *OR*, vol. 31, pt. 2: 575, 652–53, 655; Campbell, *Union Must Stand*, 136–38; Jabez Banbury Diary, November 25, 1863, Civil War Miscellaneous Collection, USAMHI.

24. Raum, "With the Western Army," 2.

4
—

BAPTIZING THE HILLS AND VALLEYS:
CLEBURNE'S DEFENSE OF TUNNEL HILL

John R. Lundberg

O n the morning of November 24, 1863, a courier from General Braxton
Bragg informed Irish-born Major General Patrick Cleburne that he
should send a brigade to protect the East Tennessee and Georgia Railroad
bridge over Chickamauga Creek. Bragg had just learned that Union forces had
crossed to the south side of the Tennessee River near the mouth of Chickamauga Creek, threatening the Confederate right. Cleburne dispatched Brigadier General Lucius Polk and his brigade to carry out the task of guarding
the bridge. In the meantime, Cleburne and his other three brigades watched
the unfolding battle for Lookout Mountain.

Just after 2:00 P.M. another courier from Bragg approached Cleburne with
orders to move the rest of his division rapidly to the Confederate right where
he would guard the high ground at the north end of Missionary Ridge. Correctly perceiving that the Federal threat had become acute, Cleburne started
his remaining three brigades north. Brigadier General James A. Smith's
brigade of Texans led the way over the rugged terrain toward the right.
Lieutenant Robert M. Collins of the 6th/10th/15th Consolidated Texas Regiment remembered: "We were put in line and started off at a double quick, to
the right. We knew from the way couriers were dashing around, the serious
look on the face of those in high place, the haste with which we were being
moved . . . that somebody was getting hurt, or we were on a race with the
Federals for some important point." As Cleburne galloped ahead of his command, he met Major D. H. Poole of Bragg's staff, an engineer whom Bragg
had sent to show Cleburne his position. The Irishman encountered Poole
atop the northernmost spur of Missionary Ridge, a prominence known as
Tunnel Hill. After rapidly examining the ground, Cleburne sent Poole back
to Bragg with the message that he could not possibly hold the hill with the
three brigades he had on hand.[1]

Cleburne did not realize at the time that he had stumbled into what would become one of the most important, and controversial, episodes in the battles for Chattanooga. Cleburne's defense of Tunnel Hill has become legendary because historians have correctly credited his stand with saving the Confederate Army of Tennessee at Chattanooga on November 25. Most scholars have pointed either to Sherman's alleged incompetence or to the difficulty of the terrain when explaining his failure to capture Tunnel Hill.[2] Historians have assumed that because Sherman vastly outnumbered Cleburne, he should have been able to take Tunnel Hill. However, once Cleburne arrived on the scene, his actions played a much larger role in the defense

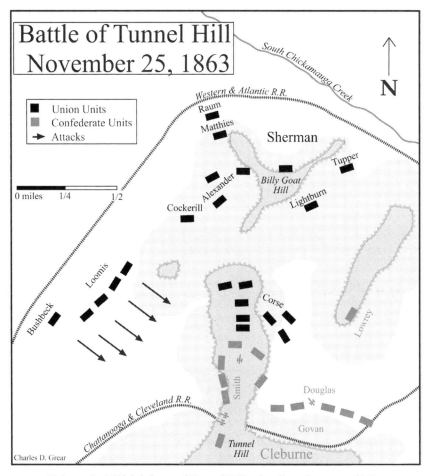

Cleburne's skillful defense of Tunnel Hill, a knoll on the crest of Missionary Ridge, blocked the persistent and stubborn efforts of Sherman's troops to exploit their position astride the northern end of the ridge.

of Tunnel Hill than historians have acknowledged. The importance of this pivotal episode in the battles for Chattanooga merits a closer, and refocused, examination of Cleburne's defense of Tunnel Hill.

By the time Cleburne reached the summit of Tunnel Hill on the afternoon of November 24, it had already been a long day for Sherman. As early as November 13, General Ulysses S. Grant informed Sherman of his plan to have him capture the mouth of Chickamauga Creek on the south side of the Tennessee River. From this position, he could outflank the Confederates on Missionary Ridge. By early afternoon of November 24, all his men had crossed the Tennessee and started south toward Tunnel Hill. Sherman's maps indicated that Missionary Ridge consisted of one continuous elevation, but they failed to show that the northernmost hill, the one closest to the river, was actually a detached spur that has since become known as Lightburn Hill, after the Union officer whose brigade was posted on it during part of the battle. Lightburn Hill was separated from Tunnel Hill by a valley approximately 150 feet deep. At about 3:00 P.M., as Sherman's men began making their way up the northern slope of Lightburn Hill, they assumed they were ascending the northern face of Tunnel Hill. Just as the skirmishers from three separate Union brigades converged on the summit of the hill, they encountered Smith's Texans coming up the other side.[3]

The impetuous charge of Smith's Texans up Lightburn Hill became the first pivotal moment in Cleburne's defense of Tunnel Hill. When Cleburne arrived on the scene with Major Poole, he understood Bragg's orders to mean that he should try to hold both Tunnel Hill and Lightburn Hill. Cleburne fully appreciated these orders because he found Lightburn Hill to be the highest ridge in the vicinity, in his words, "a high, detached ridge, which in a military point of view dominated over every point within cannon range." As Cleburne reached the summit of Tunnel Hill, Private Henry Smith of the signal corps came rushing up to inform him that the Federals were about to crest Lightburn Hill.[4]

In light of this information, Cleburne could have taken the prudent course of action and fortified his position, but instead he sent Smith's Texans into action. As the Texans rushed down into the narrow defile and up the other side, they ran into the 4th Minnesota, 30th Ohio, 47th Ohio, and 6th Iowa regiments serving as the skirmishers of three of Sherman's brigades converging on the top of the hill. Caught in the crossfire of bullets, the Texans retired down the ridge in good order, and settled into a defensive position on a small knoll at the northern end of Tunnel Hill.[5]

While the Texans skirmished and fell back, Cleburne remained busy seeing to the disposition of his other two brigades. He placed Brigadier General

Mark Lowrey's brigade of Alabamans and Mississippians south of Tunnel Hill along the crest of Missionary Ridge and had already directed Brigadier General Daniel Govan to place his Arkansans on Lowrey's left. Cleburne planned to connect his left with the right of Major General William H. T. Walker's division when the sounds of fighting to the north distracted him. He immediately realized that this continued fighting on Smith's front, although only skirmishing at the moment, meant that Sherman would probably try to turn his right flank and push Federal units in between Smith's right and Chickamauga Creek, cutting off his line of retreat as well as Polk's brigade. In reaction to this development, Cleburne ordered Govan to take his brigade and occupy a ridge spur that jutted out to the east of Tunnel Hill, between it and the Chickamauga. This ridge dominated a narrow valley that ran from north to south between the eastern slope of Tunnel Hill and the Chickamauga. These movements first showcased Cleburne's ability to react to the situation at hand and to adapt his defense to changing circumstances, something that would serve him well in his continued defense of the Confederate right.[6]

Soon after this, around 4:00 P.M., Lieutenant General William J. Hardee arrived on the scene, quickly reviewed Cleburne's dispositions, and made some adjustments of his own. He placed two of Lowrey's regiments on a ridge spur running perpendicular to and north of Govan's position. This left only two of Lowrey's regiments and a battalion on Smith's left, to cover a front of nearly a mile between Smith's Texans and Brigadier General States Rights Gist's brigade, the unit anchoring the right of Walker's division along Missionary Ridge. Hardee also took two cannon of Semple's Alabama Battery, under Lieutenant Richard Goldthwaite, and placed them with the two regiments of Lowrey's brigade on the right.[7]

Night fell on the combatants at about 6:30 P.M. that late November day, and Hardee departed to attend to the rest of his corps. Many commanders in Cleburne's place would have left well enough alone and waited for daylight to make any further adjustments to their lines, but the Irishman took a more proactive stance. Cleburne fully anticipated a daylight attack by Sherman and went about making his dispositions by moonlight with a sense of urgency. The fact that Cleburne did not wait until later in the night to arrange his division also played a critical role in preparing for his defense the following day.

Shortly after dark, Cleburne learned of the Union capture of Lookout Mountain. In anticipation that Bragg would retreat due to the loss of the Confederate left flank, Cleburne sent all of his artillery and ordinance, except for Goldthwaite's two guns, back across the Chickamauga. The Irishman impatiently waited until 9:00 P.M. for orders from Bragg to retreat but did not receive any communications. In frustration, he turned to his assistant adjutant general, Captain Irving Buck, and ordered him to find General Hardee and ask him for instructions. "Go at once to General Hardee," Cleburne instructed, "and ask what has been decided upon, and say that if we are to make a stand it is necessary that I should know, in order to get my artillery and ammunition trains in their proper place without delay." Arriving at Hardee's headquarters, Buck found the general absent. Hardee's assistant adjutant general, Captain T. B. Roy, invited Buck to await the general's return, but Buck declined. Instead, the captain rode on to Bragg's headquarters. Just as he arrived, several generals began to emerge from Bragg's tent, and he heard Major General John C. Breckenridge remark, "I never felt more like fighting than when I saw those people shelling my troops off Lookout today, and I mean to get even with them." Buck soon found Hardee, who relayed a message to him for Cleburne: "Tell Cleburne we are to fight; that his division will undoubtedly be heavily attacked, and they must do their very best." In a flourish of bravado, Buck replied, "The division has never yet failed to clear its front and will do so again." Riding back through the darkness, Buck arrived at Cleburne's headquarters around midnight, and the Irishman sent word for his artillery to return to Tunnel Hill.[8]

Cleburne set out to immediately survey his position by moonlight. On the right, he discovered a hill that lay between his right and the Chickamauga, just north of the railroad bridge. He ordered Polk to take two of his regiments and occupy this hill. He also took the two regiments of Lowrey's brigade that he had earlier posted on Smith's left and directed them to the right, to join the rest of their brigade. At 2:00 A.M., just as Cleburne finished ordering these dispositions, a lunar eclipse covered the troops of both sides in an inky blackness.[9]

Despite the absence of moonlight, Cleburne continued to adjust the position of his division. Earlier, Smith's Texans had thrown out skirmishers at the base of Tunnel Hill and constructed some slight breastworks in front of their position on the small knoll at the northern end of Tunnel Hill. Cleburne directed Smith to move his three regiments back, closer to the crest of the hill. Smith placed the right flank of the 6th/10th/15th Consolidated Texas, under Colonel Roger Q. Mills, along the military crest of Tunnel Hill, one hundred fifty yards north of the tunnel. From there, the regiment's line ran south down the crest of the hill. Sixty yards northeast of Mills's right, Cleburne placed the left flank of the 7th Texas Infantry under Colonel Hiram Granbury. Granbury's line ran "just slightly north of east," down the side of the hill. Cleburne then placed the 17th/18th/24th/25th Consolidated Texas Cavalry (Dismounted) Regiment on Granbury's right, facing the same direction. This placement put Smith's right flank within two hundred yards of Govan's line, enabling the two brigades to assist one another if needed. The Texans moved out so stealthily, and the blackness was so thick, that their own skirmishers under Captain Samuel T. Foster did not even know the brigade had fallen back. In between the right of the 6th/10th/15th Consolidated Texas and the left of the 7th Texas, Cleburne placed the four cannon of Swett's Mississippi Battery under Lieutenant Henry Shannon. Cleburne placed the guns on the crest of the hill to hold the center of Smith's line. The Irishman then placed Douglas's Texas Battery, under Lieutenant John H. Bingham, along Govan's line, in position to enfilade any attackers coming against Smith's northern front. Finally, he placed Thomas J. Key's Arkansas Battery directly over the tunnel, facing west. In the meantime, Hardee dispatched three regiments from Brigadier General John Brown's brigade of Major General Martin L. Stevenson's division to Tunnel Hill, and Cleburne placed them to the left of Key's guns, with their line running south down the crest of Missionary Ridge. In an effort to strengthen his position, the Irishman distributed axes to his men to construct breastworks, but the Confederates had to wait until the abatement of the lunar eclipse to begin their work.[10]

By daylight on November 25, Sherman had a much better grasp of the terrain and had devised a plan of attack. He faced the difficulty of attacking a now fully prepared Cleburne atop Tunnel Hill. Ideally, his attacking units would be able to attack from three different directions—approaching the prominence from the north, east, and west simultaneously—but this meant they would not be able to see each other during the movement. Therefore, even though Sherman outnumbered Cleburne roughly eight to one, his numbers would be offset by the difficult terrain.

Sherman gave responsibility for the primary attack to the division of Brigadier General Hugh Ewing. Brigadier General John Corse's brigade would attack directly along the crest of the ridge, while Colonel John Loomis and his brigade would advance down the west side of the ridge until they reached the tunnel and then turn east against the Confederate position. Finally, Colonel Joseph Cockerill's brigade would remain in reserve. Sherman also detailed two hundred men from Colonel Joseph A. J. Lightburn's brigade to reinforce Corse's brigade. Lightburn's men would advance directly on Tunnel Hill from Lightburn Hill, supporting the left of Corse's attack.[11]

At daylight, around 7:00 A.M., Sherman's advance began with the detachment from Lightburn's brigade, the 30th Ohio, plus two companies of the 4th West Virginia, who sallied down into the saddle between Lightburn Hill and Tunnel Hill. As the Ohioans and West Virginians moved forward, they encountered the skirmishers of Smith's brigade under Captain Foster. Writing in his journal, Foster recalled, "as soon as it is light enough to see anything one of my men . . . says 'Capt. I see one. Can I shoot at him.' I told him to wait until it was a little lighter and then blaze away. He fired at him in a few minutes thereafter and in so doing fired the first gun for that day." As the battle commenced, Foster told his men to keep firing but fall back slowly, moving from tree to tree. After falling back, the Texan skirmishers rejoined the rest of their brigade atop Tunnel Hill. About two hundred fifty yards from the crest of Tunnel Hill, the Federals encountered the breastworks thrown up by the Texans the night before on the small knoll at the end of the ridge. The commander of the detachment, Colonel Theodore Jones of the 30th Ohio, halted his men behind the shelter of the breastworks to catch their breath and get their bearings. Meanwhile, to Jones's dismay, Corse and his brigade had not yet reached the ridge.[12]

Despite the lack of reinforcements, the Federals began their first push on Tunnel Hill. Jones immediately sent back to Lightburn for more men, and he ordered the 37th Ohio to come to the aid of their comrades. Meanwhile, Corse had sent forward elements of two regiments from his brigade, the 40th Illinois and 103rd Illinois. With these reinforcements, the 30th and 37th Ohio advanced along the crest with Corse at their head under devastating fire from Swett's Mississippi Battery. They approached within fifty paces of the Confederate line before falling back, and the men of the 7th Texas and 6th/10th/15th Consolidated Texas leaped over the breastworks and pursued their attackers northward along the crest. The Federals fell back to the abandoned breastworks on the small knoll at the north end of Tunnel Hill and poured a galling fire into the ranks of the Texans. Near here, Colonel Mills commanding the 6th/10th/15th Consolidated Texas and General Smith both fell from their horses wounded. The Texans fell back to the top of the hill and Colonel Hiram Granbury of the 7th Texas assumed command of Smith's brigade.[13]

Undeterred, Corse took position at the head of the 40th and 103rd Illinois and led his men once more across the swale separating his knoll from the one where the Texans waited behind breastworks. This time, the Federals got all the way to the fortifications and fought the Texans with bayonets; some even made it inside the works before falling. As they began to withdraw, men from the 17th/18th/24th/25th Consolidated Texas leaped over the breastworks and pursued them back along the crest with Cleburne himself at their head. In a show of bravado, Captain Foster jumped up on the breastworks: "Yelling like an Indian when some . . . Yank . . . shot me in the right leg—the ball going crossways under my knee." Some of Foster's men helped him to the ground and tore open his pants to look at the wound before the litter-bearers carried him to the rear. The Federals fell back to the abandoned works on the small knoll at the north end of Tunnel Hill but kept their snipers active, picking off the gunners of Swett's Battery. So many of the officers and artillerymen fell from this fire, that Granbury detached some of the men of the Seventh Texas to help man the guns. Cleburne, in addition to leading the second charge, remained "omnipresent," tweaking the positions of his division.[14]

After this second attack, Sherman gave up on trying to dislodge Cleburne from the north. He also saw the futility of trying to turn Cleburne's right due to the presence of Govan's and Lowrey's brigades, leaving him with only one option: attack from the west. Fortunately for Sherman, by the time Corse's men had fallen back, Loomis had his men in position to do just that.

After some hesitation, Loomis received orders from Corse at 10:30 A.M. to advance on Tunnel Hill. Loomis, hesitating at the edge of the woods half a mile from the ridge, reluctantly gave the order to advance. However, because of an intervening hill, he could not tell where Corse's right flank rested, and he began advancing with his right flank guiding on the tunnel. This opened up a 400-yard gap between his left and Corse's right. Soon, though, Loomis received a message stating that the Confederates had repulsed Corse, and he halted his brigade half way toward the ridge, paralyzed and unsure as to what he should do next. With the Federals in this exposed position, the Confederate batteries atop the ridge began ripping apart the Union lines while Loomis's men tried to return fire as best they could.[15]

Loomis's hesitation doomed the attack, as Cleburne and Hardee shifted units to meet this new threat. At Granbury's request, Cleburne detached the 2nd/15th/24th Consolidated Arkansas under Lieutenant Colonel Edward Warfield to reinforce Granbury's Texans on the top of Tunnel Hill. On reaching the hill, the Arkansans took up prone positions in front of the left flank of the 6th/10th/15th Consolidated Texas. Cleburne ordered two cannon from Swett's Battery to reinforce Govan because of the apparent inability of Douglas's Battery to cover that front effectively, and he then replaced Swett's guns with Key's four guns, placing Key in command of all the artillery on Tunnel Hill. At the same time, Hardee ordered Brigadier General Alfred Cumming to send two regiments from his brigade on Missionary Ridge to Tunnel Hill to seize the Glass farm, a whitewashed barn, outbuildings, and slave cabins that lay north of Loomis's men. Cumming sent the 39th and 56th Georgia regiments with instructions to set fire to the farm buildings if the Union advance compelled them to fall back.[16]

In the meantime, Sherman ordered Loomis to press forward. The Federals advanced through a deep ditch and up to an embankment just under the tunnel. Here, they fell by the dozens, cut down by fire from the top of the ridge, while remaining unable to return fire effectively due to the elevation of the ridge. Unable to hold on without reinforcements, Loomis called for support from Colonel Adolphus Buschbeck's brigade, whom Sherman had earlier ordered to support him.

Loomis asked Buschbeck to reinforce his left flank, where Cumming's Georgians now held the Glass farm, and Buschbeck sent forward the 73rd and 27th Pennsylvania. The Pennsylvanians dashed forward through the artillery fire and forced the Georgians to take cover behind the buildings. As the two sides traded fire, the Pennsylvanians attempted to outflank the enemy, and Cumming recalled the Georgians to the top of the ridge. Precipitously falling back, Cumming allowed several companies to go back and set fire to the buildings, which they accomplished by igniting cartridge boxes stuffed with unused rounds. With Corse's men safely repulsed, Key turned his six cannon to the left and began tearing huge holes in the lines of the Pennsylvanians with round after round of canister. Rushing on, the Federals clambered up the side of the ridge, taking refuge just under the crest, where Key's artillerymen could not reach them. After catching their breath, the Pennsylvanians opened an accurate fire on Key's artillerymen, forcing them to abandon their guns. In addition, the Confederates of the 6th/10th/15th Consolidated Texas could not fire at them without exposing themselves. At this point, the Texans began hurling rocks down on the heads of the enemy, bashing in the skulls of some of the Pennsylvanians.[17]

With his position untenable and the Pennsylvanians still not adequately protecting his left flank, Loomis sought reinforcements and found them in the form of Charles Matthies and his brigade in the rear, and after some confusion, got the Prussian and his men to advance. Pushing forward, the Federals ran into intense artillery fire from Tunnel Hill and Missionary Ridge. Pressing on, they, like Buschbeck's men before them, veered too far to the left to protect Loomis's flank, although their presence continued to put pressure on Warfield's Arkansans.[18]

Just prior to the advance of Matthies's brigade, Cleburne had made further adjustments to his position that would pay dividends. He had already anticipated an advance against his left by placing the 2nd/15th/24th Consolidated Arkansas in position in front of the 6th/10th/15th Consolidated Texas, and now he went to work placing regiments behind the Texans. Shortly after 1:00 P.M. as Hardee watched Matthies's attack develop, he ordered Cumming to send another regiment to Cleburne, and the Georgian sent the 39th Georgia and shortly thereafter the 34th Georgia. Finally, Cumming accompanied his last two regiments, the 36th and 56th Georgia, to the right to aid Cleburne. The Irishman and the Georgians, despite their best efforts, could not convince the Texans to give up their front line positions. As one

Tennessean put it, the Texans "declined to be relieved, saying that it was the first time they had ever had a chance to fight the Yankees from behind the breastworks, and that they were rather enjoying it." Instead, Cleburne began lining up the Georgians behind the Texans. Soon, Brigadier General George Maney also arrived with his Tennessee brigade, sent by Hardee, and Cleburne placed them in line behind Cumming's men. Soon, though, the 2nd/15th/24th Consolidated Arkansas began to run low on ammunition, and Cleburne ordered Maney's regiment, the 1st/27th Consolidated Tennessee under Colonel Hume Field, into line on the right of the Arkansans. In these actions, Cleburne again showed his military acumen. Hardee had ordered up the reinforcements, but Cleburne had the foresight to place them at the point of the most danger. He also had the wisdom not to relieve the Texans, who continued to hold their own, but rather to reinforce them.[19]

Cleburne's instincts paid off as yet another Union brigade prepared to follow Matthies's men into action. Acting on orders from Sherman, Colonel Green B. Raum started his brigade forward at 2:30 P.M., across the open ground toward Tunnel Hill. Raum's five regiments started out at a run as the Confederate batteries on Missionary Ridge opened fire on them. Fortunately for the Midwesterners, this time the Confederate artillery aimed too high and most of their shells passed harmlessly overhead. Rushing forward, Raum's men came up on the rear of Matthies's men, still holding their ground in front of Warfield's Arkansans and Granbury's Texans. In coming up in the rear, Raum's men managed to avoid taking most of the incoming fire from Cleburne's defenders. Although the Confederates had managed to hold off Matthies's men, Raum and his brigade threatened to overrun their positions. The situation on Tunnel Hill had finally become untenable for Cleburne and his men. The addition of Raum's Midwesterners to their front threatened to envelope the flanks of the 2nd/15th/24th Consolidated Arkansas and the 1st/27th Consolidated Tennessee. If the Federals succeeded in breaking these regiments, the Texans, Georgians, and Tennesseans in their rear would almost surely follow, collapsing Cleburne's left flank.

In light of this dire situation, Cleburne called a meeting of his regimental commanders. On top of Tunnel Hill, Cleburne's commanders urged him to do what he already had an inclination to do: launch a counterattack. Cleburne gave the responsibility for the counterattack to Cumming's Georgians, and Granbury's regimental commanders informed the Georgians of the gap in their breastworks on the right flank of the 6th/10th/15th Consolidated Texas through which a regiment could fit. Cleburne and Cumming decided to use this gap for the counterattack, and Cumming dispatched the 56th and 36th Georgia Regiments to lead the charge. When the Georgians reached the front, they discovered that only about a third of a regiment could fit through the gap at a time. Cumming formed the 56th Georgia in front, with the 36th Georgia "ten steps" behind them. Federal fire sent the Georgians reeling back to the top of the ridge. Again, they charged, and again fell back. At this point, it looked as if the counterattack might fail, but Cleburne decided to take a huge risk. He decided to use all of the regiments on his left at once to counterattack down the side of the ridge. The rest of Cumming's brigade moved forward, and the 1st/27th Consolidated Tennessee and the 2nd/15th/24th Consolidated Arkansas fell in on their right, their front no more than twenty yards from the Federals clinging to the slope. Meanwhile, Cleburne rode over to the 6th/10th/15th Consolidated Texas and instructed Major V. P. Sanders to take the Federals in flank as Cumming charged them in front.

Exactly at 4:00 P.M. Cumming's hybrid command swept down the slope as the Texans moved out on their left. The Confederates struck Matthies's and Buschbeck's troops to their front, but the Union line might have held if not for the savage blow the Texans delivered to their right flank. In the vicinity of the still-burning Glass farm, the 6th/10th/15th Consolidated Texas used a fold in the side of the hill to surprise the 5th Iowa. The Texans appeared so suddenly that the Iowans swore that the Confederates had emerged from the mouth of the tunnel. Sergeant Albert Jernigan of Travis County, Texas, wrote: "now a scene of the wildest disorder and confusion ensues, some fly, others surrender, while others, for a brief space continue to fight, but they are soon overcome." According to Lieutenant Robert M. Collins of Decatur, Texas, his regiment "sailed into them, capturing six stands of colors and lots of guidons." Collins had earlier unbuckled his sword, and in lieu of this, went over the breastworks with a rock as a weapon. He reported that "A good many Yankees played dead that had not been touched." Collins "captured a whole company that had taken shelter behind a big chestnut log; they were more than willing to surrender." Some of the Confederates pursued so far that they had to turn and cut their way back out of the Union lines at the foot of the hill, but they had accomplished their mission. The Confederates had completely routed Raum's brigade and the remnants of the other Federal units from the face of ridge. Union artillery then opened fire on the Confederates as they made their way back to the top of the ridge. Despite the counterattack, some Union troops remained at the foot of the hill. Unsatisfied with this condition, Cleburne re-formed Cumming's men, the 6th/10th/15th Consolidated Texas, brought up the 15th Tennessee from the rear, and ordered the units to sweep down the hill again. At 5:00 P.M. the

Confederates charged again, this time clearing out the rest of the Federal units. Loomis's brigade still remained pinned down in front of the slope, but with no other option, Ewing withdrew them after dark. This ended the fighting for Tunnel Hill. Darkness soon enveloped Cleburne and his men on the hilltop. "By 8 o'clock" mused Lieutenant Collins, "quiet prevailed in the valley of Chattanooga, the pale moon looked down into the faces of many Confederates and Federals whose life blood had baptized the hills and valleys in a cause each thought was in the right."[20]

Cleburne and his men had succeeded because they never yielded the initiative and used the terrain to their advantage. Historians have assumed that because Sherman greatly outnumbered Cleburne and was a great general himself that the Federals lost the struggle for Tunnel Hill more than the Confederates won. This emphasis seems largely misplaced. Some have blamed Sherman, pointing to alleged incompetence on his part, but such was not the case. Sherman, unfamiliar with the terrain, did all he could to take the hill. He attacked from the north and west in succession, probing for weaknesses in the Confederate defenses, using up several Federal divisions in the process. Sherman's critics are driven by the fact that Union forces in the Confederate center on Missionary Ridge managed to break through with far less resistance, but they achieved this feat precisely because the other Confederate generals on the field did not, or could not do what Cleburne had done: keep the initiative and use the terrain to their advantage.

Rather, the inescapable conclusion is that Patrick Cleburne, his division, and the reinforcements who aided them had much more to do with holding Tunnel Hill than did Sherman in failing to take it. Cleburne seized the initiative on the night of November 24 when he immediately began surveying the terrain and placing his men in the most advantageous positions. Long after the rest of the army had stopped work for the night, Cleburne remained awake, positioning his men, incredibly, even in the face of a lunar eclipse. On the morning of November 25, Sherman's men floundered in their attempts to advance along the crest of Tunnel Hill because of the way Cleburne stationed his men. Sherman's thrust against the western face of Tunnel Hill achieved more success, but ultimately also failed because of the reinforcements provided by Hardee, and to a greater degree, Cleburne's skillful use of those reinforcements. Finally, when things looked the worst, Cleburne again used initiative, daring, and the terrain to deliver a crushing blow to his tormentors. Sherman certainly did not suffer from incompetence; in the end, the terrain did not stop him as much as Patrick Cleburne used the terrain against him, seized the initiative, and defeated him.

Notes

1. Irving A. Buck, *Cleburne and His Command* (Jackson, Tenn.: McCowat-Mercer Press, 1959), 164–65; Robert M. Collins, *Chapters from the Unwritten History of the War between the States: Or the Incidents in the Life of a Confederate Soldier in Camp, on the March, in the Great Battles, and in Prison* (1893; reprint, Dayton, Ohio: Morningside Press, 1988), 176–77; U.S. War Department, *The War of the Rebellion: A Compilation of the Official Records of the Union and Confederate Armies*, 128 vols. (Washington, D.C., 1880–1901), series 1, vol. 31, pt. 2: 745–53 (hereafter cited as *OR*; all references are to Series 1 unless otherwise indicated).

2. For the view that Sherman acted with incompetence, see Peter Cozzens, *The Shipwreck of Their Hopes: The Battles for Chattanooga* (Urbana: University of Illinois Press, 1996), 150–53. For the position that terrain played a larger part in Sherman's decision making, see Steven E. Woodworth, *Six Armies in Tennessee: The Chickamauga and Chattanooga Campaigns* (Lincoln: University of Nebraska Press, 1998), 184–85. Of all the major studies of Chattanooga, only Wiley Sword's study *Mountains Touched with Fire: Chattanooga Besieged* (reprinted, New York: St. Martin's Press, 1995), 240–47, gives Cleburne any credit for his stellar defense of Tunnel Hill.

3. *OR*, vol. 31, pt. 2:571–72. Other historians refer to Lightburn's Hill as Billy Goat Hill. Steven E. Woodworth, *Nothing but Victory: The Army of the Tennessee, 1861–1865* (New York: Alfred A. Knopf, 2005), 471.

4. *OR*, vol. 31, pt. 2:745–53. The high-ridge spur known as Billy Goat Hill has an elevation of about 1,100 feet, while Tunnel Hill has an elevation of just under 1,000 feet at its summit. The valley in between the two hills drops to about 850 feet in elevation.

5. Cozzens, *Shipwreck of Their Hopes*, 153.

6. *OR*, vol. 31, pt. 2: 745–53.

7. Cozzens, *Shipwreck of Their Hopes*, 154–55.

8. *OR*, vol. 31, pt. 2: 745–53; Buck, *Cleburne and His Command*, 166–67.

9. *OR*, vol. 31, pt. 2: 745–53. Craig Symonds in his *Stonewall of the West* states that Cleburne completed his dispositions before the onset of the lunar eclipse, but this would have been nearly impossible given that he had only two hours to make the complicated and myriad dispositions he did that night. What is more likely is that Cleburne had finished issuing his orders and had gotten his artillery on the west side of the Chickamauga by 2:00 A.M. when the eclipse set in. It is clear that Cleburne's men had to move to their new positions in the inky blackness. This is also corroborated by the fact that Captain Samuel Foster, commanding Smith's skirmishers, stated that is was so black, he did not know that the brigade had moved back to their new position at the crest of Tunnel Hill. If the eclipse had not set in, Foster would have seen the movement. Craig L. Symonds, *Stonewall of the West: Patrick Cleburne and the Civil War* (Lawrence: University Press of Kansas, 1997), 166. Norman Brown (ed.), *One of Cleburne's Command: The Civil War Reminiscences and Diary of Captain Samuel T. Foster, Granbury's Texas Brigade, C.S.A.* (Austin: University of Texas Press, 1980), 59–60.

10. *OR* vol. 31, pt. 2:745–53.

11. Woodworth, *Nothing but Victory*, 471.

12. Ibid., 471–72; Brown, *One of Cleburne's Command*, 61.

13. Woodworth, *Nothing but Victory*, 471–72; *OR*, vol. 31, pt. 2: 745–53.

14. Cozzens, *Shipwreck of Their Hopes*, 214–15; Brown, *One of Cleburne's Command*, 63; Buck, *Cleburne and His Command*, 169.

15. Cozzens, *Shipwreck of Their Hopes*, 217–19.

16. *OR*, vol. 31, pt. 2: 745–53.

17. Cozzens, *Shipwreck of Their Hopes*, 220–22; *OR*, vol. 31, pt. 2: 368–69.

18. *OR*, vol. 31, pt. 2: 651–53.

19. Ibid., 733–38; Nathaniel Cheairs Hughes Jr., *General William J. Hardee: Old Reliable* (Baton Rouge: Louisiana State University Press, 1965), 175.

20. *OR*, vol. 31, pt. 2: 745–53; Cozzens, *Shipwreck of Their Hopes*, 236–39; Albert J. Jernigan, Letter to His Parents, Austin, Texas, May 18, 1872, The Briscoe Center for American History, University of Texas at Austin; Collins, *Chapters*, 180–83.

5
—

WHAT HAPPENED ON ORCHARD KNOB?

ORDERING THE ATTACK ON MISSIONARY RIDGE

Brooks D. Simpson

Three times in thirteen years, the distinguished Civil War historian Bruce Catton had attempted to describe the course of events at the battle of Chattanooga on November 25, 1863. Three times he had tried to describe the situation facing Ulysses S. Grant that morning. Three times he had narrated the course of events as Grant, George H. Thomas, and several other generals pondered what to do in the face of evidence that attacks against Braxton Bragg's left and right flanks had not gone as planned. Three times he had fashioned accounts of how Grant came to order Thomas to attack Bragg's center on Missionary Ridge. And three times he had explained how an advance against the rifle pits at the base of the ridge had turned into an all-out assault that drove the Rebels off the crest and won a most improbable victory. And yet even this master of the Civil War narrative finally brought himself to make a confession: "It is impossible to harmonize all other tales of what happened that afternoon on Orchard Knob."[1]

What did happen on the afternoon of November 25, 1863? For once, the liveliest debates involve the victors. There are plenty of questions to answer. Why did Union forces assault Missionary Ridge? Who was responsible? What did Grant plan to do? What did he intend Thomas's men to do? How did changing circumstances affect Grant's thinking? And what about the advance itself? What did the commanders understand their mission to be? Was the surge up the slope toward the crest of the ridge an instantaneous impulse, or was there something else behind it? In turn, what evidence do we have with which to construct a narrative of what happened? How has the discussion over this operation evolved? What does that evolution tell us about the construction of Civil War battle narratives?

Several people on Orchard Knob left recollections of what they witnessed or did on November 25. They included newspapermen William F. G.

Shanks and Sylvanus Cadwallader, War Department observers Montgomery C. Meigs and Charles A. Dana, staff officers James H. Wilson, William F. Smith, and James S. Fullerton, division commander Thomas J. Wood, and General Ulysses S. Grant. Some of these recollections were offered shortly after the battle, while others appeared far later. Each had something to say about how the decision was made to attack Missionary Ridge, the nature of the orders given by Grant, and the overall intent of the operation. Several included vivid descriptions of the interaction between Grant, Thomas, and several of the other generals present.[2]

Quartermaster General of the Army Montgomery C. Meigs was in Chattanooga to supervise the supply situation there. His official report to Secretary of War Edwin M. Stanton of the victory at Chattanooga was widely quoted, especially his depiction of the taking of Lookout Mountain as the battle "above the clouds." At the same time, he composed a more extended narrative of events in his private journal. On the morning of the twenty-fifth, Meigs noted, "We shall have a battle on Mission Ridge"; he then became impatient for it to begin. Realizing that matters were not progressing well on either flank, Grant ordered Thomas's men to take the rifle pits at the base of the ridge and then watched as they continued on their way up. "General Grant said it was contrary to orders, it was not his plan—he meant to form the lines and then prepare and launch columns of assault, but, as the men, carried away by their enthusiasm had gone so far, he would not order them back." That comment would be overlooked by many chroniclers in the years to come, but it helps resolve one of the puzzling events of the battle, namely what Grant intended to do when he directed Thomas to order his four divisions forward.[3]

Others offered their own impressions of what had happened. Charles A. Dana's first extended description of the assault, wired that evening to Washington, mentioned Bragg reinforcing his right and Gordon Granger's obsession with operating artillery to the neglect of his responsibilities to command his troops. On the morning of November 26, Dana added that the "orders were to carry the rifle-pits along the base of the ridge and capture their occupants, but when this was accomplished the unaccountable spirit of the troops bore them bodily up" the ridge. He added, however, that it seemed Philip Sheridan and Wood had issued orders to advance.[4] In his formal report, George H. Thomas contented himself with a rather straightforward narrative, observing: "It will be perceived from the above report that the original plan of operations was somewhat modified to meet and take the best advantage of emergencies, which necessitated material modifications of that plan." He was otherwise silent as to the details of ordering the assault on Missionary Ridge.[5] Other officers, at the corps, division, brigade, and regimental level filed their own reports. Not everyone was happy with the result. William T. Sherman complained that several accounts slighted his own contribution to the victory, a sign that not everyone agreed on what had happened.[6]

Other eyewitnesses would not offer their accounts for some time. A year after the war ended, reporter William F. G. Shanks's book of essays on various Union generals appeared. The chapters had originally appeared as articles in *Harper's* magazine. When it came to Chattanooga, Shanks passed over the issue of why Grant acted as he did to describe what happened when Grant and Thomas saw the line surge up the slope. Thomas turned to Grant "and said, with a slight hesitation, which betrayed the emotions which raged within him, 'General, I—I'm afraid they won't get up.'" At first Grant offered no answer, but after taking in the situation, he calmly took the cigar out of his mouth, flicked away the ashes, and replied, "Oh, give them time, general," before returning the cigar to his mouth.[7] Shanks's description stands in marked contrast to later portrayals of how both men responded to the sight of the Union advance, and most historians skip over Shanks's account without explaining why.

Two years later, during the presidential election year of 1868, three accounts of the events of November 25 appeared. Newspaperman Albert Richardson offered a campaign biography based in part upon interviews with various people in Grant's life. Richardson's lively narrative, sprinkled with quotes, recited the notion that Bragg had reinforced his right against Sherman, leaving his left and center vulnerable; that when neither Hooker nor Sherman made progress, Grant was left to order the assault when he saw Bragg shift more forces from his center to his right; that it was left to Grant's chief of staff, John A. Rawlins, to point out to Grant that the advance had not commenced, whereupon a division commander claimed he had no orders, Thomas claimed to have issued them, and it was Granger, too busy directing the fire of an artillery battery, who had failed to implement Thomas's orders. Those orders were "to carry those rifle pits at all hazards, and then to halt for further directions." Richardson expanded upon Shanks's account of the exchange between Grant and Thomas once the ascent up the slopes commenced: when Thomas expressed alarm that the men "will be all cut to pieces," Grant replied, "Let us see what the boys will do. They are not so badly scattered as you think. You see a good deal more bare ground between them on that hill-side than you would if it were level. We will see directly. The boys feel pretty good; just let them alone." That ascent, Richardson said, was "without orders." Having praised Grant's generalship during the battle, Richardson neatly summed it, declaring that "never was commander so well aided by his soldiers. The campaign was his; the charge on Missionary Ridge was 'the Privates' Victory.'"[8]

At the same time, two people close to Grant—former assistant secretary of war Charles A. Dana and staff officer and cavalry commander James H. Wilson—collaborated on a biography. Both men had been on Orchard Knob that fall afternoon. They recounted a story that would have pleased Grant and Sherman. Yes, Sherman's attacks caused Bragg to weaken his center to strengthen his right; Grant, seeing this, waited for the right moment to order Thomas to attack; the men took the rifle pits, and then, "[w]ith one of those wild and unaccountable impulses originating in the native sagacity of men and officer alike," the men continued up the slope with the crest as their objective.[9] In light of what Wilson would later have cause to say about events on Orchard Knob, this 1868 narrative raises questions about how recollections change and deepen as circumstances change.

Finally, the first volume of what became a three-volume history of Grant's military career, penned by staff officer Adam Badeau, appeared. The same elements appeared, although Badeau relied upon a theme that Sherman had promoted and would continue to advance in years to come—that his assault on the Confederate right, far from being the planned decisive blow, had always been something of a diversion, one designed to force Bragg to weaken his center and open the way for Thomas's success. It is fair to say that this appears to have been a rationalization after the event, for Grant saw Thomas's army as performing a supporting role while he left it to Sherman to win the battle: understandably, Sherman's claim would draw fire in the years to come. Moreover, Badeau insisted that Grant knew that Hooker was making progress, and so his success was momentarily expected. Thus Grant ordered first Thomas and then his subordinates to advance, "carry the rifle pits at the foot of Missionary ridge; and, when this was done, to re-form the lines, in the rifle-pits, with a view to carrying the top of the ridge"—something the men and officers did on their own.[10]

By 1868, in short, a narrative was in place, one which featured certain key elements in explaining what happened on November 25, 1863. These accounts agreed that Grant had always intended to order Thomas forward; that he wanted to time that assault with the progress made on the flanks by Hooker and Sherman; that he (and others) believed that Bragg shifted forces from his center to his right; that the only order actually issued looked to the taking of the rifle pits, after which the attackers would regroup and await orders, presumably to ascend the slope at the proper moment; and that the men took things into their own hands and anticipated Grant's next step. Most accounts distinguished between what Grant initially desired on November 25, what motivated him to order Thomas forward, his intent to order an assault of the crest at the proper moment, and the fact that the only order actually issued concerned taking the rifle pits at the base of the ridge. Only Badeau's account, apparently influenced by Sherman, sounded a discordant note in suggesting that Sherman's attack was more in the nature of a feint or distraction than the major blow Grant had intended. In later accounts, Granger's preoccupation with artillery, the delay in getting the assault under way, and how Grant and Thomas interacted would gain more attention. Additional research into after-action reports would reveal that the decision to assault the crest was not quite the miracle of simultaneous inspiration that one might assume from these accounts and that there was no weakening of the Confederate center.

In the 1870s, Union commanders, their surrogates, and others began to contest what really happened on November 25, 1863. Chief among them was William T. Sherman, whose controversial 1875 autobiography offered an account of Chattanooga that reinforced his own belief that the battle was fought according to plan and that, far from being the featured attack, his actions on the Confederate right were designed to pave the way for Thomas's success. That, simply put, was not true. To be sure, Sherman was operating under the widely held impression that Bragg had weakened his center to reinforce his right (as it turned out, he was wrong in that regard), but anyone familiar with the course of the battle would have reason to contest Sherman's version of events.[11]

The story of how writers responded to Sherman's claims and the controversies sparked by the publication of the memoirs are worthy of study for students who want to learn more about the rivalries between Union commanders and armies. Although Sherman was not on Orchard Knob, his narrative sparked responses from people who were on Orchard Knob, intent on setting the record straight about the origins of the assault on Missionary Ridge. Thomas J. Wood, one of Granger's division commanders, offered an account in 1876 that suggested that Grant was moved to order Thomas forward to assist Sherman, whose attack had come to naught. As Wood recounts it, Grant said, "I think that if we advance and take the rifle-pits opposite our front at the base of Missionary Ridge, the movement will so menace Bragg's centre on the crest that he will withdraw force enough from Sherman's front to permit him to carry his point of attack." Wood agreed, adding that he was confident his men could take the rifle pits. The conversation did not strike him as odd, because the two men had known each other since their days at West Point. Wood wanted readers to understand "that an assault on the crest of Missionary Ridge was not intended to be a part of that particular movement, however much General Grant may have intended that such an assault should be subsequently made." That said, he challenged the notion that Grant's idea was "a radical departure from the original plan of battle": instead, it was "simply auxiliary to the dominant and ruling attack of the original plan," featuring Sherman's attack on Bragg's right.

According to Wood, Grant then walked over to Thomas, and the two discussed what to do next. Thomas called Granger over, told him to get ready to move, and Granger passed the word on to Wood (and promised to do so to Sheridan as well). Wood speculated that it was at Thomas's suggestion that Palmer's two divisions were added to the assault force. He insisted that his men "understood fully and thoroughly the whole extent and scope of the order they had received," seeking to forestall any criticism based on confusion over orders. Once the men had taken the rifle pits, they realized "that the position was untenable" and took it upon themselves to advance. As the men went up, one of Granger's aides inquired of Wood whether he had ordered the advance. Wood said no, but that, as matters stood, he believed his men would take the crest. Soon after, one of Thomas's staff officer rode up and told Wood that as the assault was already under way, "to go on with it," but to halt once the crest was taken—orders that were repeated moments later. Wood maintained, however, that left the impression that it was a "spontaneous and impulsive movement" undertaken by the men themselves.[12]

Wood expanded on this some twenty years later. He believed that had Grant's plan been implemented, a military disaster would have ensued. By that time, however, he seemed at least as interested in staking a claim to his division reaching the crest first and having been the first to advance beyond the rifle pits. He also seemed to have been far more able to set aside his earlier association with Grant in order to raise serious questions about Grant's account in his memoirs. The notion that the attack upon the crest was the natural consequence of the order to take the rifle pits, Wood argued, was "further refuted by the fact that" in Granger's two divisions "no man has ever yet been found who does not say the orders he received peremptorily ordered him to halt at the base of the Ridge. If General Grant intended the assault of the crest of the Ridge to follow immediately on the heels of the initial success, with simply a halt for reformation and without further orders, he certainly kept that intention severely to himself." One might attribute some of the passion Wood developed over twenty years to the fact that the 1896 article contained the text of an address he gave to his veterans; part of it also seemed to be fueled by anger against Grant.[13]

For if Sherman's *Memoirs* had fueled controversy about what happened on November 25, so did the writings of Ulysses S. Grant. In 1885 the general shared his views with the readers of *Century Magazine*, which had attracted much attention with its series "Battles and Leaders of the Civil War" (later published as a multivolume set). Later, basically the same narrative would appear in Grant's *Memoirs*. The story of Bragg's reinforced right, the need to offer Sherman some relief, the description of orders for an attack to take the rifle pits and then re-form "preparatory to carrying the ridge," and Grant wondering why there was a delay (in the article, Grant says he was about to ask Thomas what was going on when he saw Wood, who claimed he had not gotten any orders—a tale that omitted mention of Granger), and the men advancing "without awaiting further orders or stopping to reform" was now a familiar one. By now, however, it aroused more complaint.[14]

Joseph S. Fullerton, Granger's chief of staff, offered a different and more detailed account for what happened on Orchard Knob. He wasted no time in terming the assault "an accident," something ordered on the spur of the moment by Grant, who was desperate to achieve success somewhere on November 25. Once more, the orders were to take the rifle pits alone, although Fullerton unwittingly complicated that tale when he offered the following rendering of the orders issued to Sheridan: "As soon as the signal is given, the whole line will advance, and you will take what is before you." As Fullerton had a hand in issuing those orders (for Sheridan, unlike Wood, was not on Orchard Knob), he rendered the orders as he remembered them, unintentionally revealing their ambiguity: "You will take what is before you" leaves unanswered whether the objective was the rifle pits at the base or the main line at the crest.

Fullerton's account also insists upon the unordered attack on the crest: unlike Shanks, who had described a conversation between a nervous Thomas and a quietly confident Grant, Fullerton presented a far more quoted exchange. According to Fullerton, as Grant observed the men make their way up the slope, he turned to Thomas and angrily asked, "Thomas, who ordered those men up the ridge?" Thomas, "in his usual slow, quiet manner," replied, "I don't know; I did not." Grant then turned to Granger and asked if he had issued such an order. Granger replied that he had not, adding, "When those fellows get started all hell can't stop them." Grant "said something to the effect that somebody would suffer if it didn't turn out well, and then, turning, stoically watched the ridge." Perhaps getting the message, Granger directed Fullerton to reach Wood and Sheridan, ask them if they had ordered an advance, "and tell them, if they can take it, to push ahead." Neither Wood nor Sheridan reported that they had ordered the charge, but they seemed sure it would now succeed; however, Sheridan offered that he did not know which rifle pits—the ones at the foot of the ridge or the ones at the crest—the original orders had asked him to take. Somehow Fullerton did not incorporate the implications of that comment into his narrative or relate Sheridan's confusion to the very wording he had earlier presented. The editors included yet another account supporting the notion that the charge up the crest was not authorized, and thus the point would seem to have been made.[15]

William F. Smith also added his perspective in "Battles and Leaders of the Civil War." He had been upset with Grant for some two decades, and, although his major objective in his piece (and a subsequent rejoinder) was to claim what credit he could for the reopening of a supply line to Chattanooga in October 1863 (the so-called "Cracker Line"), he could not tolerate the claim made in an earlier number of the *Century* that "few battles in any war have ever been fought so strictly according to the plan" as had Chattanooga. Smith set out to demonstrate that this was not so, and in the process repeated the by now familiar tale of Grant's demonstration of the rifle pits being turned into a successful effort to carry the crest: "The assault on the center before either flank was turned was never seriously contemplated, and was made without plan, without orders, and as above stated."[16]

The accounts offered by Wood and Fullerton proved critical to shaping the story of a charge made not simply without orders, but almost in defiance of them. Yet one notes that Thomas remains something of a cardboard figure in these accounts and that the main characters are Grant and the men at the front, with several officers playing supporting roles. It would be left to Thomas biographer Donn Piatt to offer an explanation for which there was virtually no support in the documentary record. Eager to knock apart the stories of Grant and Sherman that leaned toward an almost perfectly executed battle plan, Piatt argued that Thomas was the victim of a conspiracy aimed at depriving him of due credit. "Grant felt uneasy and ashamed in the presence of Thomas," Piatt asserted, "and both Grant and Sherman were troubled with the thought that truth and justice would award to their subordinate in office the higher position on the roll of honor." How Piatt came to that conclusion is left unsaid. And so it goes in Piatt's account, including a far more imaginative rendering of the exchange between Grant and Thomas on Orchard Knob, for when Grant turns to Thomas to find out who ordered the advance, Thomas, "a flush of pride mounting his face at the gallant action of his men," quietly responded: "I know of no one giving such orders."[17]

As Piatt was not present on Missionary Ridge, and as he gave no source for his conversation, one might well set aside his narrative. However, in decades to come, several of Thomas's biographers, moved by a desire to vindicate the supposedly besmirched reputation of their subject, would engage in similar behavior. Richard O'Connor, in an account innocent of footnotes to offer documentation, declared that as Grant demanded to know who had ordered the assault on the crest of the ridge, Thomas "watched the advance calmly through his field glasses" and replied. "By their own, I fancy."[18] Francis F. McKinney argued that Thomas opposed the assault "until Bragg's flanks had been shattered"; Freeman Cleaves asserted that "Thomas, shrugging off Grant's sharp inquiry . . . was smiling imperturbably below."[19] It would be left to Benson Bobrick to fashion an account that sounded all too much like a mixture of Thomas B. Van Horne, Piatt, and Henry van Ness Boynton, who had completed Piatt's biography—although a check of his notes reveals his utter dependence on those accounts to the neglect of more recent scholarly studies of Chattanooga.[20]

These imaginative adventures aside, there is precious little evidence about Thomas's role in the events of November 25, 1863, and next to nothing about his thinking or emotions prior to the assault on the crest. What little we do have from eyewitnesses does not reveal him to be confident. In the words of Van Horne, who knew Thomas and who wrote extensively on his old commander and the army he led, Thomas "had been opposed to the movement as ordered when there was no prospect of support from Sherman or Hooker, and disregarding mere suggestions from General Grant made earlier in the afternoon had not sent the troops forward until positively ordered to do so."[21] That several of Thomas's biographers may have wanted to portray their subject in such a flattering light may say something interesting about their infatuation, but it does not add to our understanding of how events unfolded.

Of more interest were the accounts of newspaper reporter Sylvanus Cadwallader and former Grant staff officer James H. Wilson. Each man no longer saw Grant as he once did. Wilson had experienced a major falling-out with Grant in the 1870s, due in part to political differences, and in years to come Wilson's vitriolic treatment of Grant in private correspondence and interviews was noted by several observers. Wilson set forth two long accounts of what happened on Orchard Knob, one appearing in his 1912 autobiography, the other in a 1916 biography of Rawlins. In both accounts, Rawlins played a central role. According to Wilson, the impatient chief of staff grew testy with Granger and Thomas and then retreated to consult with Smith and Wilson on what to do next, while Grant hesitated to transform his suggestions and observations into direct and unmistakable orders. It was left to Rawlins to prod Grant to act ("in a low voice"). Walking over to Thomas, Grant asked, "Don't you think it is about time to order your troops to advance against the enemy's first line of rifle pits?" Thomas said nothing: he simply continued to survey the field through his field glasses. Again Rawlins pressed Grant to give a direct order, and this time Grant, "who had by this time also become thoroughly aroused," did so, adding that it was time for Granger to cease playing battery commander. According to Wilson, Thomas complied, and within a short period of time the advance began. Notable in this account was the absence of an exchange between Grant, Wood, Thomas, and Granger as to why nothing had happened; in light of later accounts that suggest that Rawlins was angry with Grant, Wilson's account makes it clear that while Rawlins chose to prod Grant, he was furious with Thomas and Granger.[22]

Wilson's description of the charge added nothing substantial to what was already known about the orders themselves, as he was not privy to the content or wording of the orders transmitted down Thomas's chain of command. However, he was eager to report that his study of Confederate reports showed that Bragg did not shift forces from his center to block Sherman's attack on the right. He conceded that it was an honest mistake, not an outright lie, and that the fact that Grant in the official report of the battle gave Sherman more credit for doing less and Thomas less credit for achieving more was understandable, not malicious—although this might have been due to Wilson's insistence that Rawlins drafted Grant's official reports, as if that secretarial task befitting a staff officer diminished Grant's generalship.[23] What one might note is that Wilson left out all these details in his 1868 campaign biography, mentioned above.

By the time Sylvanus Cadwallader began to prepare his recollections of his relationship with Grant from 1862 to 1866, he had come away from reading Grant's memoirs highly dissatisfied that they did not give the acknowledgement that he felt was due Rawlins, Grant's chief of staff and a close friend of Cadwallader (close enough that Cadwallader named his son after Rawlins). The resulting account, which did not appear in print until 1955 (and then in a selected edition), mentions that Rawlins was impatient at the failure of Thomas's men to advance and that he "inquired of Grant" why nothing had been done. Grant asked in turn a division commander (Cadwallader recalled that it was Absalom Baird, who was not on Orchard Knob; it was doubtless Thomas J. Wood, who mentioned Grant's question) and Thomas why nothing had happened, to which Thomas replied that he had issued orders for an advance to the corps commanders, while Gordon Granger denied he had received any such orders. Cadwallader concluded that what happened on Orchard Knob led to Grant's lack of confidence in Thomas when it came to taking the initiative in offensive operations (an estimate Cadwallader considered "just"). Elsewhere Cadwallader echoed Shanks's account of the exchange between Grant and Thomas as they observed the charge up Missionary Ridge, an exchange in which Grant appears more confident than Thomas.[24]

Thus, although Wilson, Cadwallader, and Dana remained in contact after the war, exchanging correspondence about their recollections of Grant, it would be left to Wilson alone to offer a portrayal of events on Orchard Knob that featured an explosive Rawlins railing at inactivity, and Rawlins's target was Thomas and Granger far more than it was Grant. Even the pro-Rawlins Cadwallader did not go nearly so far; when Dana's 1898 recollections appeared, the account simply repeated what was in his 1863 dispatch (perhaps a sign that ghostwriter Ida Tarbell simply inserted the wording of the dramatic dispatch).[25] Thus future accounts that would feature Rawlins's behavior would find their inspiration in Wilson's account, the last left by an eyewitness to the events on Orchard Knob.

Historians, biographers, and authors of battle studies continued to discuss what happened and why, basing their accounts on these eyewitness accounts, especially those that were prepared after 1870. Sometimes they did not weight those sources with care: in the case of several of George H. Thomas's biographers, imaginative renderings fueled by personal prejudices offered assessments not supported by the evidence they cited. Other accounts, such as J. F. C. Fuller's *The Generalship of Ulysses S. Grant*, relied on the *Official Records* to the exclusion of all else (Fuller concluded that Grant had seen the assault upon the rifle pits as a prelude to an assault on the crest and the charge itself as nothing more than "an act of common-sense").[26] Nevertheless, some accounts stand out, including three major treatments of the battle.

Most interesting was the ever-changing explanations offered by Bruce Catton, who assessed and reassessed the evidence in front of him three times. In his 1956 overview of the war, Catton offered a description of the day's events, noting that Sherman's attacks on the right "got nowhere," while Hooker's move against the Confederate left "missed fire completely." That left things up to Grant, Thomas, and the Army of the Cumberland. "What was planned and what finally happened were two different things," Catton observed. Grant directed Thomas to have his men take the rifle pits at the base of the ridge and stay there to await orders: "No one had any notion that the Army of the Cumberland could take the ridge itself." Thomas "was slow" in implementing the order to advance: he was "apparently dubious" about the whole affair. It was left to soldiers who were impatient to do something to seize the moment, the rifle pits, and then the crest on their own. It would be "a long time before the soldiers realized that they themselves were responsible for the victory."[27]

By 1965, in *Never Call Retreat*, Catton had changed his mind on a few details. Hooker "mopped up" the Confederate left, while Sherman remained stalled, leaving Grant to order Thomas to advance under the impression that Bragg was reinforcing his right. Again, the initial orders were to take the rifle pits: "A full-dress assault on the ridge itself might come later, but for the moment this move was simply a battlefield maneuver designed to keep Bragg from strengthening his right." Once more, the Cumberlanders took the base of the ridge, looked up, and decided to advance on their own, "swept forward by battlefield madness and by the impromptu orders of their own officers." Catton said nothing now about Thomas's state of mind; he cited the accounts of Wood and Fullerton; he also cited what Grant told Meigs about his intention to take the crest; and he observed in his notes that while it was clear that several generals ordered their men forward, it was "equally clear that the men got the idea independently."[28]Three years later, in *Grant Takes Command*, Catton rethought his narrative and in the process transformed it in key respects. He now flatly dismissed the story of the soldier-led charge as an "immortal legend" and took great pains to describe what he now thought had happened. Once more, Sherman stalled; once more, people thought Bragg was reinforcing his right. This time Grant postponed a morning attack by Thomas, ordered Hooker to advance against Bragg's left, and readied to send Thomas forward at the right moment, although the advance was still "supplementary," since it seemed an assault could not succeed unless Bragg was dealing with threats to his flanks. Neither Sherman nor Hooker made any headway by early afternoon, and so Grant decided to commit Thomas's four divisions. The orders were simple: Thomas's men were to "carry the rifle pits at the foot of Missionary Ridge, and when carried to reform his lines on the rifle pits with a view to carrying the ridge"—what Grant had always insisted was his intent. If Bragg reinforced his center, Sherman might break through: if Bragg had reinforced his right, then the center was weak. There were delays in moving the assault forward, but there was nothing untoward in them, and Catton said nothing about Thomas's attitude. Having taken the rifle pits, the men, "instead of carefully re-forming their ranks and await-ing further word from headquarters," simply caught "their breath and then moved on to storm Missionary Ridge itself." However, it was a simple legend that "they did this on their own hook" or that they were spurred on by the need to show Grant that they were fighters. As he concluded, "In unroman-tic fact they made the attack for the most ancient and universal of military reasons—because their officers told them to. . . . The storming of Missionary Ridge came under orders."[29]

Why, then, had anyone ever thought otherwise? Catton blamed Granger's and Wood's postwar accounts "and historians' reliance on them," noting that "these remarks prove nothing except that corps and division commanders do not always know what is going on in the combat zone." He cited several examples. One of Wood's own brigadiers, August Willich, believed his orders were to take the crest; a second, William Hazen, agreed that the orders were to stop at the rifle pits. Division commander Philip H. Sheridan "suddenly realized that his orders were vague," but before he received clarification, he concluded that he had to move forward (only to learn that Granger's orders held otherwise). Catton now moved Meigs's account of Grant's intentions from the notes to the text and said nothing about Thomas's attitude. He admitted in his notes that "this writer must confess that he simply followed the accounts of Granger and Wood," along with Joseph Fullerton's description.[30] Other historians were not so careful. Shelby Foote described a frustrated Grant and a stoic Thomas, who refused to act upon suggestions but responded promptly to orders to take the base of the ridge: then it was left to the men to take things into their own hands and rush toward the crest.[31]

As a battle, Chattanooga was neglected for some time in comparison to other Civil War battles, including the ever-present Gettysburg. Fairfax Downey offered an account of Chickamauga and Chattanooga in a volume that soon faded from attention.[32] Starting in 1984, accounts of Chattanooga began to appear. Composed in the style of the grand battle narrative that characterized much Civil War scholarship, with analysis of command decisions increasingly supplemented by descriptions offered by soldiers and junior officers on the ground, these accounts, by James Lee McDonough (1984), Peter Cozzens (1994), and Wiley Sword (1995), wrestled anew with old issues. Writing in the shadow of William S. McFeely's 1981 biography of Grant, McDonough readily adopted McFeely's skeptical perspective, arguing that although the Union general "had more substance than met the eye," he was a rather ordinary man in many ways: "War proved to be one of the things that truly aroused him."[33] No, Grant was not a dim-witted fellow whose generalship was little more than luck and superior resources, but he was no military genius, either. Taking issue with Catton, McDonough argued that Grant's biographer "became a bit carried away" in saying that Grant had always envisioned an attack against Missionary Ridge. Grant's orders to Thomas on November 24 assumed that Sherman's attack would be successful: when Sherman stalled, Grant improvised, and the orders to take the rifle pits stood alone as a diversion. After all, "if Grant had ordered an assault up the ridge against the center of the Confederate line he would have appeared reckless indeed—a general gambling contrary to sensible calculations."[34]

McDonough's explanation seemed reasonable on its face, and certainly one is hard-pressed to see what happened on November 25 merely as the fulfillment of orders given the previous evening. However, McDonough then concluded that "the final attack, as it developed, was unplanned and unauthorized by Grant." Grant had mistakenly thought Bragg was weakening his center to reinforce his right; Hooker had yet to make much progress against the Confederate left. Moving Thomas's men to the rifle pits placed them in "an untenable position." That said, McDonough also admitted that "the order to advance and take the rifle pits was not always clearly conveyed to officers who would direct the charge." Unlike Catton, McDonough was willing to speculate as to why Thomas had not implemented Grant's assault order with alacrity ("perhaps because he was skeptical of advancing even to the first line of trenches"), and he described in detail what division and brigade commanders thought they were supposed to do.[35]

Ten years after McDonough's book appeared, Peter Cozzens's study of the battle offered another version of events. Grant, he concluded, did not understand the situation when he issued his orders on November 24: he had assumed that Sherman had been successful when that was far from the case. However, Cozzens attributed to Thomas a decision to make better use of Hooker than Grant's orders permitted—"flout Grant's directive" is how he puts it. Indeed, in Cozzens's account, Thomas plays a much more prominent role, and that role is in opposition to Grant. He accepts the notion that there was a deep-seated rivalry between the Armies of the Tennessee and the Cumberland: Grant's chief of staff, John A. Rawlins, and other Grant staffers "looked to Sherman not only to deal the decisive blow of the battle, but to humiliate the Cumberlanders in the bargain," while Thomas's staff officers, led by chief of staff Joseph J. Reynolds, "shared with the Virginian the strain of uncertainty regarding their own, relatively humiliating role, and all still felt the sting of Grant's comments to the War Department that the Army of the Cumberland was too sluggish to leave its trenches." As Cozzens provides no source to substantiate his insight into such feelings and motivations, one is left to wonder how he came to ascertain such deep resentments in such a precise fashion.[36]

Cozzens's speculations can best be understood by assuming what needed to be proven, and by embracing the version of history told by the Cumberlanders. How Thomas's staff officers would have been privy to Grant's telegrams remains unanswered, and one looks for evidence to support a description of their reaction. Given that Reynolds and Grant had been friends, one would be especially curious as to why Grant would treat an old comrade this way. However, such assertions render much of what follows predictable. One sees Thomas and Hooker working together in a harmonious fashion, with Hooker moving promptly to execute Thomas's orders. "By then, Thomas was feeling much relieved, perhaps even a bit smug," according to Cozzens, because by then Grant had realized that Sherman was not enjoying any success. Once more, it is a good question as to how Cozzens knows how Thomas felt.[37]

The same characteristics appear in Cozzens's description of that happened on Orchard Knob that afternoon. As with other accounts, he relies on Wood's account of a conversation with Grant, although he frames it in terms hostile to Grant; however, when Grant approached Thomas, Cozzens tells us, Thomas was "walking the tightrope of his temper, . . . [and] made clear his objection to an attack," although he admits that "what precisely Thomas told Grant is unknown." It was left to Rawlins to prod Grant, and he "shamed him as only he could into silencing Granger and peremptorily ordering Thomas to move," which comes straight from James H. Wilson's later recollections. Even then, Rawlins had to erupt once more when Granger failed to get his men into motion, claiming he had received no such orders from Thomas, who stood but a few feet away. Cozzens reminds us that Thomas thought the attack was suicidal. Once more we read of confusion in the orders issued, including a claim that James H. Wilson, a Grant staffer, was relaying *Thomas's* wish to take the crest (it would seem that was Grant's wish, certainly if Thomas opposed the operation). Cozzens would have it both ways: according to him, Thomas opposed the attack, yet gave orders to take the crest.[38]

Comparing Cozzens's sources with his rendering of them suggests that he was not above spinning a more vivid tale, one that relentlessly cast a shadow upon Grant while spotlighting Thomas. We learn that Grant was indecisive in ordering what Thomas thought was a blunder; we learn that Thomas, having opposed the attack, indicated that he would be pleased if his generals took the crest (which would appear to do away with the notion that it was a soldiers' charge). How to resolve these apparent contradictions is left to the reader. Cozzens's take on the interaction between Grant, Rawlins, and Thomas finds little support from the documents he cites that describe these exchanges. Thus, it comes as no surprise that Cozzens concludes that Grant "never satisfactorily explained his foolish order to Thomas to seize only the rifle pits at the base of Missionary Ridge. Instead, Grant chose to lie. In both his report of the battle and his memoirs, he insisted that he had given Thomas express authority to carry the ridge itself, and implied that he fully expected that was to be done." There is simply no evidence that Grant chose to lie, and one would be left wondering how Montgomery Meigs got that version from Grant at the time of the event.[39]

Wiley Sword's lively narrative of Chattanooga also set forth the notion that the orders Grant issued on November 24 for the next day were based upon a misapprehension of what the next day would bring, and that Grant quickly set them aside. However, neither Hooker nor Sherman proved successful versus the flanks, with Thomas growing impatient over Hooker's inactivity. Grant then planned for a diversion—and nothing more—by having

Thomas advance his men to take the rifle pits, halt, and then wait. Nothing was said about taking the crest. "It was a blueprint for disaster," Sword concludes. "Grant had made a poor tactical decision, which was impulsive and not very well thought out." A check of the notes reveals that the account was built upon the recollections of Wood and Fullerton. Yes, the orders issued were confusing: "There was a sad lack of command coordination," Sword observes. Nevertheless, the advance up the ridge was "in disobedience of Grant's very specific orders." It was a "spontaneous and unauthorized charge."[40]

There have been other accounts of what happened on Orchard Knob, from Larry J. Daniel's history of the Army of the Cumberland to several biographies of Ulysses S. Grant, as well as a handful of other military studies. Daniel's account offered that Thomas was in a "sullen mood" and cited his lack of responsiveness as an example of "passive-aggressive behavior." A biography of Grant published in 2000 tried to reconcile various accounts, emphasizing that while in the end Grant's initial orders covered only the taking of the rifle pits, he had contemplated taking the crest: in the end his initial reaction to the charge was more a matter of timing and of wondering whether the advance was premature than anything else. In a study of Civil War generalship that treated Thomas well and Grant harshly, Thomas B. Buell's account of the events of November 25 agreed that the assault on the rifle pits was preliminary to a charge up the crest. Two examinations of Grant's generalship skimmed over the usual controversies (although Michael Ballard completely bought Cozzens's notion that Grant had lied about the orders he had issued to Thomas, without further elaboration); a rather straightforward biography of Thomas by Christopher J. Einolf, describing "the strange sequence of events on Orchard Knob," concluded that what happened illustrated the poor relationship between Grant and Thomas, noting that Thomas "expressed his opposition by taking a passive role," much as Daniel had suggested. However, Einolf sidestepped the usual vituperation toward Grant evident in several other Thomas biographies. Not so Benson Bobrick, who managed to overlook a great deal in preparing an account that celebrated Thomas along the lines established by Donn Piatt and others over a century before.[41]

Descriptions of what happened on Orchard Knob and the circumstances behind the assault on Missionary Ridge rest upon a finite number of primary sources. Several accounts by eyewitnesses produced years after the event appear to have been shaped by a desire to recast the story in line with a particular witness's prejudices, to avenge slights, or to make some other point—a transformation most apparent when one compares the two accounts offered years apart by Thomas J. Wood or the various stories offered over the years by James H. Wilson. Nevertheless, some of the fundamental facts seem clear. Whatever orders Grant issued on the evening of November 24, circumstances on the morning of November 25—namely, the lack of progress on both flanks—called for a change in plan. Nevertheless, it must be kept in mind that an assault up Missionary Ridge by Thomas's men was always part of the discussion, not a spur-of-the-moment decision undertaken in haste. The same challenges posed by taking the rifle pits at the base of the ridge and then advancing up the slope against the fortified crest were there on November 24 as they were on November 25, an observation rendered all the more sensible in light of evidence that Bragg did not shift forces from the center to the right to stop Sherman. That Grant thought that Sherman would strike the telling blow is evident: that this was due in part to Grant's preference for Sherman is understandable, as Grant had built up a relationship with Sherman that he did not have with either Thomas or Hooker. However, for anyone to suggest that the original plan was for Sherman to attract enough attention to weaken the Confederates elsewhere is an after-the-fact rationalization, one that Sherman eagerly embraced. Grant (and many others) accepted the argument that, whatever the original intent of the plan, Sherman's attacks caused Bragg to weaken his center. Grant was not privy to later research that such was not the case, nor was he aware that Hooker had made any progress against Missionary Ridge at the time he ordered Thomas forward.

As for the charge itself, Grant had to resort to a direct order to Thomas to initiate the advance toward the rifle pits. Given what we know, the evidence leans toward the explanation Grant gave at the time to Meigs: that after Thomas's men took the rifle pits, they were to re-form and await an order to carry the crest. Grant never issued that particular order, but that was the overall intent of the operation, and the orders to take the rifle pits implemented the first stage of a two-stage operation. Criticism of the decision to stop at the rifle pits to await orders should not be confused with evaluations of the attack upon the ridge: what the evidence suggests is that while some people may have had misgivings about the way in which Grant wanted to go about assaulting Missionary Ridge on November 25, no one questioned the idea of an assault, which was already set forth the previous day. Moreover, although there was later talk of misgivings about the idea of taking the rifle pits, for all the writing describing the relationships between Grant, Thomas, Wood, Granger, and Rawlins on November 25, no one recorded anyone raising the objection at the time that such an advance was suicidal. Over time one reads of more friction between generals on the afternoon of November 25, but one notes that neither Fullerton nor Wood said anything about Rawlins's explosions: only Wilson lavished such attention on them.

Moreover, one should conclude that whatever impatience Rawlins might have expressed toward Grant, his real target was Thomas and his subordinates for their failure to implement a plan Grant had directed to be set into motion.

There is precious little evidence bearing on Thomas's behavior on Orchard Knob and wide disagreement as to what he did and why. Most of those interpretations rest far more upon the imaginations and prejudices of authors than they do on the record. Speculation that Thomas did what he could to prevent the assault, that he waited until he knew that Hooker was approaching the ridge, or that he quietly let it be known that he'd prefer that his men push forward and take the crest, is, to be kind, problematic. Surely, if Thomas wanted his men to take the crest in defiance of Grant's orders, he forgot to tell Granger, who denied receiving any such order. Nor did he know about Hooker's whereabouts. Nor do we know what was on his mind when he saw his men make their way up the crest (and here imaginative fiction has claimed the day in several accounts). Most renderings simply overlook Shanks's account, published when both Grant and Thomas were alive: many narratives also overlook Meigs's journal.

What does come across, however, is that there was mass confusion among Thomas's subordinates as to what they were to do, and that does not speak well of that army's ability to transmit orders so as to admit of no misunderstanding. One looks in vain to the reports and accounts of corps, division, and brigade commanders for agreement as to the orders they received or what they were to do. That several commanders believed that they were to take the rifle pits in preparation for an advance up the slope suggests that at least some people comprehended Grant's overall intent. As for the assault itself, debates among participants as to who moved first, who led the way, and who reached the crest first conceal the fact that in at least several instances, lower-level commanders issued orders to advance, and that notions that the assault was the result of an instantaneous and simultaneous inspiration among enlisted personnel are understandable products of fairly vivid and ambitious imaginations—even when there might be some truth in them. For example, just days after the battle James A. Connolly recalled how Absalom Baird told him to relay an order to brigade commander Edward Phelps, calling on Phelps to advance "to storm the heights and carry the Ridge if possible." Thus, if there was confusion in the accounts of what was intended on Orchard Knob, subordinates also differed as to what they were to do.[42]

Over time, participants, observers, and most scholars fashioned their own interpretive narratives of what happened by picking and choosing whatever sources seemed to fit into a larger story that they were trying to tell. Several of these accounts substituted color, passion, imagination, and not a little prejudice for a telling of the story that relies primarily upon a fair reading of the evidence. A few attempted to extrapolate larger interpretations about the generalship of Grant and Thomas or their relationship from a particular retelling of the story. The quest to find out what in fact happened sometimes took a back seat to what people wanted to make of it. Rarely was the evidence weighed in terms of context; rarely was the possible motivation of the narrator taken into account. Instead of the telling of the story resting upon the evidence at hand, the narrative too often became a product of the story one wanted to tell, with appropriate supporting evidence presented as needed.

It is the historian's challenge to find out first what happened before determining why it happened, how it happened, or what it means. That can be a daunting task, especially when the evidence that one examines in discovering what happened often is shaped by a desire, conscious or unconscious, to shape historical memory. Moreover, sometimes these stories evolve as agendas change, as the examples of James H. Wilson and Thomas J. Wood suggest. Doubtless even the presentation of the evidence opens the presenter to the same criticism. After all, an adverb here, an adjective there, and word choices everywhere imply some sort of perspective, some form of conclusion, some inclination toward the evidence discussed, no matter how self-conscious the presenter may be of the problematic nature of the task of presenting the evidence. Many readers of Civil War literature want narrators simply to tell them what happened, as if that act in itself does not involve some sort of selection and interpretation. That is true of the events of November 25, 1863, on Orchard Knob, just east of Chattanooga, Tennessee. The best one can hope for is that the narrator proceeds deliberately and is aware of the need to be true to telling the story of what happened, so that one can trust the narrator's explanation of how it happened, why it happened, and what it means.

Notes

1. Bruce Catton, *Grant Takes Command* (Boston: Little, Brown, 1968), 499; Bruce Catton, *This Hallowed Ground: The Story of the Union Side of the Civil War* (New York: Doubleday, 1956), 297–99; Bruce Catton, *Never Call Retreat* (Garden City, N.Y.: Doubleday, 1965), 263 65, 496–97.

2. Although Grant's kinsman, William Wrenshall Smith, penned a journal of his experiences during the campaign, his observations do not significantly bear on this discussion. The journal is in the Library of Congress.

3. John M. Hoffman, ed., "First Impressions of Three Days' Fighting: Quartermaster General Meigs's 'Journal of the Battle of Chattanooga,'" in David L. Wilson and John Y. Simon, eds., *Ulysses S. Grant: Essays and Documents* (Carbondale: Southern Illinois University Press, 1981), 59–76.

4. Charles A. Dana to Edwin M. Stanton, November 25, 26, 1863, U.S. War Department, *The War of the Rebellion: A Compilation of the Official Records of the Union and Confederate Armies*, 128 vols. (Washington, D.C., 1880–1901, ser. 1, vol. 31, pt. 2:68–69 (hereafter cited as *OR*; all references are to Series 1 unless otherwise indicated).

5. George H. Thomas to Lorenzo Thomas, December 1, 1863, ibid., 96.

6. William T. Sherman to John Sherman, February 1, 1864, William T. Sherman Papers, Library of Congress.

7. William F. G. Shanks, *Personal Recollections of Distinguished Generals* (New York: Harper and Brothers, 1866), 117–18. It is noteworthy, however, that Shanks reported that when his chapters first appeared as articles in *Harper's* magazine, some people wrote to criticize his treatment of Thomas in what remained a highly favorable article. See ibid., 83–84.

8. Albert D. Richardson, *Personal History of Ulysses S. Grant* (Hartford, Conn.: American Publishing Co., 1868), 363–68. Although Richardson thought Absalom Baird was the division commander in question, it appears that it was Thomas J. Wood. Sylvanus Cadwallader would later make the same mistake.

9. Charles A. Dana and James H. Wilson, *The Life of Ulysses S. Grant* (Springfield, Mass.: Gurdon Bill & Co., 1868), 147–49.

10. Adam Badeau, *Military History of Ulysses S. Grant* (New York: D. Appleton, 1881), 1:506–9. (Originally published in 1868).

11. William T. Sherman, *Memoirs of William T. Sherman*, 2 volumes (New York: Appleton, 1875), 1;364.

12. Thomas J. Wood, letter to the *New York Times*, July 16, 1876. Wood would later tell his story again in "The Battle of Missionary Ridge," W. H. Chamberlin, ed., *Sketches of War History, 1861–1865* (Cincinnati: Robert Clarke Co., 1896), 4:23–51.

13. Wood, "Battle of Missionary Ridge," 42–43.

14. Ulysses S. Grant, "Chattanooga," in Peter Cozzens, ed., *Battles and Leaders of the Civil War* (Urbana: University of Illinois Press, 2002), 3:679–711; Ulysses S. Grant, *Personal Memoirs of U. S. Grant*, 2 volumes (New York: Charles L. Webster and Co., 1885–86), 2:74–85.

15. Joseph S. Fullerton, "The Army of the Cumberland at Chattanooga," in Cozzens, *Battles and Leaders*, 3:719–26.

16. William F. Smith, "Comments on General Grant's 'Chattanooga,'" ibid., 714–17. Smith would later confide privately that he believed Grant's plan to take the rifle pits would "lead to nothing and would, I thought, put our soldiers where they would be obliged to go on up the ridge, or pull back with nothing gained, and probably great loss of life." He carried the assault orders to Baird, who asked what he was to do if he carried the rifle pits and I told him I had received no instructions on that point." Herbert M. Schiller, ed., *Autobiography of Major General William F. Smith, 1861–1864* (Dayton, Ohio: Morningside, 1990), 80–81.

17. Donn Piatt, *General George H. Thomas: A Critical Biography* (Cincinnati: Robert Clarke and Co., 1893), 481–87.

18. Richard O'Connor, *Thomas: Rock of Chickamauga* (New York: Prentice Hall, 1948), 250.

19. Francis F. McKinney, *Education in Violence: The Life of George H. Thomas and the History of the Army of the Cumberland* (Detroit: Wayne State University Press,

1961), 293–95; Freeman Cleaves, *Rock of Chickamauga: The Life of General George H. Thomas* (Norman: University of Oklahoma Press, 1948), 199.

20. Benson Bobrick, *Master of War: The Life of General George H. Thomas* (New York: Simon and Schuster, 2009), 204–14.

21. Thomas B. Van Horne, *The Life of Major General George H. Thomas* (New York: Scribner's, 1882), 192.

22. James H. Wilson, *Under the Old Flag*, 2 vols. (New York: D. Appleton, 1912), 1:297–98; James H. Wilson, *The Life of John A. Rawlins* (New York: Neale, 1916), 172–73. Hamlin Garland was among those who observed Wilson's demeanor, as revealed in his notes for his Grant biography: see the Hamlin Garland Collection, Special Collections, Doheny Memorial Library, University of Southern California-Los Angeles, as well as the correspondence between Wilson and various publishers in the James H. Wilson Papers, Library of Congress.

Granger comes off as something of a fool in several accounts of the action on November 25: Michael V. Sheridan later noted that Granger was indeed fond of taking charge of a battery, as he had done so on November 23. See Michael V. Sheridan, "Charging with Sheridan up Missionary Ridge," in Cozzens, *Battles and Leaders*, 5:458–59.

23. Wilson, *Under the Old Flag*, 1:299; Wilson, *Rawlins*, 176–78.

24. Sylvanus Cadwallader, *Three Years with Grant*, ed. Benjamin P. Thomas (New York: Knopf, 1955), 151–55.

25. Charles A. Dana, *Recollections of the Civil War* (New York: D. Appleton, 1909), 149–50. Originally published in 1898.

26. J. F. C. Fuller, *The Generalship of Ulysses S. Grant* (Bloomington: Indiana University Press, 1958), 175–76. An appendix offered a summary of Fullerton's account; see ibid., 390–91. The volume originally appeared in 1929.

27. Catton, *This Hallowed Ground*, 364–69.

28. Catton, *Never Call Retreat*, 263–65, 496–97.

29. Catton, *Grant Takes Command*, 79–81.

30. Ibid., 499–500.

31. Shelby Foote, *The Civil War: A Narrative*, 3 vols. (New York: Random House, 1958–74), 2:851–55, 859.

32. Fairfax Downey, *Storming of the Gateway: Chattanooga, 1863* (New York: David McKay, 1969). Originally published in 1960.

33. James Lee McDonough, *Chattanooga: A Death Grip on the Confederacy* (Knoxville; University of Tennessee Press, 1984), 50–51.

34. Ibid., 163–64.

35. Ibid., 162–65, 167.

36. Peter Cozzens, *The Shipwreck of Their Hopes: The Battles for Chattanooga* (Urbana: University of Illinois Press, 1994), 200–201, 203.

37. Ibid., 204.

38. Ibid., 246–47, 260.

39. Ibid., 391; see ibid., 260, for Cozzens's use of Baird's account to suggest that it was Thomas's idea to take the crest, as relayed by Wilson.

40. Wiley Sword, *Mountains Touched with Fire: Chattanooga Besieged, 1863* (New York: St. Martin's Press, 1995), 231–32, 260–65, 359.

41. Larry J. Daniel, *Days of Glory: The Army of the Cumberland, 1861–1865* (Baton Rouge: Louisiana State University Press, 2004), 373–76; Brooks D. Simpson, *Ulysses S. Grant: Triumph over Adversity, 1822–1865* (Boston: Houghton Mifflin, 2000), 239–42; Thomas B. Buell, *The Warrior Generals: Combat Leadership in the Civil War* (New York: Crown, 1997), 290–93; Edward H. Bonekemper III, *A Victor, Not a Butcher: Ulysses S. Grant's Overlooked Military Genius* (Washington, D.C.: Regnery, 2004), 135–39; Michael B. Ballard, *U. S. Grant: The Making of a General, 1861–1863* (Lanham, Md.: Rowman and Littlefield, 2005), 164–65; Christopher J. Einolf, *George Thomas: Virginian for the Union* (Norman: University of Oklahoma Press, 2007), 213–17; Bobrick, *Master of War*, 208–14.

42. Paul M. Angle, ed., *Three Years in the Army of the Cumberland: The Letters and Diary of Major James A. Connelly* (Bloomington: Indiana University Press, 1959), 156.

6

THIS GRAND AND IMPOSING ARRAY OF BRAVE MEN: THE CAPTURE OF ROSSVILLE GAP AND THE DEFEAT OF THE CONFEDERATE LEFT

Sam Davis Elliott

The Union victory on Missionary Ridge on November 25, 1863, is a familiar story of unintended consequences. A diversionary attack against the center of the Confederate line on the ridge spontaneously became the ultimately successful effort, exposing the substantial weakness of the Confederate position and resulting in the Rebels' disorganized retreat from the ridge. The action won new fame for a rising star in the Union command, Major General Philip H. Sheridan, and the overall victory helped convince President Abraham Lincoln that Major General Ulysses S. Grant was the general needed to superintend the overall Union war effort. While an unintended consequence gave Grant a victory in the center, unforeseen circumstances made Grant put a makeshift corps under the command of a fallen star of the Union command, Major General Joseph Hooker, and placed Hooker in position to assault the Rossville Gap on the south end of the Confederate position. This little-known action came close to making the Union victory on Missionary Ridge exponentially more decisive. Ironically, only the Confederate retreat occasioned by the attack on the center prevented Hooker from enveloping the Confederate left and inflicting a much more devastating defeat on the Confederates in the ultimate battle of the Chattanooga campaign.

On the chilly evening of November 24, 1863, Hooker must have contemplated with a substantial degree of smug satisfaction a most fortunate change in his personal circumstances. Just a day before, the former commander of the Union Army of the Potomac expected to be "a spectator in the fight" while other Union commanders fought to break what was left of the Confederate Army of Tennessee's siege of Chattanooga. Instead, after a day of fighting on imposing Lookout Mountain, made dramatic by the fog and clouds that obscured the view of the mountain from the troops of both sides in the valley below, Hooker was spending the night in his newly established headquarters on the mountain itself. "A superb man in physique," Hooker was still "faultlessly clean and neat" despite a day of battle in the rain. The former commander of the Army of the Potomac was serenaded by an "irregular" fire along the lines on the mountain but had every reason to expect the complete Rebel evacuation of Lookout in the course of the night. It was a triumph that would eventually inspire Hooker to commission a richly detailed painting to commemorate his role on that memorable day.[1]

On the Confederate side of the line on Lookout Mountain that night, Colonel James Thaddeus Holtzclaw could only be less smug. A kick from a horse had disabled Brigadier General Henry D. Clayton, placing Holtzclaw, a twenty-nine-year-old lawyer turned soldier with a "clear and ringing voice" and "handsome and commanding appearance" in command of Clayton's brigade of Alabama troops. While Hooker doubtless reveled in his good fortune, Holtzclaw and his men were deployed as a covering force for the Rebel troops that Hooker had pushed around the face of Lookout that day. Before sunset that evening, the Army of Tennessee's commander, General Braxton Bragg, concluded that the position on Lookout Mountain had lost any utility. Holtzclaw's function that night was to hold Hooker's men back until the evacuation from Lookout was complete. The day's clouds and fog had given way to a clear, moonlit night. The flashing of the musketry on the slopes of Lookout Mountain could be seen from both the Rebel positions on Missionary Ridge and the Federal positions in Chattanooga, a martial scene described by one observer as "magnificently grand." Eventually, at 2:00 A.M., Holtzclaw would effect a silent withdrawal from the side of the mountain, aided by the sudden darkness of a fortuitous lunar eclipse.[2]

Prior to Hooker's seizure of Lookout Mountain, the Confederate lines that confronted the Union positions in and around Chattanooga started on the western slope of Lookout and stretched across Chattanooga Valley to the base of Missionary Ridge. A little less than halfway across Chattanooga Valley ran Chattanooga Creek, which meandered in a generally northward direction until it reached a point about a half mile from the Federal works around the town. At that point, the creek turned west and ran in a jagged fashion into the Tennessee River at the base of Lookout Mountain. From the point where the line across the valley intersected Missionary Ridge, the Rebel line stretched generally north along the line of the ridge to a jumble of hills near South Chickamauga Creek, not far from where it flowed into the Tennessee River.[3]

In his grand plan of attack, the commander of the Union forces, Major General Ulysses S. Grant, considered "the possession of Lookout Mountain of no special advantage" to the consummation of his designs. Grant anticipated employing Major General William T. Sherman's Army of the Tennessee to assault the northern end of Missionary Ridge and expected the troops under Hooker and the Army of the Cumberland, under Major General George H. Thomas, to make supporting attacks. Grant planned to move the bulk of Hooker's command across the Tennessee River at Chattanooga and launch them at the Confederate position in Chattanooga Valley, the link between the Rebel positions on Lookout Mountain and Missionary Ridge. Hooker would be relegated to making a demonstration against Lookout Mountain from Lookout Valley, on the western side of the mountain, with a reduced force. But, as Hooker observed, "man proposed and God disposed in [the] matter of battles." A broken bridge spanning the rain-swollen Tennessee hindered Grant's plan to bring Hooker's force across the river. Compounding Hooker's good fortune, a division of Sherman's Army of the Tennessee was stranded on his side of the river. The frustration of Grant's plan was thus the stroke of luck that changed Hooker's orders and gave him the three-division force he employed to attack the imposing slopes of Lookout Mountain on November 24.[4]

Hooker's conquest of Lookout made it an obvious jumping off point for an advance across Chattanooga Valley to Rossville, Georgia, just across the Tennessee state line. Near Rossville at the Rossville Gap, a road from Chattanooga crossed Missionary Ridge and intersected other roads that led into north Georgia, including La Fayette Road, over which the two armies had fought a little more than two months before at the Battle of Chickamauga. Federal possession of those roads would enable Hooker to operate on the right and rear of Bragg's position on Missionary Ridge. Although the veteran Hooker was quite aware that his next move was into Chattanooga Valley, he was so unsure of its topography that he asked army headquarters for permission to delay his advance until the fog cleared. He also requested a map.[5]

The resistance that Hooker's renewed advance would meet on November 25 was determined at a meeting held the night before between the Army of Tennessee's chief and his two corps commanders at Bragg's headquarters on Missionary Ridge, a complex of several closely grouped, small, two-room houses within an enclosure, with some appurtenant tents. At the time, the Rebel lines included Lookout Mountain, and Bragg's headquarters was located at a spot approximately 4.7 miles from the Confederate positions on the extreme north end of the ridge and approximately 2.3 miles from Rossville Gap.[6]

The problem facing the Rebel council of war was daunting. In losing Lookout Mountain, Bragg had lost the anchor to his defenses on the left. The Confederate lines stretching across Chattanooga Valley from Lookout to Missionary Ridge were subject to direct and enfilade fire from Hooker's position on the mountain. Furthermore, the Federals were for the first time able to maintain a continuous front against the Army of Tennessee stretching from Sherman's force on the north, through the Army of the Cumberland's positions before Chattanooga, to Hooker on the right. As historian Thomas Connelly observed, the Army of Tennessee also faced the problems of a rain-swollen Chickamauga Creek at its back, low morale among its soldiers, and, most important, reduced numbers in its ranks. Bragg had fewer than thirty thousand infantry and artillerymen to man his lengthy line.[7]

It was a situation that certain officers concluded would necessitate a withdrawal from Missionary Ridge. Cleburne, holding the anticipated post of danger on the Confederate right, supposed that the fall of the position on Lookout Mountain would precipitate a retrograde movement across Chicka-mauga Creek. From his brigade's position in the army's center, Brigadier General Arthur M. Manigault deduced that a retreat was likely, judging from the "movements of our trains, and the tenor of several orders I received, which, to one familiar with the movements of an army, tended to confirm me in my opinion." Division commander Major General Alexander P. Stewart wrote after the war that he also believed Bragg contemplated retreat, noting that while the position on the ridge was "naturally strong," an attempt to hold the ridge at that point in light of the Grant's large combined force was "folly."[8]

Certainly, corps commander Lieutenant General William J. Hardee came to Bragg's headquarters that evening with retreat in mind. Considering the army's reduced numbers, Hardee felt it advisable to fall back and unite with Confederate troops then preparing to attack Knoxville. On the other hand, Bragg's other corps commander, Major General John C. Breckinridge, believed that Missionary Ridge was an inherently strong position and that at any rate a retreat could not be effected before it was revealed to Grant by daybreak. Breckinridge also seemed to have his blood up, proclaiming his intention to get even for the loss of Lookout Mountain. Bragg was aware of the army's difficult situation and in fact had some days before considered the possibility of a retreat to Ringgold Gap, about eleven miles away. Yet it seemed to one of his subordinates that Bragg had a fixation on the prospect of taking Chattanooga. Whether Bragg was indeed fixated, had undue confidence in the Missionary Ridge line of defense, or simply agreed with Breckinridge's argument that it was simply too late to effect a withdrawal before daylight, he decided the Army of Tennessee would remain on Missionary Ridge the next day. His objections overruled, Hardee requested that his position on the right be heavily reinforced. Since Bragg fully (and correctly) discerned that the main Federal effort would be against his right, he assented and ordered the two divisions evacuated from Lookout Mountain to move to the extreme right. Bragg's "whole forces were concentrated on the ridge."[9]

With the transfer of the Lookout force to the right, Stewart's division now held the Army of Tennessee's extreme left. Tennessee-born Alexander P. Stewart, whose freckles and red hair indicated his Scots-Irish descent, was a veteran and a competent officer. His division contained four brigades, each of which had seen substantial service in the war. New to the division, but familiar to Stewart, its former commander, was Brigadier General Otho French Strahl's veteran Tennessee brigade. Also new to Stewart's command was the Army of Tennessee's lone Louisiana brigade, commanded by the competent Colonel Randall L. Gibson, and a Georgia brigade of recently exchanged Vicksburg prisoners, led by Brigadier General Marcellus A. Stovall. Stewart's final brigade was Clayton's Alabamians, led by Colonel Holtzclaw in their brigadier's absence, veterans not only of Chickamauga, but as of the morning of November 25, 1863, also of Lookout Mountain.[10]

During the fighting on November 24, Stewart's division occupied a line of trenches originating at Chattanooga Creek and extending east toward the base of Missionary Ridge. Bragg's decision to concentrate the Army of Tennessee on Missionary Ridge necessitated that Stewart redeploy to the ridge itself. In the course of the night, Stewart received orders to evacuate the trenches and form on the ridge. The orders also directed the Tennessean to detach two regiments and a battery to defend Rossville Gap and to "post a picket force in front of the ridge, with a reserve at its foot."[11]

Detached to Rossville under Colonel Robert J. Henderson were the two largest regiments of Stovall's brigade, the 42nd and 43rd Georgia, along with a Georgia battery. At that time, Rossville consisted of little more than the John Ross house, next to the ridge, just south of the gap. Erected in 1797, the log house with a plank façade was once the home of and named for the principal chief of the Cherokee nation. Reaching the gap at daylight, Henderson deployed his two regiments about three hundred yards in front of the gap, placing the battery between the regiments on a small hill that commanded the road through the gap. Although Henderson's southern flank was anchored on the steep slopes of Missionary Ridge, there were no supports to his south. Isolated from the main body of Stewart's division on the ridge, Henderson's detachment of approximately six hundred officers and men was effectively on an island.[12]

As the clear, chilly day wore on, Henderson's chance of getting support from the main body of his division seemed slim. The remainder of the division formed on the ridge on either side of Breckinridge's headquarters, a complex of tents on the side of a road crossing the crest of Missionary Ridge a little less than a mile south of Bragg's headquarters. At this point, the formation closest to Henderson was Gibson's brigade of Louisianans, and they were approximately a mile to the north of Rossville Gap.[13]

On the Federal side, Hooker's advance was delayed by a failure of communication with Thomas's headquarters. Although an order the night before had directed that his troops should "be in readiness to advance as early as possible" that morning into Chattanooga Valley and to cooperate with the Fourteenth Corps in a planned move on the rifle pits in front of the ridge, a directive to execute that move that was dispatched from army headquarters at 7:00 A.M. seems to have been delayed in transmission. Hooker sent a message at 9:20 that morning that he was still awaiting orders.[14]

Hooker did not have to wait long, as Thomas's order arrived to advance on the road across Chattanooga Valley to Rossville, "looking well to your right flank." Hooker moved out at 10:00 A.M., with Brigadier General Peter J. Osterhaus's division of the Army of the Tennessee in the lead, followed by Brigadier General Charles Cruft's division of the Army of the Cumberland and Brigadier General John W. Geary's division of the Army of the Potomac. Arriving at the point where the road to Rossville crossed Chattanooga Creek, Osterhaus found that the retreating Rebels had destroyed the two bridges that spanned the creek. Swollen with the same rains that had forced Grant to change his plan relative to Hooker's employment, steep-banked Chattanooga Creek was, in Grant's view, "a formidable stream to get an army over."[15]

Grant would have no doubt approved Hooker's choice of the German-born Osterhaus to lead the van of his column. Osterhaus was a veteran of service in Europe and America and had gained Grant's respect during the Vicksburg Campaign. He was gaining Hooker's as well. The former Army of the Potomac commander termed Osterhaus "a glorious soldier." His lead regiment, the 27th Missouri, fashioned a rude footbridge out of driftwood and crossed the creek. The division commander ordered the 27th forward to locate the enemy and engage him as skirmishers, while the division's pioneer detachment set to work repairing the bridge. The Missouri men moved toward the gap, forming what Colonel Henderson observed to be a "very strong" line of skirmishers. As the 27th probed forward, Henderson's line, aided by the attached four-gun battery, engaged them, with apparent effect, although the 27th's commander, Colonel Thomas Curly, claimed little injury was done by the Rebel "long arm."[16]

For more than two hours, the 27th Missouri and Henderson's Georgians engaged in what the latter characterized as "heavy skirmishing." While Colonel Curly claimed his command spent the time "pressing hard" against Henderson, he reported that both his regiment and the Rebel force before it suffered just over fifty casualties during the entire engagement. Indeed, Curly reported that notwithstanding the fire of the Rebel battery, his scant casualties resulted from sharpshooter fire. Both sides were content during this interval to trade fire from a safe distance, at least four hundred yards apart. Henderson was content to hold his position, and Curly content to occupy the Georgian's attention while the main body of Hooker's force repaired the bridge and crossed Chattanooga Creek.[17]

This impasse ended about 1:00 P.M., when, to Henderson's dismay, he saw the long lines of Osterhaus's division moving toward the ridge on either side of the gap. Osterhaus's First Brigade, under Brigadier General Charles R. Woods, advanced toward the ridge south of the gap, while the Second Brigade, under Colonel James A. Williamson, advanced toward the ridge north of the gap. James Patton Anderson's cannon subjected Woods's men to a "very severe artillery fire" but were unable to do much more than slow his advance. Understanding that an effort to flank his position in the gap was under way, Henderson sent videttes up the ridge on either side. The scouts soon reported what Henderson could see for himself: the Federals were moving quickly up the ridge on either flank.[18]

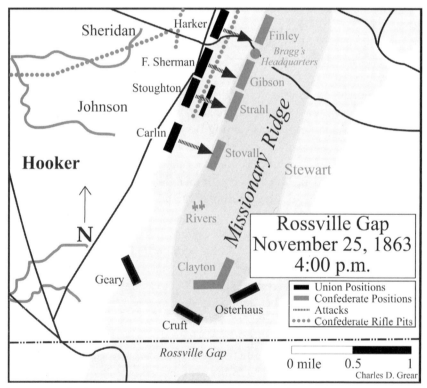

Hooker's opportune arrival at Rossville Gap, on the Confederate left flank, proved disastrous for the defenders of the ridge, facing as they were the simultaneous advance of Thomas's troops in front.

Henderson ordered a retreat, stating in his report that he had the dual goal of withdrawing Anderson's guns and positioning his two regiments at a point higher up in the gap where they might resist the flanking movements on the ridge. The weight of evidence, however, suggests that Henderson had already determined to abandon the gap on account of the clear threat of double envelopment posed by the move on his flanks and was delaying only until he could get his artillery safely away. Covered by the effective action of their skirmishers, Henderson's Georgians were able to take position farther up the gap, although they left a number of wagons, ambulances, and stores behind. Pressing behind the Rebel skirmishers, Curly's Missourians occupied the original Rebel line.[19]

Whether Henderson planned on a sustained resistance at the back of Rossville Gap, or just fought to cover his retreat, advance elements of the Federals flanking the gap on either side began enfilading his new line. Faced with this potential threat and pressed on the center by the 27th Missouri,

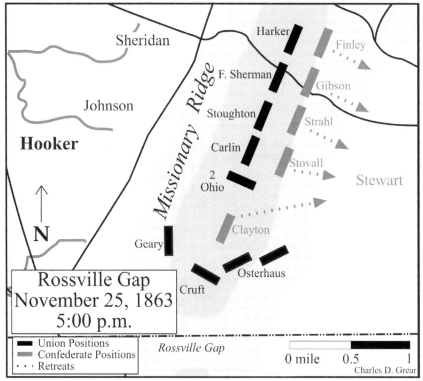

By 5:00 P.M. on November 25, the Confederate line along Missionary Ridge was crumbling, and Hooker's troops, advancing up the ridge from Rossville Gap, reaped a rich harvest of prisoners as they drove the fleeing Rebels before them.

the Rebel detachment had had enough and retreated from Rossville Gap. At the back of the gap, the road forked, one road leading to La Fayette and the other to an intersection behind the gap. At that intersection, the road again divided, one fork leading north to the rear of the Confederate position on Missionary Ridge, the other generally east below the state line past McAfee Church approximately four miles to a bridge across West Chickamauga Creek at Red House Ford. Henderson chose to march east rather than north, therefore leaving Rossville Gap unguarded without warning his comrades on the ridge to the north.[20]

With Henderson's retreat, Rossville Gap, the key to the Confederate left, fell into Federal hands. Arriving at the top of the ridge on the south (Georgia) side of Rossville "after a good deal of Klimbing," members of the 12th Missouri of Woods's brigade found the Rebels had "skedadled." Troops of Williamson's Iowa brigade advanced to the top of the ridge on the north (Tennessee) side of Rossville Gap and found deserted breastworks, but no enemy. Hooker accordingly reoriented his column to sweep up the ridge and fall on Bragg's flank. He directed Osterhaus to move his division through the gap and advance northward on the eastern side of Missionary Ridge and to "act as circumstances might demand." Osterhaus left two regiments of Williamson's brigade, the 25th and 26th Iowa, on the western side of the ridge to guard the flank. Hooker directed Cruft's small division of two brigades to move directly onto the ridge from the gap and advance "rapidly northward along the ridge until the enemy was encountered." Last in line, Geary's "White Star" Division was essentially to duplicate Osterhaus's march up the ridge, but on the west side. The batteries of all three divisions accompanied Geary, as Hooker was not sure there were roads that would enable any of the artillery to follow Osterhaus or Cruft.[21]

From Bragg's headquarters, Hooker's heavy column could be seen traversing Chattanooga Valley. Having had no word from Henderson's force at Rossville, Bragg and Breckinridge determined that the Kentuckian should make a "reconnaissance" toward Rossville, accompanied by the Army of Tennessee's chief of artillery, Colonel James H. Hallonquist. Bragg directed Holtzclaw, still commanding Clayton's brigade, to report to Breckinridge. He attached an Arkansas battery to the column, and ordered Stewart's acting chief of artillery, Captain Thomas J. Stanford, to accompany it.[22]

Although termed a "reconnaissance," Breckinridge's expedition had the dual role of supporting Henderson and of checking the obvious danger posed by Hooker's presence at or near the Rossville Gap. Breckinridge sent a member of his staff, his son Cabell, ahead to make contact with Henderson. Lieutenant Breckinridge rode his fine mare, Fannie, likely down the eastern side of the ridge, doubtless anticipating approaching Henderson's expected position in the gap from the rear. Unfortunately for young Breckinridge, the troops he encountered as he approached the gap were dressed in blue, not butternut or gray. Riding furiously, he tried to pass through a gap between the Union line of battle and some skirmishers on the side of the ridge, but soldiers of the 9th Iowa captured him. An observer noted that the slightly built young Breckinridge was neatly dressed in gray and wore both an embroidered cap and a self-confident air. Interrogated first by his captors, and then by Oster-haus himself, Lieutenant Breckinridge stated he was on his father's staff and boldly claimed the Confederates were winning the battle to that point. Sent to the rear, he put his arms around Fannie's neck, kissed her, and bade her goodbye. Osterhaus saw fit to appropriate Fannie as his own prize of war.[23]

John C. Breckinridge was moving into the very trap that had ensnared his son. The Confederate reconnaissance advanced into the area just vacated by Williamson's Iowans and then on the east side of the ridge pursuant to Hooker's plan. Believing that Henderson still defended the gap, Holtzclaw marched down the ridge with three companies of the 36th Alabama deployed forward as skirmishers, but his column moved by the flank, not in line of battle, which would have been difficult in any case on the narrow crest of the ridge. One of Holtzclaw's officers, Captain Benjamin Lane Posey of the 38th Alabama, later criticized this formation, believing a "double column at half distance" more appropriate, as it would have enabled the brigade to form a line quickly in any direction. As the skirmish line approached the end of the ridge, its soldiers observed Hooker's long column in the gap and at first seem to have confused it with Henderson's two regiments, which is, of course, was what they expected. Instead, they soon found the taciturn, businesslike Charles Cruft, with his staff and mounted escort. It was about 4:00 P.M. Finally realizing that the men in their front wore blue, the Alabama skirmishers opened a "sharp fire," scattering Cruft's escort down through the ranks of Cruft's lead regiment, Colonel Isaac C. B. Suman's 9th Indiana.[24]

Colonel Suman's quick action swiftly brought the situation under control. Throwing two companies forward as skirmishers, he formed a line of battle and moved to the top of the ridge. Holtzclaw's skirmishers opened fire, but Suman ordered a bayonet charge and forced the Rebels back, opening fire at an opportune moment, which further scattered the Confederate ranks. Holtzclaw was surprised, if not astonished, by this development. Suman's impetuous charge necessitated a rapid deployment of the Rebel column, which Holtzclaw and Breckinridge accomplished with great difficulty, man-aging, in Captain Posey's view, to change front and form a line "in some incomprehensible way."[25]

The line of the 36th and 38th Alabama was now perpendicular to the ridge. Breckinridge ordered Holtzclaw to place two regiments in echelon behind his left and advance his brigade. Breckinridge did not believe the Yankees in his front were strong, remarking to the effect "that in all events he would feel them and find them out." But Holtzclaw could not execute Breckinridge's order, as two of his regiments were at that time missing. Due to "some misapprehension of orders," the 32nd/58th and the 18th Alabama regiments were separated from the column, ending up in a field of very high "hogweeds" about a half mile up the ridge. Holtzclaw apparently rode off to find the missing half of his brigade, leaving Breckinridge to order an advance with the force present. Captain Posey accordingly moved his men forward and personally shot a Yankee officer.[26]

Each side raced to deploy its main line of battle. Suman's Hoosiers solidified their line first and advanced with fixed bayonets. In close support, the 59th Illinois moved rapidly from a column of march, made a right half wheel, and then moved forward into line, prolonging the line on the left of the 9th Indiana, Joe Hooker himself riding just behind the Illinoisan file closers. An officer of the 59th observed Suman out in front driving his line forward, beating his scabbard over the back of a reluctant soldier hiding behind a tree.[27]

Gamely blazing away at the enemy, Captain Posey was unpleasantly surprised when the Rebel line started to break. Left alone with his men, Posey joined the Confederate retreat to a line of log breastworks. Ironically, this line was constructed by Cruft's men after the retreat from Chickamauga to defend Rossville Gap from a Confederate attack in pursuit of the then-defeated Army of the Cumberland. Unfortunately for the Alabama men, the works faced in a generally eastward direction, and were almost perpendicular to the blue line of battle advancing from the south, providing almost no protection.[28]

Insofar as the 38th Alabama was on the right of the line, it necessarily was more exposed to Suman's advance than the 36th. Holtzclaw was already uncomfortably aware of Osterhaus's presence along the eastern slope of the ridge, and since the 59th Illinois was forming on the left of the 9th Indiana, it appeared that the Alabama brigade was in danger of being flanked on its right as well. Holtzclaw's immediate problem, however, was that the 38th Alabama was "getting into great confusion and reeling under the fire of the enemy."[29]

Captain Posey took it on himself to align the 38th properly outside the almost useless breastworks. He seized the regimental colors and began forming a line parallel to the advancing Yankee line. To his consternation, someone called for a retreat, leaving him alone with the colors and a few men. Posey called for the men to make a stand, and it seemed to him that the Federal advance was "whipped." Unfortunately, "another cowardly panic seized the men, and they ran off." The Federals, seeing the retreat, resumed their advance with a cheer, overrunning the first line of works at the double-quick.[30]

The disorganized retreat of the 38th Alabama on the Confederate right temporarily disrupted Holtzclaw's efforts to organize a coherent line facing Cruft's advance. Once the bulk of the 38th had streamed past, the 18th, 32nd/58th, 36th, and that fragment of the 38th that remained with Posey were able to get into "tolerable order" behind a second, more suitable set of breastworks approximately three hundred yards up the ridge and contest the Federal advance. Even at that point, a number of men did not stop at the second set of breastworks, but ran into a thick stand of trees to the rear. Clayton's brigade was discomfited by its unexpected encounter with the Yankees and the alacrity of Suman's advance. Posey noted that the commands were intermixed, seeing acquaintances from both the 32nd/58th. and 36th in the line near him. The Confederates gained time to organize a defense, however, when Suman decided to delay his advance until Federal reserves came up the ridge in his rear.[31]

With the front facing Cruft's advance temporarily stabilized, Holtzclaw focused his attention on the threat to his left, which he had discovered soon after his first contact with Cruft's column. Having passed the gap, Osterhaus began his march north on the eastern side of the ridge, toward the "terrific" sound of Sherman and Thomas's attack on the Rebel positions further up the ridge. Osterhaus observed Holtzclaw's column marching down the ridge and dispatched a warning to Hooker and Cruft. After a brief reconnaissance, Osterhaus formed his command "in an oblique line of two echelons, pushing the left [Williamson's Iowa men] well forward toward the crest of Missionary Ridge and extending with the right echelon [Woods's First Brigade] well down the slope of the hill." Osterhaus then observed the commencement of Cruft's attack, which he supposed drew the Confederates' "whole attention" to that quarter.[32]

Cruft's initial engagement with the Rebels in his front seems to have been the signal for Osterhaus's advance. Williamson led his brigade forward at a walk, then at the double-quick, "firing rapidly." Williamson's left regiment, his own 4th Iowa, was deployed as skirmishers on his left flank. Advancing obliquely up the ridge, Williamson endeavored to connect with Cruft on his left and Woods on his right. The efforts of Holtzclaw and Breckinridge to meet this threat from the east seem to have been initially successful, as the Iowa men encountered Confederates behind breastworks, doubtless the second line encountered by Cruft, and fought the Rebels for a time estimated to be anywhere from twenty minutes to an hour.[33]

On the Confederate left, Lieutenant Colonel John Washington Inzer of the 32nd/58th Alabama attempted to move his men across a hollow that Osterhaus's men were using to flank the Rebel position. Woods's brigade moved across a hollow on the Confederate flank, perhaps the very hollow that Inzer tried to guard, the Missouri men "running, yelling, shooting with furious impetuosity." Inzer experienced only partial success, as the Rebel line facing east could not be extended far enough to retard the advance of Woods's brigade.[34]

Although the men of Clayton's brigade were in immediate danger from two sides, perils awaited from other points of the compass. Pursuant to Hooker's plan, his third division, the Army of the Potomac's "White Star" Division of the Twelfth Corps, was dispatched north along the western base of the ridge. Deeply affected by the death of his son the month before at the Battle of Wauhatchie, John Geary wrote that he had "been a destroying angel ever since." Brigadier General William P. Carlin met Geary for the first time the night before when attached to his command on Lookout Mountain. Carlin described Geary as "a tall, rawboned man, with black hair," who seemed intent on relating his military history, including the singular claim that "he was the only Federal general who had ever beaten Stonewall Jackson."[35]

Geary advanced his First Brigade, under Colonel William R. Creighton, followed by his Second Brigade, commanded by Colonel George A. Cobham Jr., along the base in a column of regiments. Colonel David Ireland's Third Brigade, New Yorkers who had gained fame months before defending Culp's Hill at Gettysburg, was left to support the artillery. At Geary's direction, Battery F, 2nd Missouri Light Artillery, opened fire on the Rebel lines. The Missouri battery's fire, along with that of Battery E, Pennsylvania Light Artillery, inflicted "great damage" on Holtzclaw's command.[36]

While "no height [was] too bold" for Geary the "destroying angel," his lead brigade, Creighton's, found that their "progress up the side of the ridge was greatly retarded" by the steep western face of the ridge in that area. Not unlike Osterhaus's advance on the opposite side of the ridge, Geary's men moved obliquely up the ridge. In Cobham's brigade, there seems to have been little excitement except for watching the artillery's accurate shooting, and a stir at the start of the march when Cabell Breckinridge was escorted by as a prisoner.[37]

Fighting elements of Hooker's three divisions, Breckinridge's "reconnaissance" faced the likelihood of a sound beating as the late afternoon of November 25 wore on. Events along the Confederate main line on Missionary Ridge, however, turned the potential severity of the Alabama brigade's likely beating from merely sound to catastrophic.

Since the time of Henderson's detachment early that morning, A. P. Stewart had been plagued with indecision at army headquarters. Early that morning, Adams's brigade, under its senior colonel, Randall Gibson, was the formation closest to the troops defending Rossville Gap. By Gibson's reckoning, at about 1:00 P.M. his brigade was ordered to march to the division's extreme right flank and to report to Brigadier General James Patton Anderson, who commanded what was at that time the next division in line, located on the ridge beyond Bragg's headquarters. Gibson therefore marched from his position south of Breckinridge's headquarters, further distancing the left of the division's main line from Henderson's then-threatened position at Rossville Gap. By midafternoon, Stewart was ordered to move the whole division north along the ridge to rejoin Gibson's Louisiana men. The division's left was now Stovall's brigade of recently exchanged Vicksburg prisoners. With Henderson and the brigade's two largest regiments absent, Stovall deployed his three remaining regiments in a single line in front of and to the left of Breckinridge's headquarters.[38]

On the Union side, Ulysses S. Grant spent the morning watching his main effort against Missionary Ridge, Sherman's assault on the northern end of the ridge, do little to dislodge Bragg's right from those imposing heights. Grant anticipated employing four divisions of the Army of the Cumberland to assault the center portion of Bragg's line on the ridge once it was known Hooker had turned Rossville Gap. Although some at headquarters seemed to mistrust Hooker, the substantial hindrance he encountered in getting across Chattanooga Creek and the process of flanking Henderson out of the gap simply took longer than anticipated. George Thomas disregarded the suggestion of his chief engineer, Major General William F. "Baldy" Smith, that he should keep a staff officer with Hooker, predicting that Hooker would not apprise him when Rossville Gap was carried, "as it would not be for his interest to do so." Regardless of his motive, Hooker did not keep his superiors adequately updated on his progress, causing Thomas some anxiety. Sensing as the afternoon wore on that Bragg was focusing on defeating Sherman, Grant determined that based on what little was known, Hooker was far enough along for Thomas to launch his assault on Bragg's center.[39]

Accordingly, about 3:40 P.M., twenty minutes or so before Cruft began climbing the northern shoulder of the ridge at Rossville Gap, six guns emplaced on Orchard Knob were fired, signaling the advance of Thomas's four divisions toward the Confederate center. On the Confederate left, A. P. Stewart was just completing the disposition of his division after the last of the orders from Bragg's headquarters directing redeployment of his men. On Stovall's right, Stewart deployed two regiments of Strahl's Tennessee brigade, the other four regiments occupying rifle pits at the base of the ridge and another line part of the way up. Seeing the Federal advance, Stewart deployed one battery, the Eufala Artillery, and a section of another in a gap in the line between Strahl's right and Gibson's left. Satisfied that his line had no gaps, Stewart moved toward his extreme left to make sure it was properly posted.[40]

The sequence of events that would prove to be the undoing of Stewart's position on Missionary Ridge and, ultimately, seal the fate of Holtzclaw's detached brigade now began. It was intended that units of Breckinridge's division, then under the command of Brigadier General William B. Bate, would cover the space on the ridge in front of Bragg's headquarters. Gibson was directed to post his right about a hundred yards south of the headquarters buildings and was making plans to do so when a commotion along the crest of the ridge made him ride toward the crest, where he saw that the Federal assault had commenced. Hurrying his men into position, he saw that his two right units had obliqued to the right. Investigating, Gibson was advised that they had been directed to move in that direction by some staff officers of Bragg, a fact confirmed by Tennessee governor Isham G. Harris, a volunteer aide of Bragg's. Therefore, at the very start of the fight, Gibson's front was moved approximately one hundred fifty yards north of where Stewart supposed it to be.[41]

Riding down his line toward the right, Stewart got the first indication that things were not going well farther up the ridge. One of Bragg's staff officers approached and asked if Stewart could spare any men to restore a breakthrough somewhere to the right. Stewart dispatched one of his officers with the man to see if his division could spare any men. As Stewart rode behind Strahl's line, Colonel Francis Marion Walker of the 19th Tennessee advised him that there was a gap to the right of his line. The artillery posted in the gap between Strahl and Gibson soon exhausted its ammunition, further opening the gap between the two brigades initially created by Bragg's diversion of the Louisiana brigade.[42]

For a brief interval, it looked as if the gap might be plugged by troops of the 7th Florida, which started the day posted in the rifle pits at the foot of the ridge to the north of Stewart's position. Forced up the ridge by the relentless Federal advance, the Floridians retreated diagonally upward, although a number of them, including their commander, fell into Yankee hands during the climb. Stragglers from the 7th fortuitously reached the top right where Stewart needed them, although Private Robert Watson wrote that he was so exhausted by the steep climb that he had to lay on the ground for a few minutes to recover his breath. Rallied by members of Stewart's staff at the top, the Floridians resisted for a brief time, supported by the artillery concentrated there, but were unable to stem the Federal tide once the cannons' ammunition was exhausted. Although some of the Florida men resisted until the Federals were on the crest of the ridge, this scratch force was soon driven away. Led by the 19th Illinois Infantry, the Federals, troops of the Second Brigade of Brigadier General Richard W. Johnson's division, swept over the hill, chasing the Floridians down the eastern side of the ridge and capturing their colonel.[43]

Until the Federal penetration just south of Bragg's headquarters, Stewart's two left brigades, Strahl's and Stovall's, were successful in holding their portion of the line. Stovall's men had the good tactical sense to move forward from their position on the geographic crest of the ridge to a point where they could fire down the hill at the climbing Federals. Additionally, the Georgians had the artillery support of an Arkansas battery, located on a high eminence a few hundred yards to the south. The battery was detached to support Breckinridge's reconnaissance force, but Stewart's artillery commander, Captain Stanford, found it impractical for the battery to follow Holtzclaw to the end of the ridge. Therefore, Stanford deployed the battery to guard Stovall's left flank. The Arkansans found a position on an eminence a few hundred yards to the left of Breckinridge's headquarters and fired diagonally across the Federal lines confronting Stovall, one solid shot striking near Colonel Benjamin F. Scribner, a member of Carlin's brigade of Johnson's division. As Scribner later related, "had it been an explosive shell," he would not have survived to tell the tale.[44]

Ironically, Carlin's brigade had started the day attached to Hooker's command, having been detached to provide support for his assault on Lookout Mountain on the twenty-fourth. This gave Geary the opportunity to inform Carlin of his success against Stonewall Jackson. After a series of confusing orders that morning, Carlin rejoined Johnson's division on its right, thereby becoming the extreme right of Thomas's assault on the center of Missionary Ridge. With his right in the air, Carlin refused the regiments on that end of the line, advancing the 33rd Ohio in echelon and to the right two hundred yards behind the 94th Ohio, the 38th Indiana in the same relation to the 33rd Ohio, and the 2nd Ohio in the same relation to the 38th Indiana. Carlin advanced his men through a wooded area impeded by brush, fallen timber, and streams, and then at the double-quick across an open plain toward Rebel rifle pits and huts at the bottom of the ridge.[45]

Upon reaching the base of the ridge, Carlin's men began to take punishment from the Confederates on the ridge above them. Directing the right wing of Carlin's brigade, which had been his own until a consolidation of Federal units a few weeks before, Scribner took cover among the rude shelters built by Rebel soldiers at the bottom of the ridge, but found to his discomfiture that they proved to be little impediment to the passage of bullets. Carlin's left regiments, the 104th Illinois, 88th Indiana, and 42nd Indiana, faced fire from elements of the 4th Tennessee of Strahl's brigade, posted in a line of rifle pits about a third of the way up the ridge. Carlin's right regiments suffered from both rifles on the crest before them and the "incessantly . . . plunging fire" from the Arkansas battery. Still nervous about the extreme right flank, Carlin and Scribner detached Company A of the 2nd Ohio as a skirmish line to investigate a report of a Confederate flank attack, which proved to be false.[46]

While out with their company of Ohioans on the right, Scribner and Carlin noticed that the whole line of the brigade was moving forward. Carlin emotionally exclaimed: "My God, who will take the responsibility of this!" Returning the company to its regiment, they rushed back to the main line. Although the veteran soldiers of the 4th Tennessee were able to maintain a hot fire, Carlin's threat to their left flank, along with another threat to their right, soon required their withdrawal up the ridge to Strahl's main line. Although none had been hit while in their rifle pits, many were hit as they made the difficult climb to the top of the ridge. The 104th Illinois and the 88th Indiana moved up and occupied the line abandoned by the Tennesseans.[47]

Swept up in the excitement, the right wing of the brigade moved forward against Stovall's line. Unlike Strahl's Tennesseans, however, Stovall's Georgians were not disadvantaged by the unwise tactical disposition of troops partially down the ridge. Stanford's effective fire was a distinct advantage, as was the effective crossfire delivered because Stovall's left flank overlapped Carlin's right by at least seventy-five yards. To the south, Osterhaus's men reveled in their "fighting appellation" as "Vicksburg Rats." In contrast, Stovall's men felt the stigma of their defeat and surrender in Mississippi and fought to redeem themselves. Still in a single line, they advanced from the crest to a point on the ridge where they could deliver "volley after volley of rifle ball" on their enemies. The Federals acknowledged receiving a "heavy fire," which threw the three right Union regiments into confusion. The Federals fell back, leaving two stands of colors tantalizingly just out of the reach of the Georgians.[48]

While Carlin's left wing rested in the rifle pits formerly occupied by Strahl's Tennesseans, his right wing regrouped at the bottom of the ridge for a period estimated by one of his officers to be twenty minutes. The widening Federal penetration on the right forced first Strahl and then Stovall out of their line on the crest. In the meantime, the effective fire of the Arkansas battery on Carlin's left stopped for lack of ammunition. This fortuitous turn of events was unknown to Scribner, who once again accompanied his men under fire toward the crest, expecting that the Rebel force that overlapped them "would wrap his extended flank about us and we would be crushed and destroyed."[49]

No doubt because of this fear, and because their departure point was part of the way up the ridge, Carlin's left made it to the crest before his right. The brigade's entire line was "somewhat disordered by the ravines and ridges, rifle-pits and felled trees encountered in ascending." Carlin's extreme right regiment, the 2nd Ohio, reached the top of the ridge in the vicinity of the area where Breckinridge had maintained his headquarters tent. Still nervous about his right flank, Carlin directed the 2nd to advance obliquely to the right and assume a blocking position on a high knob estimated to be about three hundred yards away, almost certainly the very eminence occupied by the troublesome Confederate battery a few minutes before.[50]

The scene was one to confound the senses. In the valley below, an observer of the 26th Iowa, left to guard Hooker's flank, had a "grand view" of the attack up the ridge, "and the sight was sublime. We could see our troops advancing up the hill, the long lines of bayonets glistening in the sunlight." He thought the sound equally impressive: "there was such a rattle of musketry I never heard before." A soldier in Geary's column thought the sound "awful." Carlin believed the impressive sight contributed to the victory: "It was this grand and imposing array of brave men in line that struck the enemy with terror. To every man on Missionary Ridge in Bragg's army the whole Army of the Cumberland was visible at one glance of the eye."[51]

At this juncture late in the afternoon of November 25, 1863, the center and left of the Army of Tennessee had abandoned Missionary Ridge, with only Hardee and his corps on the right, and Breckinridge with Holtzclaw's beleaguered regiments on the extreme left. While Hardee and his men had the force and position to make an effective fighting withdrawal, Breckinridge's little command, nearly surrounded, had little chance to escape intact.

With Suman temporarily awaiting Cruft's reserves, Holtzclaw perceived his most immediate need was to check Osterhaus's advance on his left. He sent a message to Breckinridge asking for assistance on that flank and received a reply that the main line in their rear had broken and that Holtzclaw must withdraw. Desiring to maintain some order, Holtzclaw planned to pull back slowly and quietly under the cover of his own 18th Alabama. Breckinridge understood the direness of the situation and issued a "peremptory order to withdraw the command and make the best of [the] way to Chickamauga [Creek]."[52]

Not everyone got the order to withdraw. Seeking to stem Osterhaus's advance on the left flank, Lieutenant Colonel Inzer of the 32nd/58th Alabama saw the brigade start to "give way" and later wrote that he "*never worked so hard in my life*" as he did at that time to rally his command. Inzer saw his men fall back to a point over a hundred yards away where Holtzclaw was sitting on his horse, and he ran to the brigade commander to beg him to rally the men. Faced with Breckinridge's "peremptory" order, and doubtless having little time to explain, Holtzclaw simply declined and in a few minutes directed Inzer to face back in a column of squads. Seeing the men opposing them falling back, the Iowans of Williamson's brigade surged forward, causing what was left of Inzer's line to give way.[53]

The line facing the 9th Indiana and the rest of Cruft's men also received the order to withdraw. Captain Posey called off his men with the regimental color-bearer, starting off "slowly and in some order." The Rebels fired as they retreated in hopes of checking any pursuit, but Suman's Hoosiers, "seeing [their] advantage," sprang forward in pursuit, overrunning the second line of breastworks. Posey later wrote that he "heard the cry that the Yankees were right on us. It was true. It now became a rout." Holtzclaw's men had reached the end of endurance. They saw Hooker's three divisions moving against them and suffered the shelling of the Federal artillery accompanying Geary's column. As Holtzclaw later reported, "seeing themselves nearly surrounded by ten times their own number, discipline and courage alike were gone, and the greater portion of the command ran out like a mob, each endeavoring to be foremost."[54]

All that remained for Breckinridge, Holtzclaw, and their men was to make their escape from the ridge in the quickest way possible. Breckinridge, seeing that Carlin had carried the ridge near his headquarters, started conducting the men diagonally down the ridge away from the Yankees. Holtzclaw stayed on the crest until most of his men had streamed past and then tried to move forward to lead his column to safety. His horse was shot, temporarily incapacitating him, so he turned command of the brigade over to Colonel Lewis T. Woodruff of the 36th Alabama. Dismayed by this new responsibility in the face of disaster, Woodruff called out to Lieutenant Colonel Peter Forney Hunley of the 18th Alabama: "Oh Hunley, Hunley, help me here; help me here. Holtzclaw's left me in one hell of a fix." Although Woodruff made a brief show of trying to bring order to the chaos about him, he found that "every fellow was doing his best to keep up with the colonel in getting to the rear."[55]

Unsuccessful in his efforts to get Holtzclaw to continue the fight, Inzer moved up the ridge toward Breckinridge's headquarters and saw some men filing down the ridge to the right (the east side) through a field. His regiment's colonel and major rode by him on a single mare. At this juncture, the only escape route left to the Alabamians was a diagonal route northeastward down the side of the ridge, between Carlin's line to the north and the oblique advance up the ridge from the southeast of Woods's brigade of Osterhaus's division. Inzer turned down the hill and tried to get some men to follow him through this rapidly closing avenue of escape, when he took some fire from the direction of the top of the ridge to his left. "Hollowing" to men he believed were fellow Confederates, he shouted several times for them to stop. Turning, Inzer saw several of his officers and men at the top of the ridge, and in the noise and confusion did not recognize that they were prisoners until he joined them on top of the ridge, where to his dismay he found himself in the hands of the 2nd Ohio.[56]

With the regimental color-bearer by his side, Posey tried to conduct the group of men with him out of the trap. Unfortunately, the colors were entangled in a fallen tree, and Posey lost track of the bearer. Unlike Holtzclaw and, unsuccessfully, Inzer, Posey determined that his best chance was to work his way along the western side of the ridge in hopes of rejoining the main body of the division. The men with him started falling out with exhaustion and despair. More ominously, a man right next down was shot, and Posey saw that Geary's men were ascending the ridge on the western side. A shell burst nearly under Posey's feet, and he nearly succumbed to exhaustion. Moving onward, using his sword as a support, he hoped to escape in the gathering darkness or to hide behind a fallen log feigning being badly wounded or killed. Perhaps he could get away later. He saw a body of men at the top of the ridge who appeared in the near darkness to be wearing gray. Joining them and finding himself in among Confederates, Posey began to whirl his sword about his head, shouting "We are safe at last—we are safe at last!" An officer on horseback asked if he had surrendered. Astonished, Posey said he had not and demanded the officer's identity. It was Carlin.[57]

Years later, Carlin recalled an encounter with a Rebel similar to that described by Posey. The young man came to order arms as his officers were surrendering. Carlin asked if he, too, were surrendering, and he stated he was not. Carlin advised him to do so, "for you may be shot down if you don't." After looking around as if to confirm Carlin's advice, the young man gave up his weapon. One of Carlin's orderlies gathered up seventeen captured officers' swords. Osterhaus's men soon came up the ridge, making an acute angle between his oblique line and the line of Carlin's brigade perpendicular to the ridge, thus closing the Confederate avenue of escape. Carlin's last view of uncaptured Confederates was "that of a mounted officer, apparently a general officer, with two or three mounted men galloping off to their rear."[58]

The victorious Federals exulted with shouts and cheers that reached up and down their lines. Osterhaus threw his cap in the air and exclaimed: "Two more hours daylight and we'll destroy this army!" One of his officers, Lieutenant Colonel Jeremiah W. Jenkins of the 31st Ohio, may have taken advantage of the German's good feelings. He appropriated young Breckinridge's Fannie and rode her up and down the lines "waving his hat and rejoicing over the victory." Scribner found the joy infectious and "joined in the general exultation." Even some of the Confederate prisoners, apparently glad their ordeal was over, joined in the cheering. A Missourian heard renewed cheering when Fighting Joe Hooker rode up. An impressive victor for the second day in a row, Hooker reported: "Here our business for the day ended, and the troops went into bivouac, with cheers and rejoicings, which were caught up by other troops in the vicinity and carried along the ridge until lost in the distance."[59]

The remnants of Holtzclaw's command retreated to a pontoon bridge across the Chickamauga at Bird's Mill, where it rejoined Stewart's division. Breckinridge, shaken by his ordeal and the then-unknown fate of his son, encountered Stewart and told him of Hooker's passage of Rossville Gap and the near-destruction of the brigade. He directed Stewart to assume command at the Bird's Mill crossing, where, under the cover of Gibson's and Strahl's brigades, the crowd of retreating men was put into ranks and the wagons and artillery passed across the stream. Finally, the covering force crossed the bridge about 2:00 A.M. on November 26 and then destroyed the span, frustrating, for the time being, the Union pursuit.[60]

The defeated Confederates were horrified by their collapse on Missionary Ridge. A soldier of the 40th Georgia wrote that the "defeat was very unexpected and quite disastrous." Bragg wrote that there was "no satisfactory excuse" for the inability to hold a position, which, in his mind, "ought to have been held by a line of skirmishers against any assaulting column." Writing his hometown newspaper after his escape from Union captivity, the resourceful Captain Posey agreed with Bragg that the men failed to put up an adequate fight, but also observed that leadership was lacking, at least in Clayton's brigade. Holtzclaw, too, thought that his men had "no excuse," but correctly observed: "courage and discipline are alike unavailing when the intelligent soldier sees himself surrounded by ten times their number, and instead of a supporting column finds a heavy line of the enemy pouring a withering fire in his rear."[61]

On the Federal side, at a total cost of less than 250 casualties, Hooker's command, with the timely assistance of Carlin's brigade, had taken advantage of the weakness of the Confederate left in an effective manner. Stewart's division's casualties totaled 1,502, including 810 of the approximately 1,500 men engaged in Holtzclaw's command. The Alabama brigade suffered the capture of 700 prisoners, along with the battle flags of the 18th, 36th, and 38th regiments. The capture of Rossville Gap and the engagement with Holtzclaw was a solid Union victory, obscured to a great degree by the stunning breakthrough in the center by the Army of the Cumberland.[62]

While not as spectacular in the public eye as his capture of Lookout Mountain, or as personally redeeming, Hooker's assault on Rossville Gap had the potential for much greater results. Osterhaus's exclamation that two more hours of daylight would have meant the destruction of the Army of Tennessee had a large element of truth to it, especially from the Confederate standpoint. Holtzclaw felt that his losing fight had allowed the rest of the Confederate left time to retreat. In a similar vein, one of Breckinridge's aides wrote, with suitable emphasis, *"It was fortunate our line gave way where it did or else our left if not the whole Army would have been cut off by Hooker and his corps."* The Army of Tennessee's ranking Presbyterian elder, A. P. Stewart, did not attribute the escape from the "complete destruction that threatened us" from Hooker's flanking attack to fortune, but to the "overruling hand of a gracious Providence." The correspondent for the *Atlanta Intelligencer* perhaps summed up matters the best: "We were simply beaten by overwhelming numbers, and it is a fortunate thing that our men gave way, for had we stood, we should have been flanked on our left, and the whole army captured. So all is for the best, and we shall soon be ready for them again."[63]

Notes

1. U.S. War Department, *The War of the Rebellion: A Compilation of Official Records of the Union and Confederate Armies* (Washington, D.C., 1895–1929), ser. 1, vol. 31, pt. 2: 314, 317, 333–36, 339–40 (hereafter cited as *OR*; all references are to Series 1 unless otherwise indicated); Robert I. Girardi and Nathaniel Cheairs Hughes Jr., *The Memoirs of Brigadier General William Passmore Carlin, U.S.A.* (Lincoln: University of Nebraska Press, 1999), 113; "Painting Will Help Point Park Show Off," *Chattanooga Times*, August 20, 1986.

2. *OR*, vol. 31, pt. 2: 78, 664, 749; "Captain Posey's Narrative," *Mobile Register and Advertiser*, December 27, 1863; Edgar W. Jones, *History of the 18th Alabama Infantry Regiment*, ed. Zane Geier (Mountain Brook, Ala.: Zane Geier, 1994), 14; *Supplement to the Official Records of the Union and Confederate Armies* (Wilmington, N.C.: Broadfoot, 1994–2004) (hereafter, *ORS*), 6:156, "Battle of Chattanooga," *Athens (Ga.) Southern Banner*, December 16, 1863; C. L. Willoughby, "Eclipse of the Moon at Missionary Ridge," *Confederate Veteran* 21 (December, 1913): 590.

3. U.S. War Department, *Atlas to Accompany the Official Records of the Union and Confederate Armies* (Washington, D.C.: Government Printing Office, 1891)(hereafter, *OR Atlas*), Plate XLIX, Map 1.

4. *OR*, vol. 31, pt. 2: 31–34, 318, 340.

5. Ibid., 31–34, 96, 112–15, 318, 333.

6. Robert S. Davis, ed., *Requiem for a Lost City: Sallie Clayton's Memoirs of Civil War Atlanta* (Macon, Ga.: Mercer University Press, 1999), 104; Irving S. Buck, *Cleburne and His Command*, ed. Thomas R. Hay (Wilmington, N.C.: Broadfoot, 1987), 167.

7. *OR*, vol. 31, pt. 2: 317, 656; Thomas L. Connelly, *Autumn of Glory* (Baton Rouge: Louisiana State University Press, 1971), 273–74; Nathaniel C. Hughes Jr., ed., *Liddell's Record* (Dayton, Ohio: Morningside Books, 1985; reprint, Baton Rouge: Louisiana State University Press, 1997), 157.

8. *OR*, vol. 31, pt. 2: 748; R. Lockwood Tower, ed., *A Carolinian Goes to War: The Civil War Narrative of Arthur Middleton Manigault* (Columbia: University of South Carolina Press, 1983), 136; Alexander P. Stewart, "The Army of Tennessee: A Sketch," in John Berrian Lindsley, ed., *The Military Annals of Tennessee: Confederate* (1886; reprint, Broadfoot, 1995), 1:83.

9. *Daily Columbus Enquirer*, December 16, 1863; Buck, *Cleburne and His Command*, 166–67; Hughes, *Liddell's Record*, 154–55, 158; Connelly, *Autumn of Glory*, 273; *OR*, vol. 31, pt. 2: 664, 722.

10. *OR*, vol. 31, pt. 3:661–62; "Captain Posey's Narrative." Stewart's division had been substantially reorganized on November 12, 1863, as part of a larger shuffling of the Army of Tennessee occasioned by Braxton Bragg's desire to break up organizations that supported his opponents among the army's officer corps. *OR* 31, pt. 3: 685–86; Connelly, *Autumn of Glory*, 261–62.

11. *ORS*, vol. 6: 105.

12. Ibid., 107, 111; *OR*, vol. 31, pt. 3: 314; *OR Atlas*, Plate XLIX, Map 1, Plate XCVII, Map 3, CXXIV, Image 4; Roger C. Linton, *Chickamauga: A Battlefield History in Images* (Athens: University of Georgia Press, 2004), 14.

13. *ORS*, vol. 6:104–5; *OR Atlas*, Plate XLIX, Map 1, Plate XCVII, Map 3, CXXIV, Image 4.; Henry C. Day to Charles Day, November 20, 1863, in Charles A. Earp, ed., "A Confederate Aide-de-Camp's Letters from the Chattanooga Area, 1863," *Journal of East Tennessee History*, 67 (1995): 106, 108.

14. *OR*, vol. 31, pt. 2: 111–14.

15. Ibid., 115, 314, 336, 600; *OR Atlas*, Plate L, Map 4; Ulysses S. Grant, "Chattanooga," Robert Underwood Johnson and Clarence Clough Buel, *Battles and Leaders of the Civil War* (Reprint, New York: Thomas Yoseloff, 1956), 3:696, note.

16. Earl J. Hess, "Grant's Ethnic General: Peter J. Osterhaus," in *Grant's Lieutenants: From Cairo to Vicksburg*, ed. Steven E. Woodworth (Lawrence: University Press of Kansas, 2001), 199–202, 208–16; *OR*, vol. 31, pt. 2: 344–45, 600–601, 610; *ORS*, vol. 6: 170–71.

17. *OR*, vol. 31, pt. 2: 607, 610–11; *ORS*, vol. 6: 170–71, 176.

18. *OR*, vol. 31, pt. 2: 601, 607, 615; *ORS*, vol. 6: 171, 176.

19. *ORS*, vol. 6:171; *OR*, vol. 31, pt. 2: 601, 611. The evidence that suggests Henderson had already determined to retreat is derived from the reports of certain subordinates, who suggest the stand further up the gap was intended to last only until the artillery escaped. *ORS*, vol. 6: 174, 176.

20. *ORS*, vol. 6:171–72; *OR*, vol. 31, pt. 2: 611, 620, 627; Chickamauga and Chattanooga National Park Commission (CCNPC), "Map of the Battlefields of Chattanooga and Wauhatchie," 1896; CCNPC, "Map of the Battlefield of Chickamauga," Plate IV, 1896. Captain Anderson wrote that the road east was chosen because the road north was thought to already be in Federal hands. *ORS*, vol. 6:176.

21. *OR*, vol. 31, pt. 2: 148, 318, 400–401, 601, 615; Earl A. Hess, ed., *A German in the Yankee Fatherland: The Civil War Letters of Henry A. Kircher* (Kent, Ohio: Kent State University Press, 1983), 144; "From the Thirty-First Iowa," *Anamosa (Iowa) Eureka*, December 18, 1863.

22. *ORS*, vol. 6: 106, 156, 185; "Battle of Chattanooga," *Daily Southern Banner*, December 2, 1863.

23. *OR*, vol. 31, pt. 2: 615; "Battle of Chattanooga"; "From the 9th Iowa," *Council Bluffs (Iowa) Guardian*, January 5, 1864; "From Dr. Hudson," *Lyons (Iowa) Daily Mirror*, December 19, 1863; Alonzo Abernathy, comp., *Dedication of the Monuments Erected by the State of Iowa Commemorating the death, suffering and valor of Her Soldiers on the Battlefields of Vicksburg, Lookout Mountain, Missionary Ridge, Shiloh, and in the Confederate Prison at Andersonville* (Des Moines: State Printer, 1908); James A. Fowler, "The Most Curious Battle of the War," *National Tribune*, December 9, 1926; Wiley Sword, *Mountains Touched with Fire: Chattanooga Besieged 1863* (New York: St. Martin's Press, 1995), 307.

24. *ORS*, vol. 6:156–57; "Captain Posey's Narrative"; James W. A. Wright, "Bragg's Campaign around Chattanooga—Missionary Ridge," *Southern Bivouac*, February 1887, 546; *OR*, vol. 31, pt. 2: 147, 176, 184; "In Memoriam: Charles Cruft," Society of the Army of the Cumberland Fifteenth Reunion, Cincinnati, Ohio, 1883 (Cincinnati: Robert Clarke, 1884), 234–35.

25. *OR*, vol. 31, pt. 2: 184; "Captain Posey's Narrative."

26. "Captain Posey's Narrative"; *ORS*, vol. 6: 153, 160; John Washington Inzer, *The Diary of a Confederate Soldier: John Washington Inzer, 1834–1928*, ed. Mattie Lou Teague Crow (Huntsville, Ala.: Strode Publishers, 1977).

27. *OR*, vol. 31, pt. 2: 171, 176, 184; Arnold Gates, ed., *The Rough Side of War: The Civil War Journal of Chesley A. Mosman, 1st Lieutenant, Company D, 59th Illinois Volunteer Infantry Regiment* (Garden City, N.Y.: Basin Publishing, 1987), 128–30.

28. *ORS*, vol. 6:157; "Captain Posey's Narrative"; Wright, "Bragg's Campaign around Chattanooga," 546; *OR*, vol. 31, pt. 1: 254, 733; 31(2): 147.

29. *ORS*, vol. 6:157; *OR*, vol. 31, pt. 2: 161, 166, 171, 176, 178, 181.

30. "Captain Posey's Narrative"; *OR*, vol. 31, pt. 2: 184.

31. *ORS*, vol. 6: 157; Inzer, *Diary of a Confederate Soldier* 44; "Captain Posey's Narrative"; *OR*, vol. 31, pt. 2: 184.

32. *ORS*, vol. 6: 157; *OR*, vol. 31, pt. 2: 601, 607–8, 615.

33. "From the Thirty-First Iowa"; *OR*, vol. 31, pt. 2: 615, 620, 626–28.

34. Inzer, *The Diary of A Confederate Soldier*, 44; Abraham Jefferson Seay Diary, typescript at Chisholm Trail Museum and Governor Seay Mansion, Kingfisher, Oklahoma, 63; *OR*, vol. 31, pt. 2: 607.

35. *OR*, vol. 31, pt. 2: 400–401; William Alan Blair, ed., *A Politician Goes to War: The Civil War Letters of John White Geary* (University Park: Pennsylvania State University Press, 1995), 143; Girardi and Hughes, *Memoirs of Carlin*, 113.

36. *OR*, vol. 31, pt. 2: 400–1, 426, 453, 602; *ORS*, vol. 6:158.

37. Blair, ed., *A Politician Goes to War*, 143; OR 31(2):413–14, 426; David Mouat Memoirs, Historical Society of Pennsylvania, Philadelphia.

38. *ORS*, vol. 6: 106–7, 113, 166–67.

39. *OR*, vol. 31, pt. 2: 34, 116; William F. Smith to Henry M. Cist, November 1, 1888, Collection of Wiley Sword.

40. *OR*, vol. 31, pt. 2: 132, 147, 176, 184, 199, 238, 459; *ORS* 6: 107–8.

41. *ORS*, vol. 6: 153–54.

42. Ibid., 108–9.

43. R. Thomas Campbell, ed., *Southern Service on Land and Sea: The Wartime Journal of Robert Watson, CSA/CSN* (Knoxville: University of Tennessee Press, 2002), 87–88; *ORS*, vol. 6: 109; *OR*, vol. 31, pt. 2: 479–80, 482–84. Stewart mistakenly thought the Floridians were from the 6th Regiment. *ORS*, vol. 6: 109.

44. *ORS*, vol. 6: 137, 166–69, 177–78, 185; B. F. Scribner, *How Soldiers Were Made; or, War As I Saw It* (New Albany, Ind.: B. F. Scribner, 1887), 169–70, 179–80.

45. Girardi and Hughes, *Memoirs of Carlin*, 113–16; *OR*, vol. 31, pt. 2: 463–78; Scribner, *How Soldiers Were Made*, 179.

46. *OR*, vol. 31, pt. 2: 463–67; *ORS* 6: 143; Scribner, *How Soldiers Were Made*, 179–80; Girardi and Hughes, *Memoirs of Carlin*, 114–16.

47. Scribner, *How Soldiers Were Made*, 180–81; *ORS*, vol. 6: 143; *OR*, vol. 31, pt. 2: 466, 472.

48. *OR*, vol. 31, pt. 2: 464, 468, 476–77; R. W. Henry to "Dear Wife," December 9, 1863, Robert W. Henry Letters, Iowa Historical Society, Iowa City; Raleigh Camp to "My Dear Sister," December 7, 1863, Camp Family Papers, Woodruff Library, Emory University; *ORS*, vol. 6: 167–69, 175. Camp's letter reflects indignation at a false newspaper report that it was the "Vicksburg men" who broke on Missionary Ridge. See J. Cutler Andrews, *The South Reports the Civil War* (Princeton: Princeton University Press, 1970), 375–76.

49. *OR*, vol. 31, pt. 2: 468; *ORS*, vol. 6: 137, 167, 169, 178; Scribner, *How Soldiers Were Made*, 181–82.

50. *OR*, vol. 31, pt. 2: 464, 474; Girardi and Hughes, *Memoirs of Carlin*, 116. Lt. Rivers, the commander of the Arkansas battery, reported that he positioned his battery on an eminence about 500 yards to the left of Breckinridge's headquarters. *ORS*, vol. 6: 178.

51. "From the 26th Regiment," *Clinton (Iowa) Herald*, February 20, 1864; Lawrence Wilson Diary, addenda for November 25, 1863, Library of Congress; Girardi and Hughes, *Memoirs of Carlin*, 116.

52. *ORS*, vol. 6: 157–58.

53. Crow, *Diary of a Confederate Soldier*, 44–46; "From the Thirty-First Iowa"; *OR*, vol. 31, pt. 2: 626.

54. "Captain Posey's Narrative"; *OR*, vol. 31, pt. 2: 184–85; *ORS*, vol. 6: 158; "The Late Battles," *Memphis (Atlanta) Appeal*, December 22, 1863 (Holtzclaw letter to *Appeal*).

55. Henry C. Day to Charles Day, November 30, 1863, in Earp, "Confederate Aide-de-Camp's Letters," 112; *ORS*, vol. 6: 158; Jones, *History of the 18th Alabama Infantry Regiment*, 12.

56. Crow, *Diary of a Confederate Soldier*, 46; *ORS*, vol. 6: 162–63.

57. "Captain Posey's Narrative."

58. Girardi and Hughes, *Memoirs of Carlin*, 116; Scribner, *How Soldiers Were Made*, 182–83.

59. Scribner, *How Soldiers Were Made*, 183; "From the Thirty-First Iowa"; Hess, *German in the Yankee Fatherland*, 144; *OR*, vol. 31, pt. 2: 319.

60. A. P. Stewart to W. F. Smith, February 15, 1894, "Correspondence Relating to Chickamauga and Chattanooga," *Papers of the Military Historical Society of Massachusetts*, vol. 8, *The Mississippi Valley, Tennessee, Georgia, Alabama, 1861–64* (Boston: Military Historical Society of Massachusetts, 1910), 252–53; *ORS* 6: 109–10, 117–18, 138.

61. William A. Chunn to "My own love Lila," November 30, 1863, William Augustus Chunn Letters, Woodruff Library, Emory University; *OR*, vol. 31, pt. 2: 666; "Captain Posey's Narrative"; *ORS*, vol. 6: 159.

62. The Federal numbers are estimates from reviewing the reports of the various commands in the *OR*. Several of Hooker's formations reported consolidated casualty numbers for the three days of battle between November 24 and 27, 1863 at Lookout Mountain, Missionary Ridge, and Rossville Gap. Confederate numbers are from Stewart's report at *ORS*, vol. 6:110. For the capture of flags, see *OR*, vol. 31, pt. 2: 472, 474, 608. An account of the capture of the flag and nine soldiers of the 18th Alabama by Lt. Simeon T. Josselyn of the 13th Illinois of Woods's brigade may be found in W. F. Beyer and O. F. Keydel, comps., *Deeds of Valor: How America's Civil War Heroes Won the Congressional Medal of Honor* (1903; reprint, Stamford, Conn.: Longmeadow Press, 1992), 285–86.

63. Scribner, *How Soldiers Were Made*, 183; "The Late Battles"; Henry C. Day to Charles Day, December 5, 1863, in Earp, "Confederate Aide-de-Camp's Letters," 118 (emphasis in original); *ORS*, vol. 6: 110–11; "Battle of Chattanooga."

7

SAVING THE ARMY OF TENNESSEE:
THE CONFEDERATE REAR GUARD AT RINGGOLD GAP

Justin S. Solonick

Defeated and demoralized, Confederate General Braxton Bragg retreated toward Dalton, Georgia, on November 26, 1863. Primarily concerned with saving his fighting men, Bragg set his infantry in motion first with his wagon trains and artillery to follow. The soft November roads, still soggy from weeks of rain, made it difficult for the latter to keep up with the infantry. "The trains were toiling forward over a single narrow road, the artillery wheels cutting into the soft mud up to the axles, and requiring heavy details to prize them out, and the rear wagon was still in sight when the enemy flushed with victory and pressing forward in energetic pursuit appeared."[1]

General Patrick Cleburne had covered only about two miles since the morning's march began when an unfamiliar messenger presented himself to the Irish general. The messenger insisted that General William J. Hardee had instructed Cleburne to drive his division toward Dalton. Cleburne expressed concern at the messenger's directions. His division, the strongest intact after Grant's thrashing of the Army of Tennessee at Chattanooga, had been charged with acting as the army's rear guard and protecting the struggling wagon and artillery train. In short, Cleburne's 4,157-man division represented the sole thin gray line between the Army of Tennessee and the pursuing Union juggernaut.[2]

Cleburne argued with the messenger and explained the significance of his current mission. Should Cleburne drive toward Dalton he would have to abandon both the Confederate artillery and wagons to the Union. The messenger explained that he had been sleep-deprived for several days and that it was possible he had misunderstood Hardee's orders. Since this message constituted a verbal order and lacked the weight of written instruction, Cleburne used his better judgment and disregarded the hazardous suggestion. Later dispatches would reveal that this verbal order was indeed erroneous and that Cleburne had never been ordered to abandon his post as the Confederate rear guard.[3]

Cleburne's column reached the town of Ringgold at approximately 10:00 P.M. on November 26. Later that night the weary and hungry Confederates received orders to cross Chickamauga Creek and make camp on the opposite side in order to place this natural obstacle between his division and the Union army. The Stonewall of the West could not believe this ludicrous order. Fording the river on this freezing November night while his men stood exhausted would have proven disastrous. Determined not to lose his men to pneumonia, he decided to once again let his better judgment prevail. About that time Cleburne received further instructions from Bragg. The commanding general directed his subordinate to adopt a strong defensive position and engage in a rearguard action that would stymie the Union pursuit and allow the remainder of the Confederate army to escape. Cleburne, fearing that he might not be able to hold back the Union juggernaut, requested the order in writing so as to protect himself from later scrutiny should he fail. Cleburne's division bivouacked on the north bank of the Chickamauga and crossed the creek at 3:00 A.M. as it began the next morning's march.[4]

Bragg's written instructions arrived as Cleburne's division was striking camp. It read, "you [Cleburne] will take a strong defensive position in the gorge of the mountain and attempt to check pursuit of the enemy. He must be punished until our trains and the rear of our troops get well advanced."[5] Shortly after crossing Chickamauga Creek, Cleburne passed through the town of Ringgold. Georgians had named the town after Mexican War hero Major Samuel Ringgold who died of wounds received at the battle of Palo Alto. In 1863, two to three thousand citizens inhabited its one hundred plus brick buildings and cottages. In addition, the sleepy little town sported two churches, a hotel, and a short storehouse that functioned as a freight depot near the railroad.[6] At Catoosa Station, Bragg's messenger intercepted Cleburne with an addendum to his previous orders. The message read, "Tell General Cleburne to hold his position at all hazards, and to keep back the enemy until the transportation of the army is secured, the salvation of which depends on him."[7] Cleburne continued on his course and proceeded to inspect the terrain opposite Ringgold.

The ground just east of Ringgold appeared fated for defense. Although the town itself rests on level ground, Taylor's Ridge rises steeply above the east side of the village. The ridge runs north to south and commands the surrounding terrain. A narrow pass known as Ringgold Gap bisects Taylor's Ridge just southeast of the town and in 1863 accommodated a branch of Chickamauga Creek, the Western and Atlantic Railroad, and a small dirt wagon path.[8] In addition to the terrain's topographic advantages, woodlands abounded that would provide cover for the Confederates in both the gap and on the ridgeline.[9]

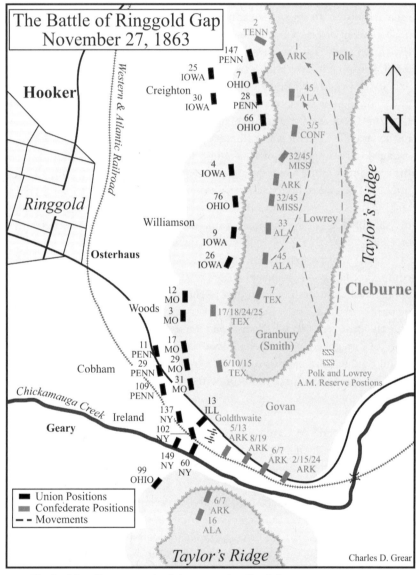

Hooker's headlong pursuit of the retreating Confederate army came to an abrupt halt at Ringgold Gap, where Cleburne's skillful maneuvering of his division in another brilliant defensive stand blocked the direct approach and then turned back repeated Union attempts to flank the position.

The battle of Ringgold Gap illuminates several axioms of war. First, success on the battlefield often relates to the tactical ability of the commander. Cleburne simply out-generaled Joseph Hooker on the morning of November 27, 1863. Adopting a strong defensive position both within the gap and atop Taylor's Ridge allowed one Confederate division to thwart a larger pursuing Federal force containing three divisions. Furthermore, the Stonewall of the West's tactical coordination and the compliance of his subordinates allowed him to respond quickly to circumstances as they developed on the battlefield. The history of the Confederate armies in the West is rife with stories of insubordination and strained relationships between commanders. Fortunately for Cleburne, this overarching situation did not apply to his division at Ringgold Gap. The action there exemplifies what a single Civil War division could accomplish on a tactical level so long as its officers worked in harmony.[10]

While Cleburne is lauded for his performance at Ringgold, his opponent, Hooker, often receives criticism. Those who chastise Hooker typically claim that his premature attack without artillery support led to his defeat. This, however, is not the entire story. The intelligence available to Hooker up until the battle indicated a demoralized Confederate army in flight. Subsequently, he pushed his attack so as to maintain pressure on the fleeing Army of Tennessee. Although artillery support certainly would have helped Hooker at Ringgold, his biggest blunder lay in the fact that he engaged his forces piecemeal as they arrived on the battlefield. Consolidating his command before he pressed the attack would have been the only way for him to dislodge Cleburne from his strong defensive position.

Finally, the battle of Ringgold Gap speaks to a larger phenomenon pertaining to Civil War combat. This war's armies were typically almost indestructible. After crippling defeat and demoralization, most Civil War armies skulked away to regroup and fight again, sometimes only a few weeks later. Rearguard actions contributed to the survivability of Civil War armies. Ringgold Gap clearly illustrates how a successful rearguard action, when trusted to competent subordinates, could save an entire army that had previously experienced defeat.

After surveying Taylor's Ridge and the surrounding countryside, Cleburne began to position his forces. First, he turned his attention to the high ground just north of the gap. Here he positioned Colonel Hiram B. Granbury's Texas Brigade, which consisted of the 7th Texas supplemented with the 6th/10th/15th Texas Infantry (consolidated). Major William A. Taylor's 17th/18th/24th/25th Texas Dismounted Cavalry (consolidated) formed a single brigade and fell in on the right of Granbury's command. Next, Cleburne detached Captain C. E. Talley's 7th Texas from Taylor's command and sent it to the summit north of the gap to protect the Confederate right flank. Subsequently, Cleburne turned his attention to occupying the ridge just south of the gap. He ordered the 16th Alabama under Major F. A. Ashford to conceal itself in the woods atop the hill and protect the Confederate left flank. The gap itself, however, still remained unmanned. Cleburne decided to plug the defile with Daniel C. Govan's Arkansas brigade, consisting of the 5th/13th Arkansas Infantry (consolidated), the 8th/19th Arkansas Infantry (consolidated), the 6th/7th Arkansas Infantry (consolidated), and the 2nd/15th/24th Arkansas Infantry (consolidated). Thus, four Arkansas regiments protected the gap itself.[11]

Next, Cleburne detached skirmishers from the Arkansas regiments and deployed them in the mouth of the gap in order to harass attacking Union troops and raise the hue and cry. In addition to infantry, the Irish general had two smooth-bore Napoleon field pieces at his disposal under the command of Lieutenant Richard W. Goldthwaite. Cleburne positioned these two guns at the mouth of the gap and concealed them behind a brush screen in order to surprise the attacking Federals. The remaining Confederate troops under brigade commanders Lucius Polk and Mark Lowrey formed the Confederate reserve and fell in at the rear behind the eastern descent of Taylor's Ridge out of the enemy's sight.[12] Cleburne and Govan confidently sat atop their horses together at the mouth of the gap and eagerly anticipated the Union advance. The Stonewall of the West had taken the best defensive posture that the ground would allow and both Union and Confederate alike would soon come to respect the natural defense Taylor's Ridge afforded. As the correspondent of the *Boston Daily Advertiser* observed, "Ringgold Gap is a strong position for defense. The slopes of the ridges are steep, wooded and difficult of ascent."[13] The combination of high ground and lethal Confederate fire at the command of Patrick Cleburne would soon exact a costly toll upon the Union army.

Shortly after daylight on November 26, Hooker set out to destroy the retreating Confederate army. Several hours later, the Union troops arrived at Chickamauga Creek only to discover that the Rebels had destroyed the bridge. Hooker sent back for pontoons, but they were slow coming up. After several hours Hooker's men found a ford and splashed through the creek. By then it was after 3:00 P.M. on the twenty-sixth. Additional time would be needed to construct a bridge suitable for artillery and wagons. Hooker moved his infantry across the river and ordered his artillery and ambulances to follow as soon as possible. By 10:00 P.M. Hooker's command caught up with the enemy. Since night battles generally proved impractical during the

Civil War, Hooker's troops bivouacked for the evening determined to engage the enemy on the morning of the twenty-seventh.[14]

Critics later chastised Hooker for rushing into battle without artillery support. The Union commander deflected these attacks, blaming the slow construction of the pontoon bridges as the primary reason he left his guns behind.[15] More to the point, evidence abounded that the Confederate army was retreating in disorderly haste. In short, Bragg's army appeared to be disintegrating before the Union advance. After the battle, Hooker wrote, "Evidences of the precipitate flight of the enemy were everywhere apparent; caissons, wagons, ambulances, arms, and ammunition were abandoned in the hurry and confusion of retreat."[16] At first glance, Hooker's statement appears self-serving; a justification for his later uncoordinated attack on Taylor's Ridge. However, other Union sources reported the same conditions that led Hooker to draw his erroneous conclusion about a disorganized retreating Rebel army. Members of the 13th Illinois and the 111th Pennsylvania describe similar scenes that confirm Fighting Joe's observations.[17] In addition, a correspondent of the *Cincinnati Gazette* accompanying the pursuing Union column wrote, "All along the road we picked up stragglers, small arms, caissons, limbers, &c., everything, in short, that marks the track of a retreating and demoralized army."[18] Thus, on the day of battle, evidence did not present itself that would have led Hooker to believe he was about to encounter stubborn resistance at Ringgold Gap.

The Union column plodded along another two miles before stumbling across a hastily abandoned Confederate campsite. Suddenly, Hooker heard firing and quickly resumed the march toward the town of Ringgold. At approximately 8:00 A.M., Union division commander Major General Peter J. Osterhaus had deployed skirmishers and engaged Cleburne's cavalry videttes, easily driving them back. The Confederate horsemen dashed into Ringgold Gap to warn Cleburne of the Union advance; the battle of Ringgold was about to begin.

Cleburne had skillfully concealed his troops in the brush line in Ringgold Gap as well as behind Taylor's Ridge. On spying the enemy in Ringgold Gap, Hooker still possessed only limited information about his enemy's deployment. Seeing only a small line of Confederate skirmishers, Fighting Joe decided to assault the gap without artillery support. According to Hooker, "The only way to ascertain the enemy's strength was to feel him."[19] Unbeknownst to the general, this series of probes in force would cost him dearly before the morning faded into afternoon.

Hooker immediately committed his lead division under the command of General Osterhaus. This was the division Sherman left behind with Hooker in Lookout Valley four days earlier when the Tennessee River persisted in breaking the pontoon bridge at Brown's Ferry and prevented the division from following the rest of the Army of the Tennessee detachment on its march to strike the north flank of Missionary Ridge. Osterhaus was a competent, veteran commander. He shook out Brigadier General Charles R. Woods's brigade first, sending the 3rd, 12th, and 31st Missouri regiments directly up the gap. Meanwhile, the 13th Illinois covered their right flank, and the 76th Ohio split wide to the left in hopes of turning the Confederate right.[20]

The three Missouri regiments advanced until they reached a railroad embankment that served as a ready-made breastwork. There they took shelter and returned the heavy Confederate fire.

On the right of his line, Woods sent the 13th Illinois dashing across an open field to seize a cluster of houses and barns in front of the gap from which Union sharpshooters might be able to neutralize the Confederate artillery. "The 13th Illinois Infantry executed the order in magnificent style," Osterhaus reported, "they charged through a hail-storm of balls, and gained the position assigned to them and held it, although the rebels poured a most murderous fire into these brave men from the gorge in front and the hill on the right."[21]

The movement came at a high cost. The Illinoisans stood and bent forward, "as though facing a hail-storm."[22] As they pressed forward, the Confederate artillery tore holes in the ranks. Color-bearer Patrick Riley went down, falling on top of the flag. Nearby, Corporal Joseph Sackett of Company C, along with a member of the color guard, rushed to where Riley lay. Acknowledging that their comrade was beyond help, they lifted up the colors, now stained with Riley's blood, and pressed forward.[23] Reaching the cluster of buildings, the Illinoisans took cover behind them as well as some piles of railroad ties. Other members of the 13th went to ground among the trees of an apple orchard. Sackett placed the colors in the fork of an apple tree and remained vigilantly prone next to the tree for the remainder of the engagement.[24]

Though its position in theory posed a threat to the Confederate line, the 13th Illinois was pinned down around the nearby cluster of houses due to rebel fire from the gap and ridgeline. The 13th's commander, Lieutenant Colonel Frederick W. Partridge, suffered a wound in the hand as a result of the intense Confederate fire. Injured, Partridge went in search of his second in command, Major Douglas R. Bushnell, wishing to turn over the command so he could fall back to the rear for treatment. The colonel made his way over to Bushnell, only to find the major dead. Suffering from pain and loss of blood, Partridge sought cover behind the railroad ties. Minutes later "a bullet from the enemy had grazed the end of a tie, and passing into his forehead lodged in the back part of his neck."[25] With Partridge fallen, command of the 13th passed to Captain Walter Blanchard of Company K, who was sheltering from Confederate small arms fire behind the log house. His new command proved equally short-lived, ending when a bursting shell shattered his knee, mortally wounding him.[26]

Casualties continued to mount among the rank and file of the 13th as well. A Confederate shot Robert Skinner as he passed from the pigpen to the barn. W. B. Howe of Company E lost four fingers on one hand and three on the other as a result of Confederate small arms fire. Meanwhile, inside the log house, Charles Beckman of Company K cried out as he "was struck and had his right arm broken while in the act of shooting out the window."[27] Beckman's companion, Ed Sheehey dealt with the stress of combat in a most unusual way. One soldier observed that he "seemed not to have any sense of danger. He was in the house; shuffled his feet and sang and swore in the thickest of the fight."[28] While the battle raged outside, a Georgia family huddled in the cellar beneath Sheehey's agitated feet, remaining undiscovered until the battle ended.[29]

Like the rest of Woods's brigade, the Illinoisans were tough, determined, and experienced, veterans of the desperate assault at Chickasaw Bayou eleven months before as well as the successful Vicksburg Campaign the preceding summer. When a bullet struck John D. Davis before he could even get off a shot of his own, he kept his rifle with him, went to the aid station in the rear, had his wound dressed and then hurried back to the front in time to get off a number of shots at the Rebels.[30] Despite the determination of its men, the 13th held on in front of the gap but could do no more.

As he had at Tunnel Hill two days before, Cleburne sought to disrupt the stubborn onslaught and launched limited counterattacks against the dogged Federals. A Confederate charge down the gap at this point in the battle drove back Woods's skirmishers but failed to budge the three Missouri regiments along the railroad embankment in his center. Cleburne's Confederates drew back up the slope, leaving a number of dead and wounded behind them.[31]

While the 13th Illinois struggled to hold onto its cluster of buildings on the Union right and Woods's three Missouri regiments held firm along the railroad embankment, the 76th Ohio made its way steadily upward, advancing along the crest of a spur that gradually ascended toward the main crest of Taylor's Ridge. Watching its progress, Osterhaus recognized that the single regiment would not be sufficient for the flanking movement he had envisioned, so he called on his second brigade, commanded by Colonel James A. Williamson. Osterhaus directed Williamson to send the 4th Iowa infantry up the slope in support of the Ohioans.[32]

About the same time that Cleburne launched his first countercharge against Woods's troops along the railroad embankment, Lucius Polk, commanding on the Confederate right, launched a similar attack against the flanking column threatening their right on the north side of the pass. Polk brought up the 1st Arkansas from its reserve position behind the ridge and hurled it at the 76th Ohio. When this force proved insufficient, Cleburne ordered Lowrey to help Polk defend the critical northern summit. In response, Lowrey led the 32nd and 45th Mississippi up from the reserve to Polk's aid. In fierce fighting, the Confederates drove the Federals back, but then were driven back themselves in turn. Hard-pressed, both Polk and Lowrey ordered the remaining regiments of their brigades to the summit of the ridge, thereby necessarily depleting the Confederate reserve behind Taylor's Ridge.[33]

The initial clash, just west of the crest of Taylor's Ridge, pitted the 1st Arkansas against the 76th Ohio in an epic struggle for control of the summit. The Confederate soldiers reached the top just before the Union troops. W. E. Bevens of the 1st Arkansas recalled, "We had the advantage of having a tree to use as breastworks, and in being able to see them. Whenever one stepped aside from his tree to shoot our men got him. Captain [Samuel] Shoup and John Baird rolled rocks down the hill and when a yankee dodged the other boys shot them."[34] According to Cleburne, desperate Confederate officers used both pistols and rocks in their efforts to beat back the attack.[35]

And it was a very desperate fight indeed. The Buckeyes drove the Arkansans back across the crest, and for a few minutes Major Willard Warner and his 150th Ohioans had the heady view of "the enemy going down the opposite slope." But it could not last. If it had been only the 1st Arkansas, the 76th might have prevailed, but the reinforcements Lowrey and Polk were bringing up lapped over both their flanks and began to drive them back. Both flanks of the 76th bent back to cope with the pressure on either side.[36]

As the fight raged on at close range, the color-bearer and four members of the color guard went down. At one point Warner took the flag himself and waved it as he led his men forward. He had handed it back to an enlisted man, however, and was leading the regiment with his sword when the new color-bearer was shot down. As an eyewitness in the 76th recounted, a Confederate soldier "snatched [the banner] from the grasp of a color-bearer as he went down."[37] The 1st Arkansas remained in possession of the colors of the 76th Ohio until the fiftieth anniversary of the war's ending in 1915 when the veterans restored the banner to its rightful owners in a ceremony in Columbus, Ohio.[38]

The 4th Iowa caught up with the 76th Ohio just in time to save it from being engulfed by the superior Confederate numbers. With the aid of the Iowans, the survivors of the 76th were able to make a fighting retreat until the two regiments met Williamson coming up to support them with two more of his Iowa regiments. This put a stop to the Confederate pursuit.[39]

The losses had been severe, especially in the 76th. "Coming down the mountain I found a number of our dead and wounded," recalled Ohioan Charles A. Willison. "Among these, one case that was most pitiable—a fine-looking boy sixteen to eighteen years old, shot through the head, the ball entering at his left ear. His dying convulsions were fearful to witness and he appeared to be in great agony, although unconscious."[40] In all, the Ohio regiment suffered 40 percent casualties during the engagement.[41]

While the Confederates had beaten back the Union turning movement led by the 76th Ohio, Williamson had in the meantime ordered the 25th and 30th Iowa farther to the left. They set a course that would lead them around the Confederate right flank farther north on Taylor's Ridge. The Iowa skirmishers were within seventy-five paces of the Rebel line when four regiments from the Twelfth Corps (147th and 28th Pennsylvania, 7th and 66th Ohio) moved up the ridge, sidestepping the Iowans and extending the Union line still farther to the left. Hooker had ordered Major General John W. Geary, commanding the division immediately behind Osterhaus's in the column, to send a brigade that would extend Osterhaus's flanking attack on the ridge north of the gap. Geary's division was a recent arrival from the Army of the Potomac. The brigade Geary ordered up the ridge was commanded by Colonel William R. Creighton.

As Creighton's regiments labored up the slope, the Rebels responded by stretching their line farther north along the ridge with the 2nd Tennessee guarding Cleburne's division's extreme right flank.[42] The eastern troops, formerly serving in the Army of the Potomac, pressed forward with their ranks neatly dressed and tightly packed in a parade-like formation. Colonel George C. Stone of the 25th Iowa hailed the Twelfth Corps men warning that such a formation was inappropriate for the terrain. The situation demanded skirmishers and a looser formation in order to overcome the steep and rocky ground. The Army of the Potomac soldiers shouted back that they "would teach Western troops a lesson."[43]

Unfortunately, events proved Stone's prophecy correct. As the Twelfth Corps men crossed the open ground in front of the ridge, the Confederate rifles exacted their toll. "I was shot," recounted Private Samuel Whitebread of the 147th Pennsylvania. "I did not feel it at first, until I took the next step, when I went down. I could feel the hot blood run down my leg and fill my shoe, and I began to realize what happened."[44] Fortunately for Whitebread, two men from Company G came to his aid and carried him to safety. After traversing the hostile terrain, Pennsylvania Lieutenant Gideon S. Stair described the chaotic situation as they climbed the hill, "[We] found the enemy in two columns. . . . After firing a few rounds we received orders to charge and again we gave the 'Yankee Yell' and away we went breaking their first line and up the mountain. . . . But . . . their second column opens on us and our men fall by the scores."[45]

The Confederate fire decimated the Pennsylvanians' ranks, forcing them to retreat back down the hill. As the Eastern men pulled back, Rebel minié balls continued to pepper them. Joseph A. Lumbard recalled that the projectiles tore "holes . . . into the earth large enough to admit the muzzle of our rifles."[46] Similarly, Sergeant Michael S. Shroyer was amazed to see three enemy bullets barely miss striking his size-ten army shoe as he made his retreat. The Pennsylvanians reached a rail fence at the base of the hill where their officers ordered them to stop. One Pennsylvanian remembered how "some of the boys when commanded to halt at the fence in coming from the hill, kept going thru [sic] and never did stop until they were safe behind the railroad in town."[47]

To the right of the 147th Pennsylvania advanced the 7th Ohio, nicknamed the "Rooster Regiment." The peculiar name became attributed to the Ohioans because of their silver rooster badge that they sported on the collar of their uniforms. The regiment embraced the name, and, before they entered an engagement, their colonel would crow and flap his arms. Responding to their maestro, the men would proceed to imitate the colonel in a spirited frenzy. The 147th's assault on Taylor's Ridge began much in the same way as both Colonel Creighton, who by now moved up to command the brigade, and Lieutenant Colonel Orrin J. Crane, who commanded the regiment, climbed up on boulders and began flapping their arms and crowing thus leading their men in the Keystone soldiers' tradition. Invigorated by their ritual, the 7th Ohio began the assault.[48]

They climbed the slope and met the Confederates near the top. According to Captain Ernst Joseph Krieger of Company K, "The regiment nearly gained the crest of the hill, within a few yards of the rebel breastworks, when their fire became too heavy and effective for flesh and blood to withstand."[49] Lieutenant Colonel Crane fell during the firefight. As Company D's first sergeant, Lawrence Wilson, recorded, "Creighton rallied the regiment and tried to reach the body of Crane, crying out that they must carry off the body, even if the charge failed; but it was impossible, the men had done all that men could do, and they were ordered to retire, which they did slowly and sullenly."[50] Another bullet struck down Creighton as the 7th retired from Taylor's Ridge. Overall, the 7th Ohio lost twelve of thirteen officers and nearly half its men.[51] Both Williamson's and Creighton's brigades remained at the western foot of Taylor's Ridge for the remainder of the battle. Geary believed the Confederates defeated Creighton's brigade because they held an almost impregnable position atop Taylor's Ridge.[52] Cleburne's use of terrain, coupled with Polk's and Lowrey's prompt response to developing threats, were the keys to the Rebels' defense of the ridge.

While Creighton's brigade had been moving against the Confederate right flank, the brigades of Colonel George A. Cobham and Colonel David Ireland occupied a reserve position approximately four hundred yards to the Union rear near the main street in the town of Ringgold. Several sources relate an unusual conversation that occurred between Generals Hooker and Geary just before the latter committed his entire division. According to one source, Hooker, after witnessing one of the Union withdrawals, barked at Geary, "Have you any regiments that will not run?" Geary is reported to have replied, "I have no regiments that will run." Hooker retorted, "Then . . . send some men into that gap and hold it until my artillery arrives."[53] Another source indicates that Hooker queried Geary about what troops he had in reserve. Geary responded, "The 3d brigade; if they fail, the position cannot be carried; they will not break, and can be relied on." Hooker is then reported to have ordered, "Lead them on!"[54] Whether or not such a dramatic conversation ever occurred is debatable, because many Civil War sources seek to praise their respective units. Regardless of the conversation's authenticity, Geary ordered Cobham to reinforce Osterhaus's division. Fortunately for the Union, Cobham's brigade arrived just in time to check the Confederate counterattack. Subsequently, at approximately 10:40 A.M., Geary ordered Ireland to reinforce the Union right flank in front of Ringgold Gap.[55]

Ireland's men entered the fray determined to check the gray tide, but their will was tested as they traversed the open ground in front of the gap and were hit with Confederate canister and musketry. The brigade deployed with its right flank near an old barn in front of the gap and its left resting along the railroad line. As it approached the gap, "The hills on both sides of the gap were lined with busy sharpshooters, and the shell and grape came plunging and hurtling into and around our position."[56] As the troops bounded across the open ground, "Capt. Charles T. Greene . . . was struck by an unexploded shell, which passed through his horse and carried away his right leg below the knee. The concussion was such that it threw him up about 5 feet, and on falling he was severely wounded."[57] According to Chaplain Richard Eddy of the 60th New York, "Corporal Conklin and Cozens of Company 'F,' went immediately to his relief, and while under violent fire, removed with their knives the fragments of the shattered limb, assisted him in applying a compress to the arteries, and bore him from the field."[58]

The 60th New York entered the gap first followed by the 149th New York and the 137th New York. Shortly after the 60th entered the gap, the Confederates flanked it, placing the regiment in jeopardy. Meanwhile, Lieutenant

Colonel Charles B. Randall of the 149th New York deployed five companies of skirmishers behind the old barn and occupied the building. Colonel James Lane of the 102nd New York, "gave directions for the men to shelter themselves by every available means, and for a few in each wing to keep up a rapid fire and careful fire whenever an enemy could be seen."[59] Shortly after the 102nd sought shelter, Cleburne's infantry appeared along the edge of the woods at the mouth of the gap accompanied by Goldthwaite's section of artillery. Frustrated by the harassing Union fire from the barn, Goldthwaite had his gunners fire four rounds of canister, which ripped through the structure, splintering the wooden walls. Fortunately for the Federals, no one was hurt. Ireland responded by deploying twelve sharpshooters from the 149th New York to deal with the wheeled Confederate menace. According to Captain George K. Collins of the 149th, "Whenever anyone came forward to work [the Confederate artillery], or remove it, he was shot by the marksmen."[60] Their relentless fire forced the Confederates to abandon the piece. However, the Rebels eventually succeeded in retrieving the guns and rolling them back to safety.

Unable to penetrate the gap, the Union soldiers sought cover wherever they could and the fighting degenerated into sharpshooting between the opposing sides. One officer ordered his men to build a makeshift breastwork in front of the gap in order to provide cover for the Union marksmen. According to Captain Collins, "The men fired upon the enemy whenever he showed himself, and he returned the compliment whenever an opportunity was afforded him."[61]

The details surrounding the end of the battle remain nebulous. Union sources indicate that their artillery arrived around noon and shelled the Confederates, forcing them to abandon their position. Confederate sources, however, indicate that they withdrew once Cleburne received word that Bragg's retreating column had successfully out-distanced Hooker's pursuing column. In all likelihood a synthesis of both versions is probably the truth. The Union troops remained pinned down in front of the gap and along the base of Taylor's Ridge until between noon and 1:00 P.M. when at last the Union artillery appeared in front of the gap. The arrival of the guns boosted Federal morale. "Our men were so elated when our artillery opened up that they wanted to rise up and cheer and charge," wrote Colonel Ireland.[62]

Meanwhile, Cleburne received a message at noon from Lieutenant General Hardee informing him that the Army of Tennessee had safely retreated and that Cleburne could withdraw. Cleburne withdrew his troops from Taylor's Ridge in good order, and by 2:00 P.M. Confederate skirmishers abandoned the gap and Taylor's Ridge, acting as the rear guard of the rear guard. After the Confederates withdrew, Union troops rushed forward and seized both Ringgold Gap and the summit of Taylor's Ridge. With the Confederates embedded atop nearby Dick's Ridge, approximately a mile to the east of the Gap, Hooker decided to hold his present position and not to engage Cleburne again.[63] The battle of Ringgold Gap was over.

Cleburne's rearguard action at Ringgold Gap earned him the official recognition of the Confederate Congress. The Stonewall of the West held his position for approximately five hours and suffered relatively light casualties.[64] Of the 4,157 men engaged, Cleburne reported his loses as 20 killed, 190 wounded, and 11 missing.[65] Union losses are harder to calculate. *The Camden Confederate* claimed that the Union suffered 300 prisoners and 1,500 killed and wounded.[66] This is obviously a gross exaggeration typical of most Civil War–era newspaper reports. Likewise, the *Milwaukee Daily Sentinel* reported that Hooker lost 1,000 men at Ringgold Gap.[67] Hooker reported 65 Union soldiers killed and 377 wounded, but he erroneously claimed that the Confederates left 130 men on the field and that the ratio of Confederate to Union casualties was three to one in favor of the Federals.[68] This is clearly an exaggeration of the Confederate losses aimed at covering his ill-coordinated and premature assault on the fixed Confederate position. Approximations of Union casualties somewhere in the neighborhood of 500 are probably closer to the truth.[69] Regardless of the actual number of Union dead, it is undeniable that more blue-clad young men carpeted the field than did the gray and butternut. As one Confederate private described, "The ground was piled with dead Yankees; they were piled in heaps. The scene looked unlike any battlefield I ever saw. From the foot to the top of the hill was covered with their slain, all lying on their faces. It had the appearance of the roof of a house shingled with dead Yankees."[70]

As the victors, the bloodied Union forces received the morbid honor of cleaning up the battlefield. Details transported wounded blue-clad soldiers to temporary hospitals in Ringgold and back to more permanent medical facilities near Chattanooga.[71] Horrific wounds resulted from the close-quarter shootouts. Although Civil War rifles contained a relatively long effective range, most firefights occurred at distances under two hundred yards. The firefights at Ringgold Gap further confirm the observation that most troops engaged at close distances. According to Surgeon B. F. Miller, "Many of the wounds received . . . at Ringgold were of a very severe character, in consequence of the relative position of the two hostile parties; so that [many] instances where bone was involved, destruction ensued for a long distance."[72]

Officers charged other details with burying the dead. According to Chaplain Richard Eddy, "The dead were buried just outside the village, nearly west from the town, on the east bank of the creek, under a small oak, about a rod from the stream, their heads lying towards the stream."[73] One soldier of the

147th Pennsylvania describes the horrific aftermath of the battle. He writes, "The sight which greeted us on the battlefield was a sad one indeed. A large number of our comrades lay stretched out in the cold embrace of death, with their eyes staring heavenward, and their hands convulsively clutching their clothing, or anything they could hold to. A large number of seriously wounded were also lying around promiscuously. The saddest case we noted was Corporal Brown . . . who had been struck in the head by a minie ball, which entered the forehead and made its egress on the top of the head having passed through his brain, and at each breath, as he drew it, the brain came out of both places. He was unconscious, but lived for several days."[74] Thus, with the disputed ground in Federal hands, the Union could claim its costly victory.

The historical evidence pertaining to the battle of Ringgold Gap allows the reader to draw several conclusions. The Stonewall of the West, Patrick Cleburne, seized victory for a number of reasons. His brilliant generalship coupled with simple good luck allowed him to hold off the Union forces that opposed him. Seizing the advantageous high ground and forcing the Union to attack the narrow defile—Ringgold Gap—allowed the Irishman to compensate for his numerical inferiority. According to Assistant Secretary of War Charles A. Dana, "It was a very dangerous defile to attack in front, and common sense plainly dictated that it should be turned . . . However, Hooker attacked in front, and the result was officially reported by him last night in the loss of 500 killed and wounded, where there was no necessity of losing 50."[75] In addition, the snake pit that was the Confederate officer corps plaguing the Army of Tennessee had not managed to taint Cleburne's division. The ability of Cleburne's junior officers to efficiently carry out his orders and seize initiatives on their own allowed the Confederates to take Taylor's Ridge before Union troops could climb its western slopes. As Irving A. Buck of Cleburne's division observed, "As with Stonewall Jackson, Cleburne's officers and men, alike, had implicit confidence in him, and hence his orders were obeyed promptly and without question. This was one of the elements of his success."[76]

As for General Hooker, some historians end their narratives about Ringgold describing how General Grant found Fighting Joe enjoying a sandwich and sipping tea at the end of the battle thereby inferring their contempt for this particular Union general, as well as highlighting his callous and oblivious disregard for the tragedy that had just befallen his men.[77] Meanwhile, others are more accepting of Hooker's mistakes suggesting that Hooker's only error was prematurely abandoning the assault.[78] Nevertheless, Hooker's own report despicably attempts to lay blame for his egregious casualties at the feet of his subordinates in order to protect his name while at the same time lauding the performance of the men in the rank and file. He writes, "The great difficulty

I experienced with my new command . . . was to check and curb their disposition to engage . . . despite my emphatic and repeated instructions to the contrary."[79] Although this claim is difficult to substantiate, one may conclude that Hooker sought reprieve for his ill-coordinated attack. While Hooker attempted to protect his reputation, many Union soldiers blamed their commander for the day's tragedy. Reflecting on the war, Major General Grenville Dodge stated that Union "troops suffered terribly in an unnecessary assault, as in a couple of hours the enemy would have been flanked out of the position."[80]

Negligence aside, more tangible reasons exist illuminating why Hooker lost the battle at Ringgold Gap. First, poor Union intelligence and Cleburne's stealthy positioning on the high ground east of Ringgold caught Hooker off guard. All of Hooker's reports up until Union forces clashed in front of the defile described a disorganized Confederate army in full retreat.[81] With such information provided, Hooker's aggressive pursuit appeared logical as all Civil War generals dreamt of capturing and destroying a fleeing enemy army. Second, Hooker attacked Cleburne without artillery support. Although Cleburne surprised Hooker, the latter exacerbated circumstances by pressing an attack without his artillery present. The fact that poor road conditions and destroyed crossing points delayed the Union guns does not excuse the fact that Hooker attempted to carry an elevated fixed defensive position without artillery support. This simply constitutes an amateur mistake that a seasoned commander like Hooker should never have made. Finally, Hooker should have consolidated his forces before attempting to carry the enemy's position. While battles are complicated and chaotic, the evidence suggests that Hooker never attempted to make a coordinated attack. Rather, he engaged his troops piecemeal as they arrived on the scene constantly attempting to either storm Taylor's Ridge or penetrate the gap itself. Both would have been more plausible had Fighting Joe waited for both his entire command and his artillery to arrive at Ringgold.

Extrapolating beyond the strengths and weaknesses of the commanders, the relatively small action at Ringgold Gap speaks to a larger phenomenon about indestructible Civil War armies. The military history of the Civil War is full of examples of armies tactically defeated on the battlefield that skulk off and are able to regroup and fight another day. One reason why this occurred is the use of effective rearguard actions during the Civil War. Rearguard actions such as the defense of Ringgold Gap illuminate how broken Civil War armies were able to retreat to safety. Although recovering from defeat always proved difficult for Confederate armies due to their limited supplies and available manpower, successful rearguard actions shielded shattered armies from their previous battle's mistakes, bought them time to escape, and contributed to the longevity of the American Civil War.

Notes

1. Irving A. Buck, "Cleburne and His Division at Missionary Ridge and Ringgold Gap," *Southern Historical Society Paper* 8 (Oct.–Dec. 1880): 469–70.

2. Ibid., 470.

3. Ibid., 469.

4. Ibid., 470.

5. Irving A. Buck, *Cleburne and His Command* (New York: Neale Publishing Co., 1908), 190.

6. For descriptions of the town of Ringgold, see "The Battle of Ringgold, Ga.," *Boston Daily Advertiser*, December 7, 1863; Albert R. Greene, "From Bridgeport to Ringgold" in *Military Order of the Loyal Legion of the United States* (Providence, R.I.: 1890), 310; and Lewis G. Schmidt, *A Civil War History of the 147th Pennsylvania Regiment* (Allentown, Pa.: Lewis G. Schmidt, 2000), 610, 619.

7. Buck, "Cleburne and His Division," 470.

8. North of Ringgold Gap, Taylor's Ridge is also known as White Oak Mountain. In their writings about the Battle of Ringgold Gap, the participants referred to the landform as Taylor's Ridge, and so it will be called in this study.

9. U.S. War Department, *The War of the Rebellion: A Compilation of the Official Records of the Union and Confederate Armies*, 128 vols. (Washington, D.C.: Government Printing Office, 1880–1901), series 1, vol. 31, pt. 2: 754 (hereafter cited as *OR*; all references are to Series 1 unless otherwise indicated).

10. For descriptions of the engagement at Ringgold Gap within the context of the Chattanooga Campaign, see Peter Cozzens, *The Shipwreck of Their Hopes: The Battles for Chattanooga* (Chicago: University of Illinois Press, 1994), 364–84; James Lee McDonough, *Chattanooga: A Death Grip on the Confederacy* (Knoxville: University of Tennessee Press, 1984), 220–25; Wiley Sword, *Mountains Touched with Fire: Chattanooga Besieged, 1863* (New York: St. Martin's Press, 1995), 334–46. For a discussion of Confederate command problems in the western theater, see Steven E. Woodworth, *Jefferson Davis and His Generals: The Failure of Confederate Command in the West* (Lawrence: University Press of Kansas, 1990).

11. *OR*, vol. 31, pt. 2: 754–55.

12. Ibid., 755.

13. "Battle of Ringgold, Ga."

14. *OR*, vol. 31, pt. 2: 319–20.

15. Ibid., 320.

16. Ibid.

17. *Military History and Reminiscences of the Thirteenth Regiment of Illinois Volunteer Infantry in the Civil War in the United States 1861–1865* (Chicago: Woman's Temperance Publishing Association, 1893), 383; John Richards Boyle, *Soldiers True: The Story of the One Hundred and Eleventh Regiment Pennsylvania Veteran Volunteers, and of Its Campaigns in the War for the Union* (New York: Eaton & Mains, 1903), 185.

18. *Daily Cleveland Herald*, December 5, 1863.

19. *OR.*, vol. 31, pt. 2: 321.

20. Ibid., 604.

21. Ibid.

22. *Military History and Reminiscences*, 385.

23. Ibid.

24. Ibid., 385–86.

25. Ibid., 386.

26. Ibid.

27. Ibid., 387.

28. Ibid.

29. For information on how soldiers coped with the stress of combat, see Earl J. Hess, *The Union Soldier in Battle: Enduring the Ordeal of Combat* (Lawrence: University Press of Kansas, 1997).

30. *Military History and Reminiscences*, 384.

31. *OR*, vol. 31, pt. 2: 604.

32. Ibid., 604, 611, 613–14.

33. Ibid., 32, 604–5, 756.

34. W. E. Bevens, "Reminiscences of a Private, Company G, First Arkansas Regiment, Infantry, May 1861 to April 1865" (N.p., n.d.), 32.

35. *OR*, vol. 31, pt. 2: 756.

36. Ibid., 612.

37. Charles A. Willison, *Reminiscences of a Boy's Service with the 76th Ohio* (Huntington, W.Va.: Blue Acorn Press, 1995).

38. "Return of a Battle Flag," *National Tribune*, April 1, 1915, 5. For information pertaining to the significance of Civil War flags, see James M. McPherson, *For Cause and Comrades: Why Men Fought in the Civil War* (New York: Oxford University Press, 1997), 84–85; Reid Mitchell, *Civil War Soldiers: Their Expectations and Their Experiences* (New York: Viking, 1988), 19–22; Bell Irvin Wiley, *The Life of Billy Yank: The Common Soldier of the Union* (Baton Rouge: Louisiana State University Press, 1992), 28–30, 93–94, and *The Life of Johnny Reb: The Common Soldier of the Confederacy* (Baton Rouge: Louisiana State University Press, 1994), 21–22, 138.

39. *OR*, vol. 31, pt. 2: 612.

40. Willison, *Reminiscences of a Boy's Service*, 80.

41. *OR*, vol. 31, pt. 2: 612, 619.

42. Ibid., 321, 616.

43. Ibid., 616.

44. Lewis G. Schmidt, *A History of the 147th Pennsylvania Regiment* (Allentown, Pa.: Lewis G. Schmidt, 2000), 621.

45. Ibid., 622.

46. Ibid., 624.

47. Ibid., 624–25.

48. Ibid., 623.

49. *OR*, vol. 31, pt. 2: 419.

50. Lawrence Wilson, *Itinerary of the Seventh Ohio Volunteer Infantry* (New York: Neale Publishing Co., 1907), 285–86.

51. Richard Eddy, *History of the Sixtieth Regiment of New York State Volunteers* (Philadelphia: Richard Eddy, 1864), 311; OR vol. 31, pt. 2: 401–4.

52. *OR*, vol. 31, pt. 2: 404.

53. George K. Collins, *Memoirs of the 149th Regt. N.Y. Vol. Inft.* (Hamilton, N.Y.: Edmonston Publishing, 1995), 215.

54. Eddy, *History of the Sixtieth Regiment*, 311.

55. *OR*, vol. 31, pt. 2: 404.

56. Ibid., 505.

57. Ibid., 439.

58. Eddy, *History of the Sixtieth Regiment*, 312.

59. *OR*, vol. 31, pt. 2: 450.

60. Collins, *Memoirs of the 149th Regt N.Y. Vol. Inft.* (Hamilton, N.Y.: Edmonston Publishing, 1995), 217.

61. Collins, *Memoirs of the 149th Regt N.Y. Inft.*, 216

62. *OR*, vol. 31, pt. 2: 438.

63. Cozzens, *Shipwreck of Their Hopes*, 384.

64. Buck, "Cleburne and His Division," 24.

65. *OR*, vol. 31, pt. 2: 757.

66. *Camden Confederate*, December 4, 1863.

67. *Milwaukee Daily Sentinel*, December 30, 1863.

68. *OR*, vol. 31, pt. 2: 323.

69. Buck, "Cleburne and His Division," 24; *OR*, vol. 31, pt. 2: 323, 757; *Camden Confederate*, December 4, 1863; *Milwaukee Daily Sentinel*, December 30, 1863; Meredith Lynn Bragg, "Holding Back the Storm: Major General Patrick Ronayne Cleburne's Division at Missionary Ridge and Ringgold Gap" (MA thesis, Texas Christian University, 1995), 42.

70. Sam R. Watkins, *Co. Aytch: A Confederate Memoir of the Civil War* (Wilmington, NC: Broadfoot, 1990), 130.

71. John Moore, U.S. Army, Medical Director of the Army of the Tennessee, "Report on the Operations of the Medical Department at the Battle of Chattanooga," in *The Medical and Surgical History of the War of the Rebellion* pt. 1, 1: 285; S. G. Menzies, 1st Kentucky Volunteers, "Extracts from a Report of the Operations of the Medical Staff in the First Division of the Fourth Corps at the Battle of Chattanooga" in ibid., 292.

72. B. F. Miller, "Extracts from a Report of the Operations of the Medical Staff in the First Division of the Fourteenth Corps at the Battle of Chattanooga," in ibid., 296. For more information on the relative effectiveness of Civil War rifles, see Earl Hess, *The Rifle Musket in Civil War Combat: Reality and Myth* (Lawrence: University Press of Kansas, 2008).

73. Eddy, *History of the Sixtieth Regiment*, 313

74. Schmidt, *History of the 147th Pennsylvania Regiment*, 627.

75. *OR*, vol. 31, pt. 2: 70.

76. Buck, *Cleburne and His Command*, 201.

77. Sword, *Mountains Touched with Fire*, 344.

78. Cozzens, *Shipwreck of Their Hopes*, 386.

79. *OR*, vol. 31, pt. 2: 332.

80. Major General Grenville M. Dodge, "Personal Recollections of General Grant and His Campaigns in the West," in *MOLLUS* 22 (Wilmington: Broadfoot, 1992), 364.

81. Cozzens, Shipwreck of Their Hopes, 1994.

Ulysses S. Grant's arrival in Chattanooga set in motion the train
of events that led to the battle. Library of Congress

Braxton Bragg had the unenviable task of facing several of the Union's best generals while leading an army whose generals were perpetual malcontents, unwilling to cooperate with him or each other. Library of Congress

Lookout Mountain looms in the distance over the railroad tracks that made Chattanooga a key strategic point. Library of Congress

A Confederate gun emplacement on the upper slopes of Lookout
Mountain gives a bird's-eye view of the toe of Moccasin Bend, the curve
of the Tennessee River just below Chattanooga. Library of Congress

Confederate general James Longstreet was responsible for holding
Lookout Valley and preventing the opening of a Union supply
line through the Tennessee Gorge. Library of Congress

William Tecumseh Sherman was Grant's most trusted lieutenant, but he ran into a difficult situation in command of the Union left at the north end of Missionary Ridge. Library of Congress

Joseph Hooker commanded on the Union right flank with success on
Lookout Mountain and against the Confederate left flank on Missionary
Ridge; he was far less successful at Ringgold Gap. Library of Congress

George H. Thomas commanded the Union troops that broke the
Confederate center on Missionary Ridge. Library of Congress

Confederates captured at Lookout Mountain were shipped north
to Union prisoner-of-war camps. Library of Congress

Hooker's attack struck Missionary Ridge at Rossville Gap, five miles south of Chattanooga. The United States Army Heritage and Education Center

Low morale showed itself in the occasional quest for the Civil War equivalent of the "million-dollar wound" or, as one Confederate soldier described his actions, "just feeling for a furlough." *Confederate Veteran*, vol. 5, p. 104.

8

FROM THE CHICKAMAUGA WITH "OLD ROSY" TO MISSIONARY RIDGE WITH GRANT: THE FALL 1863 STRUGGLE FOR CHATTANOOGA AND THE PRESS

Ethan S. Rafuse

The role the media can play in shaping popular perceptions of military operations has long been a source of consternation to those entrusted with command. The Civil War was no exception and produced its share of memorable quotes regarding the insidious effect newspapers supposedly had on the conduct of war. Just prior to the First Battle of Manassas, the commander of the Federal army informed a correspondent, with thinly veiled sarcasm, that he had "made arrangements for the correspondents of our papers to take the field under certain regulations, and I have suggested to them they should wear a white uniform, to indicate the purity of their character." General Robert E. Lee demonstrated that frustration with the press was not confined to Union commanders when he lamented that the Confederacy's great mistake was that "we appointed all our worst generals to command the armies, and all our best generals to edit the newspapers. As you know, I have planned some campaigns and quite a number of battles. . . . and sometimes when my plans were completed, as far as I could see, they seemed to be perfect. But, when I have fought them through, I have discovered defects, and occasionally wondered I did not see some of the defects in advance. When it was all over, I found, by reading a newspaper, that these best editor generals saw all the defects plainly from the start. . . . I am willing to yield my place to these best generals, and I will do my best for the cause editing a newspaper." Few expressed their views regarding the press with more bluntness or color, though, than Major General William T. Sherman, who constantly complained in letters to friends and family about "Dirty newspaper scribblers who have the impudence of Satan. They come into camp, poke around

among the lazy shirks & pick up their camp Rumors & publish them as facts
. . . reveal all plans and are worth a hundred thousand men to the enemy."[1]

Major General Ulysses S. Grant's success at Chattanooga was so complete
that it is easy in retrospect to assume there was an inevitability to the Union
victory and to see in it unquestioned vindication of the major decisions the
Union high command made during this period. But how did they appear to
observers at the time? This essay will address that question by looking at the
coverage of events in East Tennessee during the period encompassing the
defeat at Chickamauga and victory at Chattanooga in Northern newspapers.
It will describe how a number of Northern newspapers reported and analyzed
the defeat at Chickamauga and the developments that flowed from it: the
command shake-up in the Army of the Cumberland, the evolving situation
at Chattanooga, and the operations that finally produced the great Union
victory there.

This essay will focus mainly on coverage and commentary in three Cin-
cinnati papers: the *Commercial*, the *Times*, and the *Weekly Gazette*. In ad-
dition to being the largest city in the home state of much of the Army of the
Cumberland (which only a year earlier had been known as the Army of the
Ohio), as well as Major Generals Grant, William S. Rosecrans, Sherman, and
Alexander McCook, Cincinnati was the largest city in the states of the Old
Northwest from which the Federal armies that participated in the Chattanooga Campaign drew most of their rank and file.[2] Moreover, Army of the
Cumberland commander Rosecrans cultivated a strong relationship with the
Cincinnati press during the first two years of the war. This not only facilitated
its reporters' ability to cover the Army of the Cumberland's operations, but
makes their interpretation of the command shake-up at Chattanooga of particular interest, especially given the fact that correspondents for Cincinnati
papers played an active role in fueling a bitter rivalry between Grant and
Rosecrans prior to October 1863.[3]

As the Army of the Cumberland settled in at Chattanooga during the last
week of September 1863, there was no question that it had been roughly
handled at Chickamauga. As the first day of major fighting raged on September 19, the *Cincinnati Commercial* informed its readers that "the Rebels
have concentrated all their available forces in front of General Rosecrans"
and urged that he "be at once supplied with all our available forces." Should
Rosecrans be defeated, it predicted, the result would be "mischief, perhaps,
beyond remedy." On the other hand, it assured its readers, the "overwhelming defeat" of Confederate forces in "Northern Georgia would be the death
blow of the Rebellion." The *Cincinnati Times* agreed. "All eyes are centered

upon Northern Georgia."[4] Two days later, in response to reports on the fighting on September 19, the *Commercial*, under the heading "The Crisis in Northwestern Georgia," informed its readers that Rosecrans faced an enemy force "swelled to numerical superiority by General Joe Johnston's army from Alabama and [James] Longstreet's from Virginia." Although a battle of "a stubborn and sanguinary character had been fought" that day, readers of the *Commercial* and *Times* learned, the Army of the Cumberland still held its ground in the face of desperate attacks by, the former reported, an "enemy, who anticipated an easy victory" but "was completely foiled." It was "beyond doubt," though, the *Commercial* warned, that the Rebels, "having concentrated all their available forces . . . and having everything at stake will make another desperate effort."[5] "The condition of affairs is certainly critical," the *Commercial* advised its readers on September 22, "but is by no means desperate. We have confidence that our noble army and its capable leader will give a glorious account of themselves." The editors of the *Times* also expressed confidence that the Army of the Cumberland, which it proclaimed "the best body of troops on this continent," and its commander would foil the Rebels "with that same military skill which so marked his course at . . . Stones River."[6]

Of course, on September 22 the Army of the Cumberland was licking its wounds after suffering a stunning reversal of fortune at Chickamauga, initial reports of which appeared that same day in the *Commercial*. The readers of the *Commercial*, as well as readers of the *Times* and *Gazette*, which published the same report almost verbatim on the twenty-second and twenty-third respectively, learned that Rosecrans's men had fought off an attack early on September 20 against their left, but in the process of shifting forces around to support that effort, "perceiving the withdrawal of skirmishers from the front . . . of the right and center, the enemy made a vigorous attack upon that part of the line, piercing the center. . . . both Right and Center being much scattered." The left, under Major General George Thomas, though, had managed to hold its ground with help from Major General Gordon Granger's corps until the end of the day.[7] The following day readers of the *Times* and *Commercial* learned Rosecrans's entire army had fallen back toward Chattanooga after a fierce engagement with what the *Commercial*'s headline declared "The Great Combination to Crush Rosecrans." Underlining the seriousness of the situation, readers of the *Times* and *Commercial* learned from reports that nothing was being "talked of in Washington, today, except the fate of Rosecrans' army." Nonetheless, the *Commercial* advised its readers, reports indicated the Army of the Cumberland was strong enough to hold its ground against further attacks.[8]

Like the *Times* and papers in Louisville, Milwaukee, and elsewhere in the Midwest, the *Commercial* was critical of the failure to reinforce Rosecrans before Chickamauga. "The Rebels," the *Commercial* explained to its readers, "had calculated upon nothing less than the annihilation of Rosecrans' army. ... It is obvious that, after the opening of the Mississippi the best divisions of Grant's great army would have been better employed with Rosecrans." "There has been a sad lack of generalship in higher official quarters," a Louisville paper declared, "It is exceedingly to the discredit of our military authorities that the gallant commander of the Army of the Cumberland must encounter such heavy odds." "If disaster has befallen our army in the vicinity of Chattanooga," the *Weekly Illinois State Journal* predicted, the country would "earnestly inquire why Gens. Grant's and [Nathaniel] Banks' armies have been permitted to remain in comparative inactivity, or have been sent upon expeditions of doubtful importance."[9]

Nonetheless, bolstering their analysis with reference to reports in Southern papers, the editors of the *Commercial* and *Times* joined other papers in finding little cause for gloom as they considered the situation in Georgia in late September. They insisted, given the great effort the Confederates made to concentrate their forces in northern Georgia and the massive casualties they suffered, the fact that the Army of the Cumberland had not been destroyed, that Chattanooga was still in Union hands, and that Rosecrans reportedly had "no doubt of his ability to maintain himself," must have "the most disheartening influence" on the Confederacy. "If [Rosecrans] can only hold Chattanooga," the *Times* declared on September 23, "the Rebels will be foiled in their designs of repossessing themselves of East Tennessee, which will be a virtual defeat."[10]

Indeed, in his report on Chickamauga published on September 28, Joseph Miller, the *Commercial*'s correspondent accompanying the Army of the Cumberland, reported that within forty-eight hours after the battle the Army of the Cumberland was "ready and willing to fight ... completely reorganized, confident that 'we'll whip them yet.'" "The whole Southern press is urging General [Braxton] Bragg to push on and continue the fight taunting him with reminiscences of Murfreesboro and Shiloh," the *Commercial*'s editors approvingly noted in their commentary on Miller's report. "They are fully conscious that ... [t]he object of their concentration was nothing less than the annihilation of Rosecrans' army. That, and only that would compensate them for their exertions and sacrifices ... and all they have to show for it is a few miles of territory south of Chattanooga, and a few pieces of artillery."[11] The *Times* also took delight throughout the last week of September and first week of October in reporting that Confederate sources expressed disappointment at the "mere barren success" they achieved at Chickamauga and informing its readers that "Richmond is in a state of mourning for the losses Rosecrans has inflicted." "While they may outwardly proclaim a victory to their arms, they feel within themselves that they have suffered an irreparable disaster," readers of the *Times* learned on October 7. The fact that the Army of the Cumberland still held Chattanooga was also a source of comfort to the *Gazette*, which assured its readers on September 23 that initial reports that Rosecrans had been "badly beaten" had been proven false and that even though it fell back to Chattanooga, "the Army of the Cumberland has maintained its proud position."[12]

Not surprisingly, the political sympathies of members of the press were fully on display in their efforts to explain what had happened at Chickamauga. Democratic papers in Ohio and Kentucky seized on a report that a Philadelphia editor close to the Lincoln administration had remarked that the setback to Rosecrans's army "would be a mere trifle compared with the success of the democratic party in Ohio or Pennsylvania" to condemn the administration for, they claimed, sending soldiers to those states "to control the election" rather than having them on hand at Chickamauga.[13] In turn, Republican papers in Ohio and Illinois found ways to lay the blame for the setback at Chickamauga at the feet of the Democrats, with some reporting that the Confederates had concentrated their forces against Rosecrans in part out of a belief that by doing so they could achieve battlefield successes that would bolster the cause of their "allies" in the Northern Democratic Party in upcoming state elections in Ohio and Pennsylvania.[14]

In late September, the *Commercial* published a lengthy editorial on Rosecrans, whose departure from the field at Chickamauga on September 20 had understandably raised eyebrows in the North. It lauded the skill with which he managed his army and gained possession of large chunks of territory in "the very heart of the Southern Confederacy" prior to Chickamauga. It then praised him for his ability to figure out that the enemy had concentrated on him, wisdom in seeing that "the ever reliable Thomas" was given management of the army's left, and ability to thwart blows delivered by an enemy army that outnumbered his own. The editors conceded Rosecrans did not display the same "extraordinary personal daring" that he had at Murfreesboro, but argued it was unreasonable to expect him to do so at every engagement and declared themselves certain that when the history of Chickamauga was "fully written and the judgment of mankind rendered, it will appear that the name of Rosecrans has at least lost none of its luster."[15]

Readers of the *Commercial* who still had confidence in Rosecrans's mental fortitude no doubt found reassurance in reports that appeared in it and the *Times* during the first week of October that Rosecrans proclaimed, "he had taken up quarters at Chattanooga and intended to stay there. . . . Beyond this point the Army of the Cumberland will not retire while there is a foe to menace it!" That the government was moving to reinforce Rosecrans further heartened the editors of the *Times*, who on September 28 had expressed exasperation at the use of Grant's forces for anything other than the reinforcement of Rosecrans and declared the following day that if the Confederates "could not take advantage of Rosecrans' defeat on the 21st, they could not hope to do so" now that "the Government has. . . . opened its eyes to the importance of concentration."[16] If Bragg's army tried to attack Chattanooga, the *Times* informed its readers, it would have a formidable position to overcome. Federal forces had turned the ground between them and the enemy, a report in the October 1 edition of the paper confidently noted, into "a complete waste, everything has been leveled and destroyed. Houses, trees, shrubbery, fences, and all are gone. . . . Over this now desert waste, the guns of the Federals have complete control. From the embrasures of the frowning battlements, now can be seen the threatening bore of the open-mouthed cannon, ready to belch forth with flames of fire."[17]

Readers of the *Commercial*, *Times*, and *Gazette* (as well as the papers that reprinted their reports) could also take heart from a steady series of reports in late September and early October that morale in the Army of the Cumberland was high. "The army," the September 24 *Times* and September 30 *Gazette* assured their readers, "is in the best of spirits since the fact became apparent that Chickamauga was almost as much a defeat for the Rebels as for us. Gen. Rosecrans was rapturously received along the lines this P.M."[18] Indeed, declared one report in the *Commercial*, the "universal feeling in the army is that of indignation at the reports from the North that they have suffered a defeat." "The army theory of the matter," according to an October 8 editorial in the *Commercial*, "is that the battle [of Chickamauga] was for the possession of Chattanooga. They have it and claim a substantial victory." The soldiers, the *Commercial* reported on October 2, had "all confidence in the skill and ability of 'old Rosy' and will stand by him." "The army with General Rosecrans is in excellent condition and spirits," the *Times* declared on October 5, "in an impregnable position. . . . They feel a security within themselves, and are fully prepared to meet the enemy." The *Commercial* echoed the *Times*'s sentiments the following day. "No reinforcements are needed for . . . holding Chattanooga," the *Commercial* assured its readers, "the position of our army is impregnable and its spirit indomitable."[19]

Nonetheless, massive reinforcements were on the way. When it became clear in the immediate aftermath of Chickamauga that Major General

Ambrose Burnside's force at Knoxville could furnish no assistance to the Army of the Cumberland, the War Department began looking elsewhere and during the night of September 23-24 decided it would send two corps from the Army of the Potomac. These would be commanded by an officer who was then looking to reverse his fall from grace earlier in 1863, Major General Joseph Hooker. News that Hooker had received a new "important command, in a field where his brilliant fighting qualities will find their full scope" appeared in the *New York Times* only five days after Chickamauga and within a few days afterward was before readers of the *Times* and the *Commercial*.[20]

By October 7, the arrival of Hooker's command on the scene was so evident (as was the fact that early reports that he was slated to replace Burnside were false) that the papers felt free to dispense with the secrecy that had accompanied its transfer from Virginia and openly report on the fact that it was, if not in direct contact with Rosecrans, nonetheless close enough to assist him.[21] The following day, the *Commercial* published a laudatory editorial on Hooker. It praised his willingness to accept this important command (which it mischaracterized as a corps in the Army of the Cumberland rather than an independent force) and declared his doing so demonstrated he did not possess "that false and foolish pride . . . that would prevent him from serving his country in any capacity where he would be useful." While conceding it was generally believed his tenure in command of the Army of the Potomac had not been successful and that even his "best friends will not deny that he is an indiscreet talker," the *Commercial* was "sure of one thing—there is not a more gallant man or better commander of a corps. . . . We have confidence that his name will shine out in the news of the next battle."[22]

During the first week of October, the editors of the *Commercial* and the *Gazette* got an opportunity to talk to Lieutenant Colonel Henry Boynton, who had just received a medical furlough from the Army of the Cumberland. Boynton, both papers reported, had offered nothing but positive news regarding the Army of the Cumberland. "He states that the position of our army at Chattanooga is impregnable, and its spirit indomitable," the *Commercial* declared on October 6. "Chattanooga was the prize fought for, and they held it." "Chattanooga is a grand fortification," the *Gazette* reported on October 7, "and can only be reached by regular siege approaches. From this mode of operations nothing is feared. . . . we may rest assured that as Gen. Rosecrans has succeeded against great odds in defeating the plans of the Rebels, and in holding his ground, so he will succeed when he takes the next step forward." "The gloomy articles of the Richmond papers correctly represent the feeling in Bragg's army," it added confidently. "They struck for Chattanooga; they suffered tremendously, and Rosecrans remains master of the prize."[23]

On October 1, the Confederates attempted to discomfit the Federals at Chattanooga by launching a raid by approximately five thousand cavalrymen led by Major General Joseph Wheeler. Though they managed to burn hundreds of wagons carrying critical provisions for the Army of the Cumberland and compelled Rosecrans to adjust some of his dispositions, Wheeler's raid failed to achieve anything truly decisive and consequently made little impression on the editors of the *Times*. They dismissively assured their readers on October 7 that "though destroying some property" the raiders were "getting worsted and that in any case Rebel raids recently have not been paying institutions." Nor did Wheeler's efforts shake the *Commercial*'s confidence in Rosecrans and its belief that the situation at Chattanooga was satisfactory.[24] Readers of the *Commercial* could take further heart on October 6 when they read that Quartermaster General Montgomery Meigs had arrived at Chattanooga from Washington and not only repudiated reports of the Army of the Cumberland's demoralization but declared it "in excellent condition, and fully equal to any emergency."[25]

Positive reports on the Army of the Cumberland's condition at Chattanooga continued to flow from the *Times*'s and *Commercial*'s correspondents during the second and third weeks of October. "Bragg still holds Missionary Ridge and Lookout Mountain, and presents a very bold front," read an October 9 report that appeared in the *Commercial* eleven days later. "He opens artillery on us every day, and we usually return the compliment. . . . [W]e have sustained no damage that I have heard of, from this cause, except the wounding of a soldier of the 65th Ohio and the killing of a negro servant."[26] On October 14, readers of the *Commercial* learned Confederate soldiers had been taking "every possible occasion to come into our lines as deserters" and brought with them reports "that the Rebel army is in a state of mental anxiety and agitation, consequent upon the reception of news that Rosecrans is being reinforced." "Two intelligent Mississippian" deserters, one correspondent reported that day, had stated that while many in the Confederate rank and file were in high spirits over Chickamauga, "the more intelligent among the officers think they have not accomplished what they intended and are not compensated by their achievements for the loss of life and limb." Another reported that on a trip to the picket line, where the two sides were "on excellent terms," he heard a Federal soldier defiantly ask his Confederate counterpart, "If you whipped us so bad [at Chickamauga], why didn't you take Chattanooga?"[27]

It was inevitable, though, that someone would be held to account for the fact that the Army of the Cumberland had suffered a serious tactical setback. To almost no one's surprise, the first targets in the search for scapegoats would be corps commanders Alexander McCook and Thomas Crittenden, whose performance at Chickamauga—and especially their leaving the field at the crisis of the battle—immediately came under scrutiny. In a September 25 editorial commenting on Chickamauga, the *Commercial* informed its readers that it appeared it was "the extraordinary firmness and excellent management of Thomas' corps," aided by elements from Granger's corps, that saved the army from total defeat on the twentieth. In contrast, parts of McCook's and Crittenden's commands, it seemed clear, "didn't stand up to the work as might have been expected of soldiers of the Army of the Cumberland, or they were not so effectively handed."[28]

Then, three days later, the *Commercial* published Miller's report on Chickamauga, which confirmed initial impressions that Thomas had turned in a stellar performance, while the same could not be said of McCook and Crittenden. This followed on the heels of the appearance in several papers of a report—under a banner headline in one paper proclaiming "General McCook Blamed by General Rosecrans"—from the September 25 *New York Times* that Rosecrans's dispatches imputed that the battle was lost due to "disobedience of orders on the part of General McCook, who failed to occupy an important position assigned by Rosecrans. Had he done as ordered, Rosecrans' opinion is that the battle would have resulted in a splendid Union victory."[29] As if this were not enough, during the last week of September, the *Gazette* correspondent's full report on Chickamauga appeared (and would be republished in a number of other papers) describing how McCook "disappeared from the general history of the battle" almost immediately after the Confederate breakthrough on September 20 and "extricating himself from his demoralized and routed corps, he headed toward Chattanooga, and . . . disappeared entire from the field."[30]

By the time these reports were published, though, McCook's and Crittenden's fates had already been sealed. On September 28 the War Department issued orders announcing that McCook's and Crittenden's commands would be consolidated into a single corps under Granger's command and the two generals' conduct would be subjected to a court of inquiry. The *Times* informed its readers of the War Department's actions on September 30 and implicitly approved of it by declaring, "Had they displayed the generalship of Thomas . . . the day would have been ours." The *Commercial*, however, made no mention of the command shake-up until October 1, when it reprinted a report from the September 29 *New York Times* on the War Department's actions.[31]

When the newspaper finally printed a copy of the official order relieving McCook and Crittenden and consolidating their commands on October 6, the *Commercial*'s editors still, as they had when they first reported the news, refrained from offering commentary on it. Two days later, though, the *Commercial* told its readers that an official from the Sanitary Commission who had just left Chattanooga reported that while the Army of the Cumberland did not view Chickamauga as a defeat, it was "believed that if McCook's and Crittenden's corps had been efficiently commanded the Rebel army would have been by this time a wreck at Atlanta." And certainly the *Times* did nothing to help McCook's cause on October 10 when it published a report on Chickamauga that appeared in a Chicago paper in which its correspondent snidely described how at the crisis of the battle, "McCook, like the Arabs, had 'silently passed away' toward Rossville" while other officers stood their ground. "If half the accounts in regard to the conduct of these Generals is true," the editors of the *Milwaukee Sentinel* declared, "they should be punished in such a manner as to afford an instructive example for others."[32]

Crittenden and McCook, of course, were furious at the aspersions cast on their characters and military ability after Chickamauga and received steadfast support from the *Louisville Journal*, a paper whose political sympathies rested with Kentucky's long-time senator John Crittenden, father of General Crittenden. "The many friends of McCook and Crittenden cannot easily believe that a just court will find cause to censure them," its editors defiantly declared, adding, if "General Crittenden . . . is not a brave man, the race of brave men is extinct among us."[33] And as the two generals passed through Louisville during the second week of October, readers of the *Commercial* learned their friends in that city were confident they would "triumphantly refute any allegations against them, which may be made before the approaching Court of Inquiry."[34]

On October 16, the *Commercial* printed the bitter farewell order McCook issued to his corps upon relinquishing command in which he declared they had been "slandered and maligned by news scribblers, who, unfortunately, in our country, mould the public mind." Alongside his letter appeared commentary by one of its correspondents. "Outside the 14th Army Corps," he reported, "there seems to exist a feeling of hostility toward General McCook, for his conduct in the late battles." The specific complaint was that McCook had left the battlefield for Chattanooga on September 19 and was not on the field after that (which was false) and, as had been reported earlier, that Rosecrans had censured McCook "and blames him in a measure, for our defeat." The correspondent disputed this latter assertion and sympathetically opined that he thought the "prejudice against McCook arises from a misapprehension as to the part he was obliged to play." After reaching the rest of the army's position behind the Chickamauga, he noted that McCook's units had been parceled out to other parts of the field and thus "the truth is there was no corps to command, and . . . [t]he worst that can be said of McCook is that he lost his temper seeing his corps distributed among the other corps, and went to the rear because he saw nothing for him to do in the front."[35]

A few days later, the correspondent for the *Times* also weighed in on the situation with McCook and Crittenden. He declared that while the consolidation of their corps and their removal from command "may not prove agreeable to the officers to whose lack of ability or skill the disaster at Chicamauga [*sic*] was owing, but it will, doubtless, prove beneficial to the army." He then blasted McCook for his bitterness toward the press and declared his complaining to be "in very bad taste . . . for it argues both ingratitude to the professors of the quill and a flaw in his character as a military commander." Though he would not go so far as the editors of the *Louisville Journal* in its treatment of the general, the *Times* correspondent was more charitable toward Crittenden, whose farewell address to his troops he characterized as "more large and philosophic than his companion . . . and is therefore more commanding of respect and public consideration."[36]

Yet McCook was not alone in his bitterness toward how newspaper correspondents had conducted themselves in regard to Chickamauga. On October 16, the *Commercial* published a report from a correspondent with the Army of the Cumberland stating there existed "a feeling of intense indignation in this army against the correspondent of the *New York Herald*, who rushed himself into telegraphic notoriety in Cincinnati at the expense of our bravest and best men and officers. The correspondent of the *Gazette* is in bad odor too."[37] A few days later, another correspondent's report, this one dated October 9, appeared in the *Commercial* reporting McCook's bitter "denunciation of army correspondents" and stating that the general specifically blamed "Mr. [William F.] Shanks, of the *Herald*, for his removal." "It is a bad commentary on the President's discretion," the correspondent added, "to say that an unauthenticated newspaper paragraph was his only guide in such an important action as the displacement of two Major Generals."[38] Indeed, the *Commercial* felt impelled on November 27 to speak up on McCook's behalf in response to reports of the battle of Chickamauga that cast what it described as "the most cruel aspersions upon the conduct of this gentleman." While conceding McCook "may not be a General whose capacity is equal to the most efficient direction of an army," it also proclaimed "the great charges of cowardice and imbecility that have been made against him . . . so freely circulated throughout the country, are clearly unwarranted, and it is time to do him simple justice by making the truth known."[39]

While McCook and Crittenden battled the cloud Chickamauga had cast over their reputations, no such anxiety existed in regard to Thomas.

"'Thomas' stock has gone up so much since the battle of Chickamauga," the *Commercial's* correspondent in Chattanooga proclaimed, "that I believe the soldiers would, at his bidding, storm the gates of an institution supposed to be due south from heaven." Rosecrans, too, continued to hold the confidence of the men. "Our men ask for no more inspiration," the correspondent declared, "than the presence of 'Rosey' and Thomas. What they will not do under their leadership must be put down under the list of impossibilities for the Army of the Cumberland."[40]

Thus it is not surprising that the *Commercial* was immediately inclined on October 21 to dismiss as a "canard" a report in a New York newspaper that Rosecrans had been removed from command of the Army of the Cumberland. When the telegraphic news came in later that day, though, the *Commercial* found that the report was true. The day before, its readers learned, the War Department had consolidated the western military departments under Grant's command while Rosecrans received orders directing him to turn command of the Army of the Cumberland over to Thomas and report to Cincinnati.[41]

As might be expected, such a dramatic development sparked a flurry of reporting seeking explanations. Of the dozen papers consulted for this essay, the only ones that outright endorsed Rosecrans's removal were the *Chicago Tribune* and the *Northwestern Gazette*. The former did so fairly tepidly, emphasizing more its faith in Lincoln's wisdom than its ability to find fault with Rosecrans, though it did not hesitate to publish and call its readers' attention to highly critical reports on Rosecrans that appeared in Washington and New York papers. The latter paper refused to repeat the more outrageous explanations for the move in favor of its own: "Rosecrans is a good strategist, but a bad tactician; and . . . it absolutely required a general in command of his late army who combined the two qualities." Given the fact that Grant and Rosecrans were widely perceived to be rivals, it is not surprising that a paper published in Galena, Illinois, the former's place of residence immediately prior to the war, would respond favorably to the command change that firmly established Grant's ascendancy.[42]

In Cincinnati, Rosecrans's removal from command received a much different reception. The *Times* immediately responded on October 21 with a lengthy editorial criticizing the move. It pointed to Rosecrans's performance at Murfreesboro and in the operations that captured Tullahoma and Chattanooga as vindication of the "universal gratification" that greeted his appointment to command. "Overwhelmed by numbers at Chickamauga, he managed his army with admirable skill," it exclaimed, "and though he lost the day, he robbed the Rebels of the spoils of victory by defiantly holding Chattanooga." And the *Times* did not hesitate to point out where it believed the blame for Rosecrans's removal lay: General in Chief Henry W. Halleck. "Such is the man," it declared after running through Rosecrans's military accomplishments, "who has been sacrificed to gratify the malice of General Halleck, who will not permit a successful rival to command the army. . . . The means employed to secure the removal were contemptible, and will add to the public indignation [toward] Halleck and his clerks, the President and the Secretary of War."[43]

Nonetheless, the consolidation of the Western commands under Grant did meet with almost universal approbation from papers throughout the Old Northwest. This move, the *Times* declared on October 21, "will give him many advantages; and that he will avail himself of them, and be successful, is the ardent wish of every patriot." "The organization of the new Military Division is certainly a most commendable movement," the *Ohio State Journal* informed its readers, "Gen. Grant . . . has shown himself a man well fitted for giving direction to military movements on so grand a scale as the command of such a division implies. In addition to rigorous and persistent powers of execution, he has manifested capacity for enlarged combinations which it is given to but few Generals to possess." The selection of Thomas to command the Army of the Cumberland was also well received.[44] Thomas's stellar performance at Chickamauga was widely reported in the aftermath of the battle and on September 25 inspired the *Commercial* to publish a profile under the heading "Major General Thomas, the Hero of the Battle of Chickamauga." "Thomas will rank in history," a report on Chickamauga that appeared in the October 10 *Times* proclaimed, "among the coolest, quietest, most modest of heroes. . . . Kind, calm, brave, God made him for a leader, and he honors the manufacture." "That this officer has won high renown on the hotly contested field of Chicamauga [*sic*], every lover of his country is proud to acknowledge," another *Times* correspondent declared after learning of the command change.[45]

On October 22, the *Commercial*'s Washington correspondent informed readers that a paper in the capital was reporting Rosecrans's removal as the consequence of the general's possessing "an affliction of an apoplectic character" but was quick to dismiss this report and others indicating that the decision may have been made on anything other than "purely . . . military grounds."[46] The following day, the *Times* and *Commercial* both informed their readers that the *Washington Chronicle* had published "astounding intelligence in regard to the removal of Rosecrans. . . . It is that three charges have been made against the late popular commander. The first is preferred by Crittenden and McCook, to the effect that Rosecrans left the battle-field during the crisis and fled to Chattanooga. . . . It is reported that subsequently, through the influence of opium, he became insensible." The second charge was that Rosecrans had disobeyed orders before Chickamauga "to remain at Chattanooga until reinforcements should arrive." Finally, it was complained that Rosecrans had defied orders to advance from Murfreesboro the previous June. As if this were not enough, New York papers, the *Commercial* and *Times* informed their readers, reported that Rosecrans, Crittenden, and McCook had been accused of being asleep in Chattanooga during the battle of Chickamauga, even though they had learned "semi-officially, that in regard to Crittenden this statement is false. . . . The blame connected with the failure at Chickamauga will fall wholly on Rosecrans." On October 24, the *Commercial* published a report from the *New York Times* that the decision to remove Rosecrans was also a result of the fact that his relationship with General in Chief Henry Halleck had been bad.[47]

The editors of all three Cincinnati papers responded strongly to the rumors, especially those that appeared in the *Chronicle*, in part because their tone and the information contained in them indicated the paper was in close contact with officials in the War Department. On October 23, an editorial in the *Times* declared it was "strange that the hundreds of citizens of Cincinnati who have visited Rosecrans' headquarters . . . know nothing of the faults imputed to him" and confidently predicted that "such slanders will only recoil upon the heads of those who utter them." Three days later, the *Times* published a report from a flabbergasted correspondent, who opened his report by stating, "The removal of Gen. Rosecrans from command . . . cannot be regarded in any other light than that of calamity." Grant's appointment, he noted, had been received "with satisfaction by all his military admirers, and if his plenitary [*sic*] appointment is necessary to the success of the country, in God's name let every voice be raised in favor of his accession." But, he declared, it was the "decided impression in the army that. . . . taking Gen. Rosecrans from the Department of the Cumberland" had severely shaken "the confidence of the army in the judgment of the rulers to pass upon interests and honors so near and dear to those who have fought and bled."[48]

The following day, a report from a correspondent in Chattanooga sent right after Rosecrans's removal appeared in the *Times* that informed its readers, "There is wailing and weeping in the Army of the Cumberland . . . for the heroic Rosecrans has become another victim to the . . . *mean, vindictive, personal spite of the Secretary of War and General Halleck.*" Secretary of War Edwin Stanton, the correspondent explained, had been angered by Rosecrans's refusal to be goaded into commencing operations, and the fact that the general had been vindicated by such operations as the one that captured Tullahoma, which was declared to have "only one parallel—that of

'Napoleon before Ulm.'" Halleck, the correspondent added, could not tolerate Rosecrans's success "because his plans of conducting war and the affairs of his department are widely different from the bungling, tardy strategy of ... the 'plagiarist of Jomini.'" Thus, he argued, Stanton and Halleck undermined Rosecrans by preventing the timely arrival of available reinforcements so they could generate an excuse to remove him from command.[49] The *Cincinnati Times* took further aim at Halleck in a November 12 editorial in which it complained that "officers have been ordered to remain in their positions when they considered it advisable to advance, and they have been ordered to move when it was most disadvantageous. . . . The working and untiring officer in the field has found his energies paralyzed by the great 'Brains' at the War Department." Criticism of Halleck was not limited to Cincinnati papers. "All the world knows we are for Old Abe," the *Chicago Tribune* assured its readers before expressing hope that the president would finally "put out that beetle-headed Halleck."[50]

The *Gazette* proclaimed on October 28 that it would prefer to ignore the "atrocious" article in the *Chronicle* and "let the reputation of General Rosecrans rest upon his great services" but could not do so. The editorial writer expressed outrage at the report that Rosecrans's removal was partially a consequence of charges that McCook and Crittenden had leveled against him for leaving the field at Chickamauga. "Crittenden and McCook are in disgrace," the paper declared. "Who would give any weight to such a charge by these men in such circumstances, smarting under their own disgrace ... and ready to drag anybody down to cover their own failures?" If Rosecrans was guilty of anything in regard to these two men, the *Gazette* concluded, it was of being "magnanimous toward them and forbearing; as to General McCook, too forbearing." (The paper bolstered its case by printing an article elsewhere in that same edition on the operations leading up to and during Chickamauga that was critical of McCook; although when official reports from Chickamauga appeared in mid-November, it moderated its criticism of McCook on this point.) If, as the report in the *Chronicle* indicated, strategists in Washington had been displeased with Rosecrans's management of its army, the *Gazette* declared, that meant they presumed "to give orders in detail to conduct a campaign ten or twelve hundred miles off—a thing which would be mere folly." Nor did the *Gazette* blanch at taking on reports that Rosecrans could not remain in command due to physical, character, or mental defects. "If the commander of Rich Mountain, Iuka, Corinth and Stones River," it declared, "has a mental disease, it is to be hoped that it can be transmitted; and if the military direction at Washington could be inoculated with it, the prospects for the country would be much improved."[51]

A few days later, the *Commercial*, while also critical of the *Chronicle*'s explanation of Rosecrans's removal, nonetheless deemed it necessary to explain to its readers that for some time there had existed a rivalry between the high commands of Grant's Army of the Tennessee and the Army of the Cumberland. (The *Commercial* conveniently left out the role it and other Cincinnati papers had played in exacerbating this rivalry by taking Rosecrans's side in his disputes with Grant over operations in northern Mississippi the previous fall that produced the battles of Iuka and Corinth. Nor did it see fit to acknowledge that it had provided a forum to a correspondent who suggested Grant's judgment had been impaired at critical moments during those operations by alcohol.) Once it was determined to reinforce Rosecrans, a move that made a long-overdue concentration of authority over the Western armies necessary, the paper reported, "at once the old sore feeling between Grant's and Rosecrans' departments was apparent." Thus, while lamentable, the replacement of Rosecrans was an inevitable consequence of the fact that "Thomas had won the confidence of the army and country, at Chickamauga, and had no controversy with Grant." On top of this, the paper noted, "in Washington there has long existed a feeling of distrust of General Rosecrans, and confidence in General Grant, that has been curiously tenacious." Rosecrans's "splendid victory" at Corinth and "display of the qualities of a hero and a General" at Stones River had not, the paper declared, impressed Washington, while its inability to appreciate the difficulties the general labored under logistically after Murfreesboro and its continual harassing of him had provoked Rosecrans. "Rosecrans didn't like to be meddled with," it declared, "He thought he knew the business of his department better than it was known at Washington, and esteemed a good many of the dispatches of General Halleck and Secretary Stanton, obtrusive and impertinent; and we expect he replied to them in a 'mind your own business' sort of style. . . . a thing not likely to be forgotten at Washington . . . to General Rosecrans' disadvantage."[52]

To further bolster their criticism of Rosecrans's removal, during the first week of November several papers called their readers' attention to an October 26 editorial in a Richmond newspaper that proclaimed the general "the greatest Captain the Yankee nation has yet produced. . . . Lincoln is helping us. He has removed from command the most dangerous man in his army, and put fools in his place." This further fueled a conviction on the part of the *Gazette*, as it remarked in an editorial on the same page in which it presented Richmond's perspective, that Rosecrans must be viewed by the country "as one of our best and most successful Generals, who failed to win a complete victory at Chickamauga because he was not properly sustained by the Government."[53]

On November 3, however, the *Commercial* published a report from its correspondent in Chattanooga that suggested a mixed perspective on the recent changes in command was developing in the Army of the Cumberland. "The removal of McCook and Crittenden," he declared, was widely deemed to be justified and "took no one in the army by surprise." It also ended any speculation in the army as to command changes and while the displacement of Rosecrans with Thomas came as a great surprise to the army, its main reaction to it was, as far as the correspondent could tell, total apathy. This surprised the correspondent, as he declared, "I had always been led to believe that Rosecrans possessed the esteem and confidence of officers and men to an extent amounting to enthusiasm." Yet now that Rosecrans was gone, he noted a number of fair weather officers who had previously expressed faith in Rosecrans were now making "not a few harsh criticisms of his campaigns . . . clamorously assert[ing] that 'they knew it would come to this.'"[54]

The following day, a report from a correspondent in Chattanooga appeared in the *Times* that further filled readers in on the command changes, the factors behind them, and how they were received by the army. As the other reports had, this one stated Rosecrans's removal had come as a surprise to the army and that his popularity with the rank and file, while not doubted, "has been somewhat lessened since Chicamauga [*sic*]." The correspondent told readers he had encountered Rosecrans as he departed from the army and that in addition to his staff, the general was accompanied by Assistant Secretary of War Charles Dana. The role Dana played in undermining Rosecrans through his letters to Washington was apparently not known to the correspondent, although he noted that Dana "receives the credit of the removal of McCook and Crittenden." (The extent of Dana's influence was evident two days later, though, when this same correspondent filed a report in which he noted in Chattanooga, "Common report says that a few words from him will accomplish the removal of any officer however high in position.") He then stated that, "In regard to Crittenden, we find there is but one opinion, and that is in his favor. The confidence of his men in him is of the strongest and most enduring character." Such was not the case with McCook. "McCook's conduct is more seriously criticized," the report stated. "His whole course since the war commenced is strongly condemned—by many officers and men."[55]

On November 10, the *Commercial* found itself once again revisiting the question of Rosecrans's removal as a consequence of the publication in the *New York Tribune* of a November 5 letter from Washington containing a lengthy indictment of Rosecrans's performance in command. As the

Commercial perceived—undoubtedly correctly—the letter, "if not directly 'inspired,' was written by a well-informed person, to whom the gossip of the War Department is familiar." After dismissing reports that Rosecrans was drunk, consuming opium, suffering epileptic fits, or other physical and mental maladies as "wholly, maliciously false," the *Tribune* explained his dismissal was grounded in four factors: his delays after Stones River and in the summer operations around Tullahoma in defiance of the demands of the War Department, his mismanagement of operations that led to Chickamauga, his leaving the field at Chickamauga after the disaster of September 20, and his abandonment of Lookout Mountain shortly after his arrival at Chattanooga. All of this combined, the *Tribune* declared, to make his justifiable removal on purely military grounds "only a question of a convenient occasion." The *Commercial*, walking a delicate line as a proadministration paper that was also sympathetic to Rosecrans, disputed many of these charges and instead called attention to the inability of Washington to "satisfactorily explain their neglect to reinforce the Army of the Cumberland . . . after the fall of Vicksburg and before Chickamauga."[56]

The *Commercial* two days later further picked up this theme by declaring, "We have only to consider what would have been the result . . . had General Rosecrans been reinforced before the advance beyond the Tennessee River, by fifty thousand soldiers from the Mississippi. It requires no military education, no acute faculties of observation . . . to inform any sane mind that the result would have been the utter overthrow of the army of General Bragg . . . and that our grasp would have been as firm today upon Rome and Atlanta, and all the important cities of Central Georgia, as it is upon those of Middle Tennessee. . . . The consideration of these mistakes and their results is certainly not flattering to the management of our war office." That same week, the *Gazette* also responded to the lengthy list of criticisms of Rosecrans its correspondent reported he had been exposed to in Washington. In addition to providing readers once again with what to them was already a familiar case for Rosecrans's decisions in the episodes that were being cited as cause for his removal from command (which once again included pointed criticisms of McCook), the *Gazette*'s correspondent and editors took explicit aim at Halleck, finding it quite hypocritical for him to be criticizing the pace of Rosecrans's operations when his own had been characterized by considerable sloth.[57]

As they digested news of Rosecrans's removal, readers of the *Commercial* continued to receive regular reports on the situation at Chattanooga. On October 26, the paper published a report from its correspondent with the

Army of the Cumberland, in which he reported that when news of Republican John Brough's decisive victory over Peace Democrat Clement Vallandigham in a hotly contested Ohio gubernatorial race reached troops from the Buckeye State it "caused a good deal of hearty cheering" and was "hailed with delight by men from Illinois, Indiana, Iowa and Kentucky as well." Otherwise, he reported quiet, muddy roads after three days of rain, and recent Confederate moves suggested they planned a siege, which had prompted local residents to begin "migrating rapidly."[58] Five days later, the *Commercial* published an October 20 report from a correspondent that Bragg had fortified Lookout Mountain and Missionary Ridge, evidently with an eye on a siege and bombardment. The latter, he reported, had been expected for three weeks and its delay was attributed to difficulties the Confederates were having transporting supplies. The men of the Army of the Cumberland, he noted, were well provided with tents and clothing, and demonstrating impressive architectural skills in their use of materials from local buildings to improve their dwellings. This, he declared was in sharp contrast with the enemy, who were reported to have few tents or blankets and thus must have suffered greatly from a recent "cold winter rain that appeared to come directly from the North pole." Still, supplies were a concern, as indicated by the hundreds of horses with the army that were reported to have recently died of starvation and the "pitifully gaunt and lean" appearance of those still alive, which had been gnawing on army wagons in desperate search of nutrition. Although the railroad bridge at Bridgeport was operational, *Commercial* readers learned, it was "absolutely necessary to the maintenance of this army, that railroad communication be established to Chattanooga," which could "only be done by the removal of Bragg from Lookout Mountain; and the only question . . . is, whether this can be done [by Hooker's force] without bringing on a general engagement."[59]

Of course, by the time this report appeared on October 31, the problem of the supply situation in Chattanooga was well on the way to being solved. Four days earlier, Federal forces had launched what *Commercial* readers learned on November 2, what Washington papers were describing as "a brilliant movement . . . under the direction of General [William F.] Smith, Chief Engineer, Department of the Cumberland" against Brown's Ferry that opened the "Cracker Line" and in which Hooker's forces advanced from Bridgeport to link up with the Army of the Cumberland. "This is an important achievement," the *Times* informed its readers on October 29, "and frees our army from all apprehension from short supplies and unites both Hooker and Thomas; and by this time, we presume, Sherman, with his two corps, is not far off. The Rebels have lost all opportunity to profit from Chicamauga [*sic*], if they ever had any."[60]

A few days later, *Commercial* readers learned that during the early morning of October 29, Hooker repulsed a Confederate counterattack at Wauhatchie in what Washington papers were reporting as "a severe fight" in which "Hooker report[ed] . . . the conduct of our troops to be splendid. They repulsed every enemy attack made on them, and drove the enemy from every position they assailed. . . . General Thomas' operations at the mouth of Lookout Valley are spoken of as a great success and their brilliancy can not be exaggerated." Although it incorrectly suggested that Union troops had occupied Lookout Mountain, the *Commercial* was correct when it crowed on October 31 that the Federal success was "an event of considerable significance. The mountain was supposed to be a place of first-class importance."[61]

That same day and on November 2, the *Times* published reports on the operations in Lookout Valley, which one of its correspondents declared "puts a new aspect upon affairs. . . . The last grip of the Rebels has been loosed, and now the Army of the Cumberland is relieved from a serious pressure, the pressure of the Rebel thumb upon our alimentary canal." "The repulse of the Rebels by Gen. Hooker was spirited and decisive," the *Times* declared on November 2, and "settles the supply question, and with it the Chattanooga question."[62] During the first week of November, the *Times* and *Commercial* provided more detailed accounts of the operations of late October that, in what a *Commercial* headline declared "A Neat Job," opened and secured the "Cracker Line." Hooker and his command, readers of the *Times* were informed, had gone into the fight at Wauhatchie telling onlookers that "Old [James] Longstreet was the same old fellow wherever met, and that they were ready to meet him under any sky or under any circumstances" and that throughout the engagement "Fighting Joe Hooker was ever looking to the interests of his men, who in this, their first fight in Tennessee, sacrificed none of their pristine fame." "If the remainder of the campaign now begun shall be so well completed," a Milwaukee paper crowed, "the country will have reason to rejoice." In a report that also appeared in the *Louisville Journal*, one correspondent from the *Times* described with great satisfaction seeing written in chalk on the side of an old house the statement, "In the year of our Lord, A.D. 1863, the Yanks drove the rebs out of this valley; bully for them!"[63]

Of course, in discussing the importance of these operations in opening the so-called Cracker Line, the papers indicated to their readers that their earlier assurances that the Army of the Cumberland's situation was completely secure had not been entirely accurate. In a report filed on November 4, a correspondent for the *Gazette* insisted that concerns over the Army of the Cumberland's earlier supply situation had been unwarranted. "I don't believe a single man in this army has actually suffered for want of food since the battle of Chicamauga [*sic*]," he declared, "Even the animals of the army are in better trim than I was led to believe." Other papers more accurately described the earlier situation. On November 24, an evidently relieved Illinois paper informed its readers that "the soldiers who dieted for awhile on an ear of corn a day, have now good and full rations." For his part, the *Commercial*'s correspondent conceded during the first week of November that "two weeks ago there were doubts in many good military minds as to our ability to hold" Chattanooga, and he traced the progress in eliminating those doubts to Grant, who "seems to have settled the question in our favor. His first move on coming here was a Vicksburg feat in miniature." He also reported that the Federals did not have full possession of Lookout Mountain, but did hold "the important part, from which the river and railroad was commanded." On November 9 readers of the *Commercial* learned of the arrival of a supply boat from Bridgeport at Brown's Ferry two days earlier carrying supplies, mail, and, perhaps most important from the troops' perspective, "Paymasters . . . with funds to pay the troops." The following day, a report in the *Times* assured readers that "brighter days will dawn for the Army of the Cumberland. Plenty of coffee, sugar, bread and an occasional sugar cured ham will consign to oblivion the reminiscences of former want."[64]

During the three weeks after the operations at Brown's Ferry and Wauhatchie, the correspondents for the *Gazette* and *Commercial* at Chattanooga had little of interest or importance to report, although the manner with which Grant assumed direction of the situation excited favorable comment from the *Times*'s correspondent. "Grant is daily seen on his horse riding through the camps and becoming thoroughly posted regarding the position of affairs," readers of the *Times* learned on November 3. "He is the same hardworking, stern-looking soldier he was at Vicksburg, and is complete master of the situation." "The old hero of Vicksburg looks like he means business," a report in the next day's edition declared. "We trust Gen. Grant's usual good fortune will not desert him." That Grant's efforts during his first two weeks in command had made an impression on the army was evident in the report the *Times*'s correspondent filed on November 5, in which he reported soldiers in the Army of the Cumberland were speaking of Rosecrans in a way that led him to declare reports (not mentioning that he had filed such a report a week or so earlier) of discontent over his removal "wholly false."[65]

Meanwhile, the papers kept their readers fully informed during the first three weeks of November of how the Federals at Chattanooga were utilizing the newly secured Cracker Line to accumulate supplies. The detachment of Longstreet's two divisions to operate against Knoxville in early November was also reported, with the *Times*'s editors speculating that Bragg was trying to "get between Grant and Burnside, with a view of crushing the former, and compelling the later to evacuate Chattanooga" and that this "exceedingly critical movement" would create an opportunity for Grant to strike a strong blow around Chattanooga—assumptions that mostly proved inaccurate.[66] Otherwise, correspondents at Chattanooga had little exciting to report during the first half of November, other than that the Confederates were doing little more than continuing to "throw shell occasionally" at Chattanooga with "nearly all fall[ing] short" and deserting by the dozens. The *Times* and *Commercial* also informed their readers during the second and third weeks of November that papers in Richmond were expressing consternation over the situation at Chattanooga and dismay at the prospect of an advance by Grant's forces. In contrast, a report in the November 13 *Times* declared, "Grant and Thomas, with their iron legions, have the confidence of all."[67]

Five days later, readers of the *Gazette* and the *Commercial* reported the arrival of Sherman's force on the scene on November 17. The progress of Sherman's march had been a source of interest for many papers ever since it commenced in late September, with the editors of the *Times* reporting on October 2 that "Sherman's corps is on the move—destination contraband. Of course, it is contraband, but who [is] so obtusive [*sic*] as not to know where it is going." By late October, though, the *Times* was beginning to express consternation, if not serious concern, about Sherman's progress. On October 31, it advised its readers that ten days had passed since it received word of Sherman and his two corps' movement toward Chattanooga and presumed that the task of repairing railroads as he moved east was the cause of the delay. Nonetheless, the *Times* editors were sanguine that Sherman "is, like John Brown's host, marching along, and that, if he has not yet joined Grant's main army, he is, at least, within supporting distance."[68]

Needless to say, once Sherman's force reached Chattanooga, it was a source of great gratification to the press. The *Commercial* informed its readers the following day that Sherman's arrival "has greatly disquieted the Rebels, and . . . will speedily cause the determination of the question whether there is to be a grand struggle" for Chattanooga. Indeed, readers of the *Commercial* had already been primed to expect much from Sherman by a report in its November 4 edition that Grant declared shortly after Sherman's arrival in Chattanooga that he was "the best soldier in the United States Army, and that he was worth to the Government $1,000 a day [more] than any other man in its employ." "Any one who knows the two Generals knows that Sherman is General Grant's right-hand man," a correspondent for the *Times* reported less than a week after Sherman's arrival, "and I do not hesitate to say that when the present campaign is ended, his name will stand foremost among its heroes. . . . I regard his advent in this department as an almost unfailing sign of success."[69] As if these reports of the growing power of the Federal force at Chattanooga were not enough to inspire confidence among the Northern public, the Cincinnati papers also continued to publish reports of extensive desertion from Bragg's force, which the *Times* declared on November 20 was "now more numerous than at any time since the expulsion of Bragg from Middle Tennessee."[70]

While none questioned that Chattanooga was where the fate of East Tennessee was to be decided, the press also provided a steady stream of reports regarding the situation at Knoxville, where Burnside's forces were being pressed by Longstreet's command. On November 20, the *Times* informed its readers that upon Longstreet's approach, "strong skirmishing and sharp fighting took place" that compelled Burnside to concentrate his forces in a defensive position at Knoxville, but the editorialist assured them, "Burnside is well-posted." For its part, the *Commercial* expressed anxiety over Burnside's situation and understood why some were wondering why none of the forces at Chattanooga had been sent to his assistance on November 23, while also being quick to assure readers that it was "not to be supposed . . . that the forces under Thomas, Hooker, and Sherman, are wasting their time. . . . We are in hourly expectation of receiving intelligence of the most important character."[71]

The following day, readers of the *Commercial* learned that the paper's eager anticipation in regard to events at Chattanooga was justified. On November 23, Grant initiated offensive operations by ordering Thomas's command to conduct a reconnaissance in force that resulted in the seizure of a piece of high ground known as Orchard Knob just outside the town, a development that the *Commercial*'s correspondent reported to the paper in time to make the next day's edition.[72] The following day, the *Times* published its account of Thomas's capture of Orchard Knob, along with an editorial advising its readers that "the advance of Longstreet against Burnside moved the pugnacity of Grant, and he has been pressing Bragg with a squeeze or two of his Boa Constrictor. . . . A general battle is expected today." That same day, readers of the *Times* and *Commercial* both learned of the movement of Sherman's command to a position on the far left of the Union line at Chattanooga from where it could operate against Bragg's right. Meanwhile, the papers reported Hooker was "at work on our right, attempting to carry the Lookout Mountain range, a very difficult operation if the enemy are in force. Thomas is at work from Chattanooga direct." While it had little doubt that the forces under Grant's command were superior to the enemy's in numbers, the *Commercial* cautioned on November 25 that the Confederates still had "a strong and well fortified position."[73]

Of course, that day the Battle of Chattanooga reached its climax when Thomas's command stormed Missionary Ridge and, in combination with Hooker's operations after seizing Lookout Mountain on the twenty-forth, rendered Bragg's position untenable and forced him to retreat from Chattanooga. The following day the *Commercial*, *Gazette*, and *Times* exuberantly reported the great victory to their readers. On November 23, they learned, Sherman and his command had crossed the Tennessee River a little over a half-dozen miles above Chattanooga "and carried the upper end of Mission[ary] Ridge." Meanwhile, "Hooker ascended from Lookout Valley" on the twenty-fourth, "carried the intrenchments on the Point, half way up the mountain, driving the enemy . . . before dark, taking some cannon and about two thousand prisoners." While Hooker "swept on triumphantly" up and over the Confederate left on Lookout Mountain, the *Commercial* reported, "The enemy massed on their right, and abruptly repulsed Sherman. While they were doing this, however, their center was carried by four divisions of the old Army of the Cumberland." "General Grant has again covered himself with glory," the *Times* crowed on November 26. "There is no estimating the importance of the victories of Grant near Chattanooga. The army of Bragg has been badly crippled and worse demoralized. . . . [N]othing could withstand the impetuosity and valor of our troops."[74]

As further reports came in of the scale of the victory, on November 27 the *Times* published on its front page a map of the "Scene of Grant's Brilliant Victory over Bragg." That same day the *Commercial* delightedly proclaimed in a headline the victory was "More Complete than at First Supposed," and then described the effort to follow it up, which ended after a sharp engagement between Hooker and a strongly posted Confederate force at Ringgold on the twenty-seventh. The *Commercial* declared "the conduct of our troops was magnificent. They have won immortality. . . . Our magnificent victory will fall with a stunning, crushing effect upon the languishing Rebellion." It also praised Grant and declared "with such an army as he has and with such corps commanders as Thomas, Sherman, and Hooker, nothing in the Southern Confederacy can stand before him." The performance of Hooker's command especially attracted praise from the *Times*, which mistakenly reported on November 27 that the assault on Missionary Ridge had been made by divisions operating under his direction.[75]

In the days that followed the papers continued to file reports on the battle. On November 28, the *Commercial* published an editorial declaring that the news from "Grant's army is in the highest degree satisfactory. Fears were entertained that the proportions of the victory at Mission[ary] Ridge would be found to dwindle as the particulars were received, but, on the contrary, they increase with every scrap of news that reaches us." "Prisoners," the paper's correspondents crowed, "say it is impossible for the Rebel leaders to make their troops stand. . . . [T]elegrams say that wherever we reach portions of Bragg's army, in arms, they instantly throw them down, and scatter like frightened sheep." While it had no news from Burnside, the *Commercial* was confident, justifiably, that the events at Chattanooga had ensured "that Burnside will come out all right." "Since Grant's successes," the *Times* informed its readers, "Longstreet will be compelled to retreat or unconditionally surrender." This proved to be the case, as Longstreet was finally compelled to abandon the siege of Knoxville after being repulsed in his assault on Fort Sanders, one of the principal forts guarding the town, on November 29.[76]

Finally, on November 30 and in the days that followed, subscribers of the *Gazette* were able to read full reports of the fighting at Chattanooga submitted by its correspondent with the army, as were readers of the *Times* on December 1 and readers of the *Commercial* on December 2. All three published these alongside a number of other first-person accounts, including the one submitted by Quartermaster General Meigs on November 26. (A number of papers republished Meigs's report as part of their coverage of Chattanooga, with the *Ohio Statesman* calling attention to a *New York Times* report that Meigs's description of Hooker's fight for Lookout Mountain on November 24 as "above the clouds" echoed descriptions of a 1797 French victory at Col de Tarvis.) While they added a few additional details, these reports largely confirmed the general outline of the battles that had appeared earlier and offered little commentary or fuel for controversy.[77] All three Cincinnati papers dramatically described the Army of the Cumberland's decisive charge up Missionary Ridge. "Thus ended in a magnificent feat of arms," the *Gazette* declared, "a series of as brilliant operations as this war has yet witnessed." "Never was work done more completely," the *Times* correspondent concluded, "never did valor receive a more complete reward. Just as the firing ceased, the moon rose red and resplendent and her first mild rays were hailed by the boys as was the Sun of Austerlitz by the great Napoleon."[78]

That the Army of the Cumberland's storming of Missionary Ridge was not Grant's work did not receive much notice in initial press reports on the battle—although Cincinnati's *Times* published reports that this had been the case almost immediately after the battle. It was also suggested in the *Gazette*'s initial report, but readers could be forgiven if they missed it in between headlines crowing about "Brilliant Generalship." On November 28, though, a report appeared in the *Chicago Tribune* from its correspondent stating clearly that the troops that successfully assaulted Missionary Ridge had "acted under no orders from superior officers" when they did. Readers received further confirmation that this had been the case when a report from Washington appeared in the *Commercial* on December 3, and the *Gazette* published a November 26 dispatch from a correspondent stating that the troops that charged the ridge disobeyed orders in doing so and vividly described the scene at Grant's headquarters at the "crisis of the battle" when Sherman's attack had been stymied and the Army of the Cumberland made its advance.[79]

The accounts in all three papers accurately presented the contrast in the accomplishments of Hooker's and Sherman's efforts in the battle, with the *Commercial*'s correspondent declaring Hooker's assault on Lookout Mountain "magnificent" and both it and the *Times* mistakenly reporting that the troops that stormed Missionary Ridge (which the *Times*'s correspondent reported "saved what of Sherman's Corps he had with him") the following day did so under Hooker's command. All three papers made a point, however, of laying out the difficult tactical problem Sherman faced on Tunnel Hill, leading a *Gazette* correspondent to declare "our left wing blameless" for its lack of progress and to credit Sherman's compelling the Confederates to weaken their center for helping make Thomas's attack on Missionary Ridge possible. All three papers also noted the lighter opposition Hooker faced in his operations around Lookout Mountain, but offered little analysis or commentary regarding the two commanders beyond that. "Our army was magnificently handled," the *Gazette* concluded without qualification, assigning neither credit nor blame to anyone in particular in an editorial on December 2. "[It] fought splendidly and achieved a complete victory." Nonetheless, it was with great satisfaction that the editors of the *Times* proclaimed on November 12 that, "Since the battle of Lookout Mountain, Hooker stands higher than ever" and speculated that he might soon once again find himself in command of the Army of the Potomac.[80]

While complaining about the press has long been and no doubt will always be a popular pastime among military men, there is no question that it plays an important, indeed essential, role in wartime, for as journalist Kenneth Payne observed in a recent consideration of the media's impact on contemporary military affairs, "winning modern wars is as much dependent on carrying domestic and international public opinion as it is on defeating the enemy on the battlefield." This certainly was the case during the Civil War, a conflict that was, as Abraham Lincoln correctly pointed out in July 1861, "essentially a people's contest."[81] During the months that saw the Northern war effort recover from a stunning defeat at Chickamauga to achieve an even more spectacular triumph at Chattanooga, the newspapers studied here appear to have fulfilled their role of providing a connection between the battlefield and the home front well. They effectively provided readers with the information they needed to understand events and, where merited, differing perspectives to support the debate over them and the men who shaped them that is vital in a republic.

Of course, no man stood so high in the eyes of the Northern press and public after the great victory Chattanooga as its principle architect. "Grant . . . looks satisfied with the work of the past week," declared one correspondent. "He is justly regarded as our greatest and most successful warrior." That further honors were soon to come was confirmed in early December when the *Times* informed its readers that Congressman Elihu Washburne had announced he would introduce a bill "to give Gen. Grant the position of Lieutenant-General, to which his victories and talents entitle him." Not surprisingly, few were as enthusiastic in their praise of Grant as was Galena, Illinois's *Northwestern Gazette*, which eagerly anticipated passage of Washburne's bill and declared the victory at Chattanooga as its proved once again that the quiet man who had left the small river town a little over two years earlier to fight for the Union was "a complete master of the art of war." "Napoleon Bonaparte, Caesar and Alexander," it predicted, "will have to take back seats among military heroes, if this war continues much longer."[82]

Notes

1. Sir William Howard Russell, *My Diary North and South* (London, 1863), 187; B. H. Hill, "Address . . . before the Georgia Branch of the Southern Historical Society at Atlanta, February 18th, 1874," *Southern Historical Society Papers*, edited by R. A. Brock, 52 vols. (Millwood, N.J., 1876–1959), 14: 496; Brooks D. Simpson and Jean V. Berlin, eds., *Sherman's Civil War: Selected Correspondence of William T. Sherman, 1860–1865* (Chapel Hill: University of North Carolina Press, 1999), 217, 395–96.

2. According to the 1860 census, Cincinnati was the seventh largest city in the entire country with over 50,000 more residents than Chicago, its nearest competitor in the Old Northwest. *Statistics of the United States (Including Mortality, Property, &c.,) in 1860; Compiled from the Original Returns and Being the Final Exhibit of the Eighth Census under the Direction of the Secretary of the Interior* (Washington, D.C.: Government Printing Office, 1866), xviii. The other papers consulted were the *Cleveland Herald, Galena (Ill.) Weekly Northwestern Gazette, (Centreville) Indiana True Republican; (Portage) Wisconsin State Register; (Springfield) Weekly Illinois State Journal, (Columbus) Ohio State Journal, Chicago Tribune, Mahoning (Ohio) Sentinel, (Columbus) Ohio Statesman, Milwaukee Sentinel*, and *Aurora (Ind.) Commercial*. All but the last four were clearly Republican in their political sympathies.

3. William M. Lamars, *The Edge of Glory: A Biography of General William S. Rosecrans, U.S.A.* (New York: Harcourt, Brace & World, 1961), 260–62. It was also hoped at the outset of this project that it might provide an opportunity to engage

the findings of Eric T. Dean Jr. and Brooks D. Simpson on how the press shaped and reflected public expectations and interpretations of particular military campaigns. The differences between the situation here and the ones Dean and Simpson looked at were so great, though, that this hope was not fulfilled. Eric T. Dean Jr., "'We Live under a Government of Men and Morning Newspapers': Image, Expectation, and the Peninsula Campaign of 1862," *Virginia Magazine of History and Biography* 103 (January 1995): 5–28; Brooks D. Simpson, "Great Expectations: Ulysses S. Grant, the Northern Press, and the Opening of the Wilderness Campaign," in *The Wilderness Campaign*, edited by Gary W. Gallagher (Chapel Hill: University of North Carolina Press, 1997), 1–35.

4. *Cincinnati Commercial*, September 19, 1863; *Cincinnati Times*, September 19, 1863.

5. *Cincinnati Commercial*, September 21, 1863; *Cincinnati Times*, September 21, 1863.

6. *Cincinnati Commercial*, September 22, 1863; *Cincinnati Times*, September 22, 1863.

7. *Cincinnati Commercial*, September 22, 1863; *Cincinnati Times*, September 22, 1863; *Cincinnati Gazette*, September 23, 1863.

8. *Cincinnati Times*, September 22, 1863; *Cincinnati Commercial*, September 23, 1863.

9. *Cincinnati Commercial*, September 23, 24, 1863; *Cincinnati Times*, September 21, 24, 1863; *Milwaukee Sentinel*, September 23, 1863; *Louisville Journal*, September 21, 22, 1863; *Weekly Illinois State Journal*, September 23, 1863.

10. *Cincinnati Times*, September 21, 23, 24, 1863; *Louisville Journal*, September 21, 30, October 21, 24, 1863; *Milwaukee Sentinel*, October 3, 1863; *Weekly Illinois State Journal*, September 23, 1863; *Ohio State Journal*, September 24, 1863; and, *Chicago Tribune*, September 26, October 6, 1863; *Cincinnati Commercial*, September 24, 25, 26, 1863.

11. *Cincinnati Commercial*, September, 27, 28, 1863. The practice of pointing to the fact that Rosecrans held Chattanooga and rendering it thus impregnable to capture, while emphasizing the severity of damage that Bragg's army had suffered to minimize Confederate accomplishments at Chickamauga was common among papers in late September and early October. *Northwestern Gazette*, September 29, 1863; *Mahoning Sentinel*, September 30, 1863; *Cleveland Herald*, September 22, 25, 1863; *Wisconsin State Register*, September 26, 1863; *Milwaukee Sentinel*, September 24, 25, 1863; *Ohio State Journal*, September 24, 25, October 5, 17, 1863; *Chicago Tribune*, September 23, 24, 25, 26, October 7, November 30, 1863.

12. *Cincinnati Times*, September 24, 25, 26, October 6, 7, 1863; *Cincinnati Gazette*, September 23, 1863. Citing Confederate sources to bolster a positive spin on Chickamauga was common among the papers examined here. See also the *Ohio Statesman*, October 14, 1863; *Ripley Bee*, October 15, 1863; *Cleveland Herald*, September 30, October 6, 1863; *Milwaukee Sentinel*, September 25, 30, October 10, 1863; *Louisville Journal*, September 27, October 2, 1863; *Northwestern Gazette*, October 6, 1863; *Wisconsin State Register*, September 26, October 10, 17, 1863; *Ohio State Journal*, October 6, 1863; and, *Chicago Tribune*, September 25, October 5, 1863.

13. *Mahoning Sentinel*, October 21, 1863; *Ohio Statesman*, October 3, 1863; *Louisville Journal*, September 27, 29, 30, October 2, November 10, 1863.

14. *Ohio State Journal*, September 26, October 10, 1863; *Cleveland Herald*, September 22, 25, 26, 1863; *Chicago Tribune*, September 25, 1863.15. *Cincinnati Daily Commercial*, September 29, 30, 1863.

16. *Cincinnati Times*, September 28, 29, October 1, 1863; *Cincinnati Commercial*, October 2, 3, 4, 1863.

17. *Cincinnati Times*, October 1, 1863.

18. *Cincinnati Times*, September 23, 1863; *Cincinnati Gazette*, September 30, 1863.

19. *Cincinnati Commercial*, October 2, 6, 1863; *Cincinnati Times*, October 5, 1863.

20. *Cincinnati Times*, September 26, 1863; *Cincinnati Commercial*, September 28, 1863.

21. *Cincinnati Commercial*, October 7, 1863; *Cincinnati Times*, October 10, 1863.

22. *Cincinnati Commercial*, October 8, 1863. The *Commercial's* remarks closely paralleled those that appeared in a Louisville paper a week earlier on the occasion of Hooker's passage through that city. *Louisville Journal*, October 1, 1863. See also the positive commentary on Hooker and the transfer of his command in *Northwestern Gazette*, September 29, 1863; *Wisconsin State Register*, October 17, 1863; *Milwaukee Sentinel*, October 1, 1863, and the report of the excitement the passage of Hooker's forces through Centreville, Indiana, stirred up among its residents in the *Indiana True Republican*, October 1, 1863.

23. *Cincinnati Commercial*, October 6, 1863; *Cincinnati Gazette*, October 7, 1863.

24. *Cincinnati Times*, October 7, 1863; *Cincinnati Commercial*, October 6, 1863. See also the accounts and minimization of the accomplishments of Wheeler's raid in the *Louisville Journal*, October 8, 13, 1863; *Ohio State Journal*, October 20, 1863; *Milwaukee Sentinel*, October 6, 1863. According to historian Peter Cozzens, as a consequence of Wheeler's raid, in particular its overrunning of a large wagon train on October 2, supplies for three of Rosecrans's divisions were lost and the entire army's supplies of ammunition were dangerously diminished. It also compelled Rosecrans to disperse reinforcements that were arriving from Virginia to guard the railroad against Wheeler. Peter Cozzens, *The Shipwreck of Their Hopes: The Battles for Chattanooga* (Urbana: University of Illinois Press, 1994), 19–20.

25. *Cincinnati Commercial*, October 6, 1863.

26. *Cincinnati Times*, October 12, 14, 1863; *Cincinnati Commercial*, October 13, 20, 1863.

27. *Cincinnati Commercial*, October 14, 1863. Given the fact that similar stories had been planted using deserters by the Confederate army just before Chickamauga with serious consequences for the Army of the Cumberland, it might well have been appropriate to point this out to help readers understand just how seriously to take reports about and by Confederate desertions. Peter Cozzens, *This Terrible Sound: The Battle of Chickamauga* (Urbana, IL, 1992), Steven E. Woodworth, *Six Armies in Tennessee: The Chickamauga and Chattanooga Campaigns* (Lincoln: University of Nebraska Press, 1998), 62, 67.

28. *Cincinnati Commercial*, September 25, 1863.

29. *Cincinnati Times*, September 26, 1863; *Cincinnati Commercial*, September 28, 1863; *Northwestern Gazette*, September 29, 1863. In fact, Rosecrans made no such official charge against McCook and Crittenden.

30. *Cincinnati Times*, September 25, 1863. *Cincinnati Gazette*, September 30, 1863; *Chicago Tribune*, September 27, 1863; *Cleveland Herald*, September 26, 1863.

31. *Cincinnati Times*, September 30, 1863; *Cincinnati Commercial*, October 1, 1863.

32. *Cincinnati Commercial*, October 6, 8, 1863; *Cincinnati Times*, October 10, 1863; *Milwaukee Sentinel*, October 3, 1863. That same day the *Weekly Illinois State Journal* also published first-hand accounts of Chickamauga in which McCook's actions were portrayed in a decidedly unfavorable light. *Weekly Illinois State Journal*, October 7, 1863.

33. *Louisville Journal*, October 5, 1863. In mid-October, the paper reported with relief and a sense of vindication that reports by what it described as a "pusillanimous scribbler" that Rosecrans was going to bring charges against McCook and Crittenden were false. It also published a series of editorials asserting that reports by "reliable army writers" had "confirmed all we predicted in reference to the gallant conduct of Crittenden" and that apparently "General McCook himself need be under no apprehension as to the result of any Court of Inquiry." For these reports, and further evidence of its steadfast support for Crittenden and to a lesser extent McCook, see *Louisville Journal*, October 14, 15, 16, 17, November 9, 10, December 7, 1863.

34. *Cincinnati Commercial*, October 14, 1863.

35. Ibid., October 16, 1863. On October 3 an article extolling McCook's military record and claiming the fact the general was a Democrat played a large role in his demise that appeared in the *Dayton Empire* was republished in the *Ohio Statesman*. The *Statesman* itself certainly did the general's cause no favor when a few days later it attacked reports in "Abolition papers" that the McCook family was "adverse" to Clement Vallandigham, the Democratic candidate for governor of Ohio in 1863 and notorious antiwar Copperhead leader. *Ohio Statesman*, October 3, 7, 1863.

36. *Cincinnati Times*, October 23, 1863.

37. *Cincinnati Commercial*, October 16, 1863.

38. Ibid., October 20, 1863. See also the scrutiny to which Shanks's account of Chickamauga was subjected to in the *Louisville Journal*, September 29, 1863; *Milwaukee Sentinel*, October 1, 1863; and *Northwestern Gazette*, October 6, 1863. One New York correspondent was so taken aback by what he described as "ill-natured" remarks in the September 29 *Gazette* regarding his reporting on Chickamauga that he sent a note defending his actions to the editors of the *Cincinnati Commercial*. *Cincinnati Gazette*, September 29, 1863; Cincinnati *Commercial*, September 30, 1863.

39. *Cincinnati Commercial*, November 27, 1863.

40. Ibid., October 19, 1863.

41. Ibid., October 21, 1863.

42. *Chicago Tribune*, October 21, 22, 1863; *Northwestern Gazette*, October 27, November 3, 1863. For what may be characterized as neutral stances on Rosecrans's removal see the *Wisconsin State Register*, October 24, 1863; *Cleveland Herald*, October 22, 1863; *Milwaukee Sentinel*, November 12, 1863, and one paper that switched to it after initially objecting to the move, see *Weekly Illinois State Journal*, November 18, 1863.

43. *Cincinnati Times*, October 21, 1863.

44. *Chicago Tribune*, October 21, 22, 1863; *Mahoning Sentinel*, November 4, 1863; *Louisville Journal*, October 21, 27, December 5, 1863; *Weekly Illinois State Journal*, October 7, 28, 1863; *Ohio State Journal*, October 24, 1863; *Cincinnati Times*, October 21, 26, 1863.

45. *Cincinnati Commercial*, September 25, 1863; *Cincinnati Times*, October 10, 26, 1863. See also the profiles of Thomas in the *Ohio Statesman*, October 11, 29, 1863;

Weekly Illinois State Journal, October 21, 1863; *Cleveland Herald*, October 23, 1863; and, *Milwaukee Sentinel*, September 26, 1863.

46. *Cincinnati Commercial*, October 22, 1863.

47. *Cincinnati Times*, October 23, 24, 1863; *Cincinnati Commercial*, October 23, 24, 1863.

48. *Cincinnati Times*, October 23, 26, 1863.

49. *Cincinnati Times*, October 27, 1863. Much of Halleck's reputation as a military intellectual, reflected in his nickname "Old Brains," rested on his 1846 book *Elements of Military Art and Science*, a work the *Times* accurately pointed out was largely a translation and rehash of the writings of the popular Swiss military theorist Baron Antoine Henri Jomini. For discussion of Halleck's writings, see Herman Hattaway and Archer Jones, *How the North Won: A Military History of the Civil War* (Urbana: University of Illinois Press, 1983), 13–14; John F. Marszalek, *Commander of All Lincoln's Armies: A Life of General Henry W. Halleck* (Cambridge: Harvard University Press, 2004), 42–46; Russell F. Weigley, *American Way of War: A History of United States Military Strategy and Policy* (New York: MacMillan, 1973), 84–89; and, Brian McAllister Linn, *The Echo of Battle: The Army's Way of War* (Cambridge, Mass.: Harvard University Press, 2007), 23–25.

50. *Cincinnati Times*, November 12, 1863; *Chicago Tribune*, October 6, 15, November 23, 1863. Halleck's value as a lightning rod for critics of the administration's treatment of Rosecrans was also evident in the sharp criticism of the commanding general contained in the *Louisville Journal*, October 27, 1863; *Ohio State Journal*, October 21, 22, 28, 1863; *Milwaukee Sentinel*, December 22, 1863. While they had no kind words for Halleck, in responding to Rosecrans's removal the editors of the *Ohio Statesman* resisted efforts to place principle blame for the state of affairs on the general. Instead, they admonished their readers not to forget where true responsibility for it lay, properly reminding them that nothing could have been done without Lincoln's "consent and express authority," and proclaimed that the true "power behind the throne" was not Halleck, but "the Jacobin radical Abolition faction, which is determined to 'rule or ruin.'" A few days later, the paper called its readers' attention to parallels in the administration's treatment of Rosecrans and George McClellan, neither of whom were enthusiastic about approaches to the war championed by the Radical Republicans. *Ohio Statesman*, October 29, November 3, 1863.

51. *Cincinnati Gazette*, October 28, 863. The *Gazette* further expanded on its critique of the way Washington had been managing its armies the following week in an editorial entitled, "Dispersion versus Concentration—Strategy versus Common Sense." The reverse at Chickamauga was not due, it asserted, "to any want of generalship in the immediate field. . . . Rosecrans did all that man could do." Rather, it was a consequence of Washington pursuing a policy of dispersion that prevented Rosecrans from being reinforced, rather than a "common sense" policy of concentration. *Cincinnati Gazette*, November 4, 1863. Dismay at Rosecrans's removal and outrage at aspersions on his character and military record contained in reports in New York and Washington papers were not confined to the Cincinnati papers. Many of the papers examined for this study that commented on the matter responded negatively to both. See *Mahoning Sentinel*, October 28, November 4, 11, 1863; *Louisville Journal*, October 21, 24, 1863; *Weekly Illinois State Journal*, October 21, 22, 1863; *Ohio State Journal*, October 21, 1863.

52. *Cincinnati Commercial*, November 3, 1863. In April 1863, a correspondent for the *Gazette* also wrote a personal letter to Secretary of the Treasury Salmon Chase on Rosecrans's behalf in which he proclaimed Grant "a poor drunken imbecile" who was "shamefully jealous of Rosecrans." Lamars, *Edge of Glory*, 154–80, 261–63; Brooks D. Simpson, *Ulysses S. Grant: Triumph over Adversity, 1822–1865* (New York: Houghton Mifflin, 2000), 153–56, 177–78.

53. *Richmond Examiner* of October 26, 1863, quoted in *Cincinnati Commercial*, November 2, 1863; *Cincinnati Times*, November 2, 1863; *Cincinnati Gazette*, November 4, 1863; *Ohio Statesman*, November 2, 1863.

54. *Cincinnati Commercial*, November 3, 1863.

55. *Cincinnati Times*, November 4, 13, 1863.

56. *New York Tribune*, November 5, 1863, reprinted with critical commentary in editorial section, *Cincinnati Commercial*, November 10, 1863. The following day, the *Chicago Tribune* republished the letter with commentary much different in tone and content, November 11, 1863.

57. *Cincinnati Commercial*, November 12, 1863; *Cincinnati Gazette*, November 11, 1863. Several weeks later, the *Gazette* also took aim at Halleck's treatment of Rosecrans in his annual report, released in mid-December, declaring, "The reader will observe that this is a studied effort to disparage the achievements and movements of Gen. Rosecrans" and "a species of unfairness" toward the general. *Cincinnati Gazette*, December 16, 1863.

58. *Cincinnati Commercial*, October 26, 1863.

59. Ibid., October 31, 1863.

60. *Cincinnati Times*, October 29, 1863; *Cincinnati Commercial*, November 2, 1863.

61. *Cincinnati Commercial*, October 31, 1863. This same Associated Press report also appeared in the *Louisville Journal*, November 2, 1863.

62. *Cincinnati Times*, October 31, November 2, 1863.

63. *Cincinnati Times*, November 3, 1863; *Milwaukee Sentinel*, November 13, 1863; *Louisville Journal*, November 7, 1863.

64. *Cincinnati Times*, November 3, 10, 1863; *Cincinnati Commercial*, November 4, 9, 1863; *Cincinnati Gazette*, November 18, 1863; *Northwestern Gazette*, November 24, 1863. On November 21, a report appeared in the *Times* informing its readers that, "Full rations are now issued to the men, which fact, together with the supplies of greenbacks scattered by the Paymaster, has shed happiness through the camp." *Cincinnati Times*, November 21, 1863. In downplaying the seriousness of the supply situation at Chattanooga before the opening of the Cracker Line, and continuing to do so afterward, the *Gazette* was alone among the papers consulted for this essay. See the discussion of this matter in the editorials and correspondent reports in the *Mahoning Sentinel*, November 18, 1863; *Louisville Journal*, November 7, 1863; *Chicago Tribune*, October 13, November 2, 3, 11, 1863; *Aurora Commercial*, November 26, 1863; *Ohio State Journal*, October 31, November 2, 3, 1863.

65. *Cincinnati Times*, November 3, 4, 1863.

66. Ibid., November 9, 1863. In fact, Grant did hatch a plan to take advantage of the Confederate move but was forced to abandon it when Thomas demurred from executing it. Cozzens, *Shipwreck of Their Hopes*, 106–8; Woodworth, *Six Armies in Tennessee*, 171–72.

67. *Cincinnati Times*, November 7, 9, 10, 13, 17, 1863; *Cincinnati Commercial*, November 16, 18, 19, 1863.

68. *Cincinnati Times*, October 31, November 2, 1863. The *Times* evidently based its reporting on the progress of Sherman's march on an Associated Press report of October 30, which also appeared in the *Louisville Journal*. *Cincinnati Times*, October 2, 1863. For this report, and takes on Sherman's movements as they were in progress, see *Louisville Journal*, November 2, 13, 14, 16, 1863; *Northwestern Gazette*, October 6, 13, 1863; *Ripley Bee*, October 15, 1863; *Milwaukee Sentinel*, November 10, 1863. After Chattanooga, highly favorable assessments of Sherman's march, which one report declared "one of the most remarkable feats in the history of army marches" appeared in the *Chicago Tribune*, December 1, 1863; *Milwaukee Sentinel* December 12, 1863; and *Wisconsin State Register*, December 5, 1863.

69. *Cincinnati Commercial*, November 4, 1863; *Cincinnati Times*, November 24, 1863.

70. *Cincinnati Gazette*, November 18, 25, 1863; *Cincinnati Times*, November 7, 20, 1863; *Cincinnati Commercial*, November 20, 1863.

71. *Chicago Tribune*, November 20, 23, 25, 1863; *Ohio State Journal*, November 24, 1863; *Milwaukee Sentinel*, November 20, 24, 1863; *Cleveland Herald*, November 23, 25, 1863; *Cincinnati Times*, November 17, 20, 1863; *Cincinnati Gazette*, November 18, 1863; *Cincinnati Commercial*, November 23, 1863.

72. *Cincinnati Commercial*, November 24, 1863.

73. *Cincinnati Times*, November 25, 1863; *Cincinnati Commercial*, November 25, 1863.

74. *Cincinnati Gazette*, November 26, 1863; *Cincinnati Commercial*, November 26, 1863; *Cincinnati Times*, November 26, 1863.

75. *Cincinnati Times*, November 27, 28, December 2, 4, 1863; *Cincinnati Commercial*, November 27, 1863.

76. *Cincinnati Commercial*, November 27, 28, 30, December 2, 3, 1863; *Cincinnati Times*, November 27, 1863.

77. *Cincinnati Gazette*, November 30, 1863; December 2, 9, 1863; Cincinnati Times, December 1, 1863; *Cincinnati Commercial*, December 2, 3, 1863; *Northwestern Gazette*, December 8, 1863; *Ohio State Journal*, December 2, 1863; *Ohio Statesman*, December 3, 1863.

78. During the first week of December, the *Chicago Tribune, Milwaukee Sentinel,* and *Cleveland Herald* republished the *Cincinnati Gazette's* accounts of the battle, while two days later, the *Ripley Bee* provided its readers with a condensed version of it. Its authoritative stature among newspaper reports on the battle was further confirmed by its appearance two years later in the multivolume compilation of documents from the war edited by Frank Moore. *Chicago Tribune*, December 1, 2, 3, 1863; *Milwaukee Sentinel*, December 2, 1863; *Cleveland Herald*, December 1, 1863; *Ripley Bee*, December 3, 1863; Frank Moore, ed., *The Rebellion Record: A Diary of American Events* 12 vols. (New York, 1865), vol. 8: 228–36.

79. *Ohio State Journal*, November 26, 28, 1863; *Mahoning Sentinel*, December 2, 1863; *Cleveland Herald*, November 27, 1863; *Cincinnati Times*, November 27, December 4, 8, 12, 1863; *Chicago Tribune*, November 26, 18, 1863; *Cincinnati Commercial*, December 3, 1863; *Cincinnati Gazette*, November 28, 30, December 9, 1863.

80. *Cincinnati Gazette,* November 30, 1863; December 2, 9, 1863; *Cincinnati Times,* November 27, December 4, 8, 12, 1863; *Cincinnati Commercial,* December 3, 1863. For the uniformly positive (and for the most part properly so) analysis of Chattanooga and the commanders, see also *Louisville Journal,* December 2, 3, 4, 5, 1863; *Chicago Tribune,* November 26, 28, 30, December 2, 5, 1863.

81. Kenneth Payne, "The Media as an Instrument of War," *Parameters: U.S. Army War College Quarterly* 35 (Spring 2005): 81; Abraham Lincoln, "Message to Congress in Special Session," July 4, 1861, in Roy P. Basler, ed. *The Collected Works of Abraham Lincoln,* 9 vols. (New Brunswick: Rutgers University Press, 1953–55), 4: 438.

82. *Cincinnati Times,* December 8, 1863; *Northwestern Gazette,* December 1, 8, 1863.

9

"WHAT I AM DOING I DO NOT CONSIDER DESERTION":
TRANS-MISSISSIPPIAN REACTIONS TO
CHICKAMAUGA AND CHATTANOOGA

Charles D. Grear

The combined battles of Chickamauga and Chattanooga transformed the Civil War in the western theater. More important, the events changed the way many Confederate soldiers felt about the conflict. Historians have chronicled the impact of Chickamauga and Chattanooga on the morale of Confederate soldiers throughout some parts of the South, but soldiers from the trans-Mississippi—specifically Arkansas and Texas—had stronger reactions to the events that underscore the differences of this little-studied region of the Civil War. Though trans-Mississippi regiments fighting in these battles had already experienced waves of demoralization, another tide of frustration flooded their ranks during and after these battles, resulting in an unusual spike in desertion. There have been several noted studies on desertion, such as Mark Weitz's *A Higher Duty: Desertion among Georgia Troops during the Civil War* and *More Damning than Slaughter: Desertion in the Confederate Army* and Ella Lonn's *Desertion during the Civil War*. However, their focus, like that of many Civil War studies, is on the men from the eastern and cis-Mississippi western theaters. Compared to their cis-Mississippian comrades, trans-Mississippian Confederate soldiers were less likely to desert out of a desire to quit the army. Instead their priorities and motivations changed. Additionally their departure from the cis-Mississippi theater during and after the battles of Chickamauga and Chattanooga had a significant impact on the South's ability to maintain its ranks for the remainder of the war.[1]

Early in the war, the Union threat to trans-Mississippi Confederate states was limited because of the great distance from the rival capitals, the Western states' lack of industry to support the war, and their small populations. With their immediate homes relatively safe, the men of these states enlisted to serve in army units east of the Mississippi River. When the battles of Chickamauga and Chattanooga concluded, demoralization spread through the ranks of the trans-Mississippians. Factors influencing morale included the hardships of army life, feelings of defeat, frustration with commanding officers, witnessing too much bloodshed, and being denied permission to visit their homes. Most of these men wanted to return to protect their homes and families in the West. Many of these soldiers nevertheless chose to remain in the cis-Mississippi theater and fight for the Confederacy there. Others decided to continue the fight but only in the defense of the families and homes they left behind when they joined the Confederate army.

The reasons men joined the Confederate army varied; the defense of slavery was only one of them. On another level, men enlisted to fight to defend their homes, families, and land from what they had been told was an invading army. However, trans-Mississippians' motivations were especially complicated since their concept of "land" generally had more than one meaning. In previous decades, the slogan "Gone to Texas" had resonated throughout the United States and many foreign lands. By 1861, Texas boasted a booming population, three-quarters of which had taken their first breath somewhere east of the Sabine River. Similarly Arkansas's population more than doubled in the decade before the war, the majority coming from the cis-Mississippi Southern states. These transplanted Easterners felt multiple attachments—to their original hometowns in the East and also to their current homes in the West.

When the war began, trans-Mississippians had to decide which of these lands to defend. For instance, a man might feel compelled to defend some locality "back East," far from his current residence in the West, if he had family or friends who still lived in the region, particularly if he perceived them to be threatened while his current residence seemed safe. Early in the war, many trans-Mississippians enlisted to defend their old hometowns and regions, believing that their current homes at the extreme west of the Confederacy would not be a major priority for the authorities in Washington, D.C. Obviously, some soldiers had no desire to fight east of the river and joined home guard units, only to receive orders sending them across the river. Among those who found ways to remain in the trans-Mississippi region in defense of their homes were James Webb Throckmorton, future governor of Texas, and nearly two-thirds of the 11th Texas Cavalry.[2]

The responsibility to protect family members, even extended family, was an extremely important value for Southern men. Although family members might reside in different states, their familial bonds remained tremendously strong. Moreover, given the absence of strong institutions such as public houses, fraternities, or theaters throughout the South and the lack of urban centers and factories, combined with the relative social isolation of the predominantly rural and agricultural lifestyle in the South, kinship bonds were even more important. In essence, outside of the family there were few organizations available to Southerners and fewer associations to take up their time away from home. Familial bonds among trans-Mississippians produced a strong desire, even a sense of duty, to defend parents, grandparents, aunts, and uncles left behind in westward migration.[3]

The trans-Mississippi units engaged in the battles of Chickamauga and Chattanooga include some of the most famous of the war and some with the most at stake in fighting east of the Mississippi. These include the Texas Brigade (1st, 4th, and 5th Texas Infantry; 18th Georgia Infantry; and 3rd Arkansas Infantry), which had won the admiration of General Robert E. Lee through its exploits with the Army of Northern Virginia, and Terry's Texas Rangers (8th Texas Cavalry), the most famous and feared Texas cavalry unit in the western theater. Others such as the 6th and 10th Texas Infantry, the 15th, 17th, 18th, 24th, and 25th Texas Cavalry (Dismounted), and the 19th and 24th Arkansas had a burning desire to prove themselves to their Confederate comrades because of the disgraceful surrender they had endured at Arkansas Post earlier that year on January 11. Similarly the 7th Texas Infantry had surrendered at Fort Donelson. The last thing these men wanted to do was to further stain their honor and reputations. Lesser known regiments like the 15th Texas Infantry and 1st, 5th, and 13th Arkansas Infantry desired to maintain the strong reputations they had earned through the course of the war. For all these reasons, the last moniker these soldiers wished to have attached to them in the fall of 1863 was deserter.[4]

John Baynes writes that the subject of his book *Morale* "is concerned with the way in which people react to the conditions of their existence."[5] Maintaining morale is extremely important in warfare, even more important than tactics, because commanders face extreme difficulty getting their soldiers to fight hard or remain in the ranks for the duration if their hearts are not engaged in the struggle. Soldiers experience demoralization from the accretion of different annoyances and irritations over a period of time: isolation from their homes, lack of supplies, harsh weather conditions, resentment of command, and perhaps most important, perceived threats to the homes and families they left behind when they went off to fight the war. Demoralization touched soldiers from every state in the Confederacy, but the reactions of the trans-Mississippians differed from the men from east of the river.[6]

The story of their demoralization began well before the battles of Chickamauga and Chattanooga. Unlike their counterparts in the East, the Western Confederate armies suffered a string of defeats from Forts Donelson and Henry to the salient loss of control over the Mississippi River with the capitulation of Vicksburg. Defeat at the Gibraltar of the South started a slide of morale. Major Khleber Miller Van Zandt of the 7th Texas Infantry expressed the feelings of the men in his command when he wrote, "I suppose the fall of Vicksburgh and the consequent possession of the whole of the Miss. River by the Feds made you all feel pretty blue, did it not? And so it would many of us I judge, . . . It is indeed a dark hour to us."[7] Little did Van Zandt know that the sun had only begun to set on the Confederacy.

Vicksburg was more than a city for trans-Mississippians; it secured the sole remaining open line of communication between them and their families. Less than a month before the fall of the city, Frederick W. Bush of the 1st Arkansas Infantry penned to his wife, "I think us Ark boys would fight mighty hard, to keep them from cutting off Communications between us and Arks."[8] Without letters to support the soldiers and, more important, to inform them of their families' condition, it was difficult for the men to continue the fight. Benjamin F. Burke of Terry's Texas Rangers elaborated this point less than a month after the fall of Vicksburg: "Vicksburg . . . has cut our further communication off from Texas east of the Miss. river. There has never anything happened during the war that I regreted as bad as the fall, of Vicksburg."[9]

To trans-Mississippians, the Mississippi River was an important psychological barrier. As long as the Confederacy controlled the river, it was a bulwark between Texas and the bulk of the Union army. A Texan wrote, "Our lines once broken, whether on the Mississippi or the Arkansas, or the Red River, would have thrown open the approach to the invasion of Texas, by an ever alert and powerful foe."[10] Once control of the river fell to the Federals, the Westerners began to fear a Northern invasion into their state. That fear directly affected Texans and Arkansans serving in the Confederate army who believed that the Lone Star State was secure as long as the Mississippi River remained an obstacle to Union forces. As the Arkansan Bush expressed it, "if we can hold Vicksburg all is saved."[11]

Vicksburg had a huge impact on the morale of Texans in the Army of Tennessee. Desertion increased throughout the Confederate army after the simultaneous defeats at Vicksburg and Gettysburg, but to trans-Mississippians, Vicksburg was the more pernicious because in taking the Mississippi River the enemy now blocked their way home. The day after the fall of Vicksburg, Christian Wilhelm Hander, a captured German soldier from Waul's Texas Legion, recorded in his diary, "What will happen to us, everybody is asking and in unison we say, 'To Texas we want to go.'"[12] Feelings of uncertainty and longings to return home to the Lone Star State spread across Texas units, and dozens of men in the 9th Texas Cavalry deserted. James C. Bates wrote from Vernon, Mississippi, on September 3, 1863, "About 30 men have deserted the Brigade within the last two weeks—ten of them from my old co. . . . The men of this Brig are very much dissatisfied & want to get west of the Miss." Some of the men simply returned to their homes, but many joined other Confederate units serving in the trans-Mississippi. Bates explained this to his mother: "You will probably hear before this reaches you of the desertions in this Regt. . . . Saying they will enter the service on that side of the river does [not] paliate their offense, but it is on the other hand, an aggravation of it."[13] Similarly a soldier in the Second Arkansas Mounted Rifles noted after Vicksburg that "Dessertions are frequent."[14] Despite this downturn in Confederate morale, many trans-Mississippi soldiers remained in the ranks, holding onto the hope of new fortunes for their fledgling country.

The most prominent group of Westerners feeling the sting of demoralization after Chickamauga and Chattanooga was the famed Texas Brigade. Transferred to Georgia with Lieutenant General James Longstreet to help General Braxton Bragg, commander of the Army of Tennessee, many of these men felt resentment toward their commanders and the Confederate Congress for not granting them furloughs to visit homes and families. Zack Landrum, a disgruntled member of the 4th Texas Infantry, wrote his mother in August 1863, "The Government will not grant furloughs to none of the troops that came [from] west of the Mississippi, not even to visit any of their relations in any of the states unless they claim their home to be there, so as to me getting a furlough is 'played out.'"[15] Their frustration over the denial of furloughs motivated some soldiers during the battle of Chickamauga to expose their extremities, especially their hands, in hopes of getting a minor wound and being sent home on furlough. Joseph B. Polley of the 4th Texas Infantry commented on such an instance during the thick of the battle of Chickamauga when a comrade, Tom, "stepped behind a tree, and, while protecting his body, extended his arms on each side and waved them frantically to and fro, up and down." When asked what he was doing, Tom replied, "'Just feeling for a furlough' . . . and continued the feeling as if his life depended on it."[16] Though he gave his best effort, Tom never caught his furlough at Chickamauga.

Leading the charge for furloughs after the battle was the brigade's commander, Brigadier General Jerome Robertson. In several letters, Robertson outlined what he believed was unfair treatment to soldiers who hailed from west of the Mississippi, complaining that they were not allowed to visit family while in service. To buttress his chances for returning to Texas, Robertson took his plan to the Confederate Congress. On December 12, Robertson urged the War Department to allow his men a furlough until the following spring so that they could return to Texas. Ultimately, the Texas Brigade's commander noted, each man could serve as a "recruiting officer" by returning with "one or more recruits."[17] Unfortunately for the Texans, their furloughs never materialized, but their aspirations continued to plague the ranks. Men sent petitions to the governor of Texas after Chickamauga and other pleas for the balance of the war.[18]

Other stressful experiences such as witnessing the carnage of war also took their toll on morale. The carnage of Chickamauga had an especially detrimental effect on the men who had already endured the war for over two years. It was their first major engagement since the fall of Vicksburg, and it produced scenes of death, destruction, and mutilated bodies that haunted the minds of those who witnessed them. Isaiah Harlan of the 10th Texas Infantry described the impression to a companion back home: "I have seen dead men enough. I never want to witness such a scene again as I did on the battle ground of Chickamauga." Being counted a victory did nothing to diminish the horror of the battle. "There is no prospect that I can see that the war will close without other bloody battles yet to come," wrote Harlan.[19] As in other battles such as Shiloh, many soldiers spent the night "on the battle field strung out on the skirmish line among the dead and wounded."[20] Members of Terry's Texas Rangers rode across the moonlit battlefield and saw that "everywhere lay the wounded and dying and the slain of both armies. The screams of the mangled artillery horses made the night hideous with their heart-rending appeal for relief, and the pitiful moans of those brave fellows."[21] The ride had a powerful effect on the column's leader, George Washington Littlefield, veteran of numerous engagements. In the following months his letters reveal a new sense of mortality, a deepened sadness, and obsession with death. Many men after witnessing such bloodshed divorced themselves from youthful ideas of glory on the battlefield, replacing such thoughts with grim reflections on the realities of a protracted war.[22]

Following the Southern victory at Chickamauga Creek, Major General William S. Rosecrans consolidated his Union army and occupied and reinforced the Chattanooga defenses the Confederates had abandoned during the Chickamauga Campaign. Realizing the futility of an assault, Bragg positioned his troops on the surrounding high ground and laid siege to the Union army. Generally, sieges are not especially good for morale because of the tedium and inactivity that go with waiting the other side out. Compounding the Confederates' plight was their position in the mountains. Though they had uncontested supply lines, the logistics were complicated and deliveries extremely slow for various reasons: the railroad line from Atlanta was frequently in need of repairs, the army had a shortage of wagons, and teamsters had to traverse rough, mountainous terrain with thick undergrowth, to reach the camps. These compounded problems made it difficult for the few wagons the army had to transport supplies from the nearest railroad to the hungry soldiers. Good morale depended in part on having adequate supplies of good food, proper equipment, shelter, clothes, and medical supplies. Before Chickamauga the Army of Tennessee was generally healthy and well provisioned, but after the battle supplies became more restricted, which further dampened the spirits of the men, as one Texas soldier commented: "Most of the boys think they would starve almost if they could not get something more."[23] Similarly W. S. Boothe of the 25th Texas Cavalry wrote, "we donot draw rations enought hardly to keep us alive."[24] William G. Young of the 15th Texas Cavalry (Dismounted) gave the most dramatic account of their privation: "We thought we had a hard time of it but we now see the difference between having plenty and starvation. We are now very near our last crumb. The boys are as proud of an ear of corn as you would be to find the finest maverick in the woods. You have no idea how quick the boys run to a Yankee when they shoot him down. The first thing is to see whether he has any grub, then they strip him of everything he has. If it was not for getting into a fight the boys would have to go naked. The boys have lost all feeling for mankind."[25]

Compounding the decline in morale was inclement weather. Cold weather came early that year with the first frost of the fall coming on September 19. Though Southern soldiers welcomed the relief of the cooler fall months, such weather also brought rain. Constant rains caused the surrounding area to flood and turned the camps into quagmires. Flooding and mud hampered logistics even further, making swollen creeks difficult to ford and roads impassable, worsening the already uncomfortable conditions of camping in the mountains. With only tents to protect them from the elements the men suffered. Waterlogged clothing and boots amplified the cool weather and made it nearly impossible for the men to find any reprieve. Their trials did not end there. Lack of food and supplies combined with inclement weather brought pestilence to the camps. Disease ravaged the camps, thus lowering morale even further. Philip Daingerfield Stephenson, an eighteen-year-old soldier of the 13th Arkansas Infantry, later opined, "The state of things had much to do with the disaster that was soon to overtake us on Missionary Ridge, yet I have never seen it refered to."[26]

Deficient supplies and squally weather were not the sole reasons for grumblings in the camps. One topic that dominated campfire talk was dissatisfaction with their commander, General Bragg. Colonel Adam Rankin Johnson, a Texan commanding the remnants of John Hunt Morgan's Kentucky cavalry brigade, unabashedly labeled Bragg "the old man," for ordering the dismounting of his cavalry. Nineteenth-century cavalrymen, and certainly these Texans, resented being dismounted because their horses entitled them to a higher status than infantry; much as it had done for medieval knights. In many cases, when Texans received news of their dismounting they suffered from "the Hippo," depression, and others deserted. Disgruntled over the order, Johnson consulted Brigadier General Nathan Bedford Forrest, who quickly ordered him "to get them [Kentucky cavalry] as far as possible from 'the old man's clutches." Obeying to his immediate superior, Johnson led his men at a forced march, with a few remaining Texans, to Athens, Tennessee. Once there he solicited letters of commendation from prominent Confederates to aid in his appeal to the War Department to countermand Bragg's orders. The ever stubborn and resourceful Johnson successfully removed himself from the old man's influence and kept his men in the saddle.[27]

Contributing to the enlisted men's low opinion of Bragg was his perceived mismanagement of the army. Already distrustful of their commander, the men continued to blame Bragg for all their misfortunes. The Arkansan Stephenson reminisced that "Bragg's actions therefore in the days just before the battle were to us, odd!"[28] Isaiah Harlan commented further that "there is such a lack of confidence & determination amongst the people and army here. A great many are despondent both in and out of the army and they have cause to be so. Bad generalship and shortsighted legislation have brought us to the very brink of destruction."[29] Even during the retreat from Chattanooga the men "felt disgusted with themselves and degraded. So humiliated, demoralized, and as they ran becoming more and more under the power of that subtle and most powerful of all contagions, *panic*, they lost all morale, became for the most part a mere mob, and arrived at Dalton execrating and denouncing Bragg with curses loud and deep."[30] Regardless if Bragg truly deserved the disdain of the soldiers, their pent-up frustrations with their commander erupted with the disastrous loss at Chattanooga.

Complicating trans-Mississippians' reactions to the Battle of Chattanooga were their experiences during the fighting itself. This was particularly true of those soldiers who fought at Tunnel Hill under the command of Major General Patrick Cleburne. The fighting at Tunnel Hill, on the far right of the Confederate line, proved successful for the Rebels. Stephenson of the 13th Arkansas recalled, "With us, the fight was insignificant and our loss trifling" with only a couple of charges and most of the fighting at a distance. "Indeed the day was a glorious day to us on the right! No defeat there, nor giving way, nor anything like a 'rout.' It was *victory*. We closed the day in high spirits, full of fight, confident of the morrow."[31] With the fog of war hiding the true results of the battle, Confederate soldiers on the right "were under the impression that the Confederates had gained a great victory at

Missionary Ridge and were thunderstruck when at night we were ordered [to] withdraw and cover the retreat of the demoralized army."[32] They "were bewildered and indignant at the move."[33] Successfully defending the right flank of the army, only to learn it was for naught, added to their frustrations at fighting a seemingly never-ending war. Soldier Aaron Estes captured this sentiment when he wrote, "I wish this horable war would end. It is awful to think about. It looks like it will never end till all the [men] is killed."[34]

The great distance separating the Texans and Arkansans from their homes and families out west had initially seemed, a blessing, since the remoteness of their homes from the seat of war assured the security of loved ones. Erasmus E. Marr, a private in the 10th Texas Infantry, commented to his sister in June 1863, "Texas is the most fortunate state in the confederacy on account of its distance from the seat of war and of consequence has never been over run by large armies and been subjected to worse cavalry raids If you could but see a country that has been like subjected you would be thankful that it was your lot to be elsewhere."[35] Henry V. Smith of the 25th Texas Cavalry (Dismounted) echoed the sentiment from his camp outside of Chattanooga: "How thankful to God that, if our fathers husbands and sons are and must be engaged upon the battlefield our homes and innocent one are far away for personal harm and danger."[36]

Despite the semblance of sanctuary, the men's experiences east of the river, particularly the continual defeats between the Appalachians and the Mississippi, along with the spectacle of destruction wherever the armies traveled, created a profound concern for their homesteads. Intensifying their anxiety during the fall of 1863 was the fact that for the first time their homes seemed to be seriously threatened by war. Though their angst had risen numerous times during the war, defeat at Chattanooga crushed the remaining hopes buoyed by victory at Chickamauga and intensified their uncertainties of the impending spring campaign. The Union-controlled Mississippi River had now become a barrier that virtually severed communications with their homes, and at the same time the Father of Waters had ceased to be a physical obstacle to the Northern army, which could now, at least in the imaginations of anxious Texans and Arkansans, range deep into their home states. In the months leading to the Chattanooga Campaign, Texans thwarted Union invasion of their state at Sabine Pass and prepared for an impending Union campaign up the Red River into East Texas. Throughout the rest of the fall, Union Major General Nathaniel P. Banks ordered numerous insignificant assaults along the Texas coast at Brownsville, Rio Grande City, Aransas Pass, and Matagorda Island. News of Banks's landings on the coast created a strong reaction among the men of the Texas Brigade. First Lieutenant Watson Dugat Williams recorded that "we have lately heard that the enemy are holding Brownsville and Mustang Island. Efforts are being made by Gen'l Robertson to get his Brigade transferred to the Trans-Miss. Dept."[37] Although these early Union probes disturbed Texas troops, the Red River Campaign posed a greater threat to their home state.[38]

Arkansas's conditions were just as bleak, with Fort Smith and Little Rock captured just days apart in September 1863. Despite limited postal service and letters carried to and from home by friends, the trans-Mississippians heard rumors of the conditions back home by interrogating everybody they crossed returning from the region. Alex Spence of the 1st Arkansas Infantry exulted over the victory at Chickamauga but kept "hearing the Yankees have possession of Arkadelphia. I hope it is not so, for I know how they destroy everything as they go." Spence's concern over the Union invasion of Arkansas was a constant topic in his letters carried by a friend to nearby Washington, Arkansas, asking for verification of the rumors, until he received confirmation of Union occupation of his hometown in early February.[39]

Separated from home, having just lost a major battle, and fearing their homes were threatened by impending invasion and occupation, the trans-Mississippians were no longer concerned about fighting the Union army in the cis-Mississippi theater, and thoughts of home and family occupied their minds. Consequently, morale plummeted to its nadir. The topic the soldiers wrote most about during the months immediately after Chattanooga was their desire to go home. When Texans heard of threats to the Lone Star State it too produced a strong reaction. "It is said that the feds are preparing to invade Texas," wrote Isaiah Harlan of the 10th Texas Infantry from Chattanooga. "If this be so I would like very much to be there to meet them on Texas soil."[40] Isaac Dunbar Affleck of Terry's Texas Rangers produced a more dramatic response to the danger of a Union invasion of Texas. "I am ready to do any thing and sacrefice every thing, but honor if it will only end this war. I have but one time to die and although I am not prepared to meet death, I am ready to give my life in defence of Texas, and our home if it is required."[41]

Major Van Zandt of the 7th Texas Infantry acted on his desires. Immediately after the Battle of Chattanooga, he wrote his wife, "I shall take steps to get away from here as soon as practicable. If I don't succeed in one way I will try an other. Col. [Hiram B.] Granbury has made application to the Secty. of War to send me to Texas to gather up men there, and accompanied his application with the Surgeons certificate of my condition. If the Secty of War will grant it then I will go to Texas under his orders, but if he disapproves then I shall have to adopt some other measures, either to get a leave of absence or resign. I would not have any hesitancy about resigning, and would adopt it as the least objectionable course to pursue."[42] To his delight, he received informal notice that he would be furloughed to recover from "Chronic lar-yngitis" and collect deserters in Texas. Ironically he never received formal orders allowing him to return to the Lone Star State, and thus technically he was a deserter as well. Van Zandt never returned east. Instead he resigned his commission, a privilege only an officer had, and served as collector of "tax in kind." More important, he returned to his family and "set about the task of providing for their comfort and making plans for the future."[43] Lieutenant James R. Loughridge of the 4th Texas Infantry discovered an ingenious way of getting back to Texas by becoming "a member of the State Legislature for the County of Navarro, Texas." He quickly resigned his commission and was back in Texas "in time for the meeting of the Legislature."[44]

Van Zandt and Loughridge discovered honorable means to return to the trans-Mississippi to protect their homes. Others were not as fortunate and resorted to desertion, the definitive expression of demoralization. Generally men were reluctant to desert in fear that their community would find out about their actions. Soldiers, when possible, continuously communicated with their family and friends back home, and they were not shy about ex-posing the actions of the neighbors who had enlisted with them, especially when it involved desertion. Alexander C. Crain of the 16th Texas Cavalry reported to his wife, "You must not say any thing about it but Mr. Frankling is a diserter."[45] If rumors such as this circulated through the community, a man's honor would be tarnished and his neighbors would view him as a coward. This was detrimental to a man's future back home because people would no longer associate with him, and he would thus face sharply restricted employment and business opportunities. The Southern culture of honor di-rectly influenced Confederate views of desertion. Rufus K. Felder of the Texas Brigade wrote to his mother, "We have just summed up the number dead & deserted. They amount to over seventy. The boys back there are put down on the muster rolls as deserters, and should be dealt with as such. It is a shame that we should be here fighting & suffering so much for our country and so many at home equally able to do duty running about enjoying themselves, as if there was no war going on or our country in no danger. They ought to be frowned upon by the community and be made to leave home in disgrace."[46]

In many cases, when men wrote home about deserters they would define their reasons; such as the dismounting of a cavalry regiment, hardships at home, conscripts forced into the ranks, and the lack of necessary supplies. Stephenson of the 13th Arkansas Infantry remembered that while in winter camp in Dalton, Georgia, "Desertions were increasing alarmingly. The men were in rags and half starved."[47] Others like Henry Cole and a friend con-templated deserting back home to Arkansas because they felt isolated from their families after receiving a letter asking them to return and alleviate their loved ones' suffering. One of their comrades convinced them to remain with their unit for fear they would be caught and executed for desertion.[48]

Despite the negative views and consequences of desertion, the culmination of demoralization overwhelmed many trans-Mississippians to abandon their units and return to their home states. "Many from our Brigade are deserting," noted A. B Hood of the 5th Texas Infantry."[49] Jeremiah Caddell of the 4th Texas Infantry wrote, "There is a good many of the boys in this Brigade will take what they call a French furlough and come home."[50] It was much the same in the Arkansas regiments. "Our reverse at 'Missionary Ridge' last Nov is to be regretted indeed," wrote an Arkansas soldier. "Since then our Army has been gradually lessening. Disease and battle has done its work with us. I am sorry to say there has been a great many desertions."[51]

Superficially, their demoralization and subsequent desertion appeared typical to Confederate soldiers throughout the South whose homes were threatened, but their reactions to the situation differed greatly. The archetypal Confederate soldier from east of the Mississippi deserted when demoralized. The most common factor was Union army occupation of a soldier's hometown. With a direct threat to their homes and family the men simply returned home or surrendered to nearby Union soldiers, deeming the war useless if fighting it could no longer keep the Yankees out of their home county. Typical of this type of desertion were the men of the 8th Georgia Infantry, fighting in Lee's Army of Northern Virginia. Two of its companies came from Rome, Georgia, in the northwestern portion of the state. Once Sherman's troops passed through the region in early spring, men from those companies began deserting in greater numbers, never to fight in the war again. Additionally, in November 1863, the number of Georgians in the Army of Tennessee deserting increased significantly. They left the army because of the loss at Chattanooga and their close proximity to their homes made it easier to return to their loved one.[52] These desertions did not escape the attention of the trans-Mississippians. Erasmus E. Marr of the 10th Texas Infantry noticed during the month after the campaign that, "There is a right smart of disertions here amongst the troops and expecially the Georgians and Alabamians[.] Georgia is nearly whipped her citizens are disheartined worse than the Tennesseans that are now driven from the foot of their soil and more of her soldiers disert than of all the other states."[53]

The reaction of deserting trans-Mississippians differed significantly. Obviously, desertion was a more ambitious decision for trans-Mississippians because their trip home was fraught with greater danger. Many deserting cis-Mississippians found safety within Union lines, taking the oath of allegiance and sitting out the rest of the war north of the Ohio River. Deserting trans-Mississippians, however, made their way back to their home states, striving to avoid Union soldiers, Confederate patrols rounding up apostates, and, most important, the Union brown water navy patrolling the Mississippi River. Most trans-Mississippians did not leave their units in order to quit fighting. Instead they thought of themselves as continuing to battle the enemy but now doing so directly in defense of "hearth and home." With the trans-Mississippi relatively devoid of Union incursions, they had an added incentive not to surrender to the enemy. By joining General E. Kirby Smith's army west of the Mississippi, they hoped to keep the invading Union army away from their homes and families and escape the depredation and hardship the people in the cis-Mississppi were presently experiencing. While encamped at Tunnel Hill, Westerners contemplated their role in the future of the conflict. Harlan of the 10th Texas Infantry described the topic that Texans debated. "There is still a good deal of gloom and despondency existing in the army, at least in portions of it, and yet many of those whose terms are about to expire are reenlisting for the war. Our officers have been throwing out feelers to ascertain how our Brigade stands on that subject. Most of them are unwilling to volunteer again on this side of the Mississippi river. There is a general disposition amongst them to go to the other side. Some of them are deserting and going over. They profess to be going over on account of the difficulty of getting news from their families on this side, stating that they will go in to the service again as soon as they get back to Texas."[54] Similarly Alex Spence of the 1st Arkansas Infantry in his first letter to home since the defeat in Tennessee, informed his parents of his hope of joining Smith's army. "I assure you as I am anxious to get to Arkansas once more," Spence wrote. "These are 'hard and trying times' with us. . . . The general belief is that we will be Kept on this side of the River, but if there is *any possible chance*, I am going to cross the Mississippi."[55] It was the most forceful statement in all the letters Spence would write during the war.

Desperation to return home during this time encouraged soldiers to write openly in justification of their desertion. In a letter home, Robert Hodges of the 24th Texas Cavalry (Dismounted) told his family, "I have been imposed upon until I have become desperate, I take no interest in anything that is going around here. I am determined to cross the river at all hazards. I would not be surprised if I were not in the Trans-Mississippi Army, the next time I write. . . . I would be the last one to desert my country's cause. What I am doing I do not consider desertion nor do I think any sensible mind can view it in that light." Hodges considered his actions heroic and not treasonous. He believed he was not deserting but instead relocating his enlistment to a different army in another theater of the war. Hodges did desert with thirteen other men, only to be caught while crossing Alabama and returned to their command. Fortunately for them, they were not executed. For Hodges and other trans-Mississippians the war east of the river no longer mattered. Instead their priorities and loyalties narrowed with the defeat at Chattanooga. The importance of defending the Confederacy as a nation diminished and was replaced with the defense of their immediate homes, the remaining attachment not soiled by invading armies.[56]

The culmination of many factors during the battles of Chickamauga and Chattanooga demoralized soldiers from Texas and Arkansas. Being isolated from their homes, enduring an intense period of hardship, inclement weather, witnessing bloodshed on a large scale, and experiencing what they interpreted as poor leadership eroded the spirits of even the most optimistic warriors. Though many of the men weathered the rough times and remained with the Army of Tennessee and Army of Northern Virginia, a significant number of them did not. Reasons for their desertion are numerous, but the desire to defend their homes back west appeared time and again in their letters and memoirs. The protracted war and the sense of isolation created by the loss of the Mississippi River and the emergence of threats to their homes and families persuaded these men to reconsider the reasons they continued to fight. Ultimately, they considered their loved ones' lives worth more than the cause of the Confederacy. Their decision, though honorable, had an impact on the Confederacy. The loss of manpower exacerbated the Confederacy's situation in the cis-Mississippi and hobbled its chances of defending against Sherman's capture of Atlanta and his march to the sea. Once the men crossed the Mississippi River, they refused to return, leaving an army with dwindling enlistments vulnerable to the constantly approaching and ever-growing Union army in the heartland.[57]

Notes

1. Mark Weitz, *A Higher Duty: Desertion among Georgia Troops during the Civil War* (Lincoln: University of Nebraska Press, 2000); Mark Weitz, *More Damning than Slaughter: Desertion in the Confederate Army* (Lincoln: University of Nebraska Press, 2005); Ella Lonn, *Desertion during the Civil War* (Gloucester, Mass.: Peter Smith, 1966). Louisiana is excluded from this study because the experiences of its troop differed significantly from those of Texans and Arkansans. Unlike the latter states, which had some battles and a limited occupation before September 1863, significant portions of the Pelican State had been occupied by the Union army starting April 1862, the most notable places being its capital, Baton Rouge and the economic hub of the state, New Orleans. Consequently the context for the experiences of Texas and Arkansas soldiers during the battles of Chickamauga and Chattanooga was more pronounced than for the men of Louisiana.

2. Randolph B. Campbell, "Statehood, Civil War, and Reconstruction, 1846–76," in Walter L. Buenger and Robert Calvert, eds., *Texas through Time: Evolving Interpretations* (College Station: Texas A&M University Press, 1991), 166; J. D. B. DeBow, *The Seventh Census of the United States: 1850* (Washington, D.C.: Robert Armstrong Public Printer, 1853), xxxiii; Joseph C. G. Kennedy, *Population of the United States in 1860: Compiled Returns of the Eighth Census* (Washington, D.C.: Government Printing Office, 1864), iv, lxii; Charles D. Grear, *Why Texans Fought in the Civil War* (College Station: Texas A&M University Press, 2010), 38–40, 72–98; Richard McCaslin, "Conditional Confederates *Military History of the Southwest* 21(Spring 1991): 87–99; Richard B. McCaslin, "Dark Corner of the Confederacy: James G. Bourland and the Border Regiment," *Military History of the West* 24 (1994): 59; Kenneth Wayne Howell, *Texas Confederate, Reconstruction Governor: James Webb Throckmorton* (College Station: Texas A&M University Press, 2008), 78–80; Ella Lonn, *Desertion during the Civil War* (Lincoln: University of Nebraska, 1998), 16.

3. Carolyn Earle Billingsley, *Communities of Kinship: Antebellum Families and the Settlement of the Cotton Frontier* (Athens: University of Georgia Press, 2004), 7, 14–15; Frank L. Owsley, *Plain Folk of the Old South* (Baton Rouge: Louisiana State University Press, 1949), 90, 94–95.

4. John Dollard, *Fear in Battle* (New York: AMS Press, 1976), 1, 47; Singleton B. Bedinger, *Texas and the Southern Confederacy* (Taylor, Tex.: Merchants Press, 1970), 51; Ralph A. Wooster, *Lone Star Regiments in Gray* (Austin: Eakin Press, 2002), 47, 132; Thomas A. DeBlack, "1863: 'We Must Stand or Fall Alone,'" in Mark K. Christ, ed., *Rugged and Sublime: The Civil War in Arkansas* (Fayetteville: University of Arkansas Press, 1994), 63. In his book, Dollard surveys interviews with 300 veteran soldiers of the Abraham Lincoln Brigade that volunteered to fight in the Civil War in Spain. He concluded that 74 percent of the soldiers that belonged to a famous unit made them feel like a much better soldier, thus boosting morale.

5. John Baynes, *Morale: A Study of Men and Courage, The Second Scottish Rifles at the Battle of Neuve Chapelle 1915* (New York: Preager, 1967), 92.

6. Weitz, *More Damning Than Slaughter*, xvii–xviii.

7. Baynes, *Morale*, 92–93; Van Zandt to wife, June 16, 1863, Khleber Miller Van Zandt, Seventh Texas Infantry, Texas Heritage Museum, Hill College, Hillsboro, Texas. (Hereafter cited as THM.) Other defeats such as the surrender of Fort Hindman (*Arkansas Post*) had an impact on morale. The most notable from this battle were the former member of the W. P. Lane Rangers (Texas) who after their release from Camp Butler in Illinois, received orders to report to Bragg. Most of the men deserted after the Battle of Chickamauga and defended the Lone Star State with Morgan's Cavalry. William W. Heartsill, *One Thousand Four Hundred and Ninety-One Days . . . ,* edited by Bell I. Wiley (Jackson, Tenn.: McCowat-Mercer Press, 1953), xv–xviii, 2–14. A good concise overview of the western theater is Steven E. Woodworth, *Decision in the Heartland: The Civil War in the West* (Westport, Conn.: Praeger Press, 2008).

8. Daniel E. Sutherland, *Reminiscences of a Private: William E. Bevens of the First Arkansas Infantry, C.S.A.* (Fayetteville: University of Arkansas Press, 1992), 124.

9. Burke to father and mother, July 31, 1863, Benjamin F. Burke, Eighth Texas Cavalry File, THM.

10. Anne J. Bailey, *Between the Enemy and Texas: Parsons' Texas Cavalry in the Civil War* (Fort Worth: Texas Christian University Press, 1989), 3;

W. H. Getzendaner, *A Brief and Condensed History of Parsons' Texas Cavalry Brigade Composed of Twelfth, Nineteenth, Twenty-First, Morgan's Battalion, and Pratt's Battery of Artillery of the Confederate States, Together with the Roster of the Several Commands as far as Obtainable—Some Historical Sketches—General Orders and a Memoranda of Parsons' Brigade Association* (Waxahachie, Tex.: J. M. Flemister, 1892), 21.

11. Sutherland, *Reminiscences of a Private*, 124.

12. Ella Lonn, *Desertion during the Civil War*, 18; Chuck Carlock and V. M. Owens, *History of the Tenth Texas Cavalry (Dismounted) Regiment* (North Richland Hills, Tex.: Smithfield Press, 2001), 243–44; July 5, 1863, Civil War Diary of Christian Wilhelm Hander, Center for American History, University of Texas–Austin.

13. Richard Lowe, ed., *A Texas Cavalry Officer's Civil War: The Diary and Letters of James C. Bates* (Baton Rouge: Louisiana State University Press, 1999), xii, 263, 264, 265, 271, 272.

14. Wesley Thurman Leeper, *Rebels Valiant: Second Arkansas Mounted Rifles* (Little Rock, Ark.: Pioneer Press, 1964), 182.

15. Landrum to Mother, August 4, 1863, Zack Landrum, Fourth Texas Infantry File, THM.

16. J. B. Polley, *A Soldier's Letters to Charming Nellie* (New York: Neale Publishing, 1908), 165, 179; Weitz, *More Damning than Slaughter*, 247. The Confederate government enforced this policy because of the distance and difficulties the Texans had getting home.

17. Jerome B. Robertson to Texas Delegation in the Confederate States Congress, in Jerome B. Robertson, *Touched with Valor: Civil War Papers and Casualty Reports of Hood's Texas Brigade*, ed. Harold B. Simpson (Hillsboro, Tex.: Hill Junior College Press, 1964), 54–55.

18. Hendrick to Mother, November 8, 1863, James Henry Hendrick, First Texas Infantry File, THM; Stephen Chicoine, "'. . . Willing Never to Go in Another Fight': The Civil War Correspondence of Rufus King Felder of Chappell Hill," *Southwestern Historical Quarterly* 106 (April 2003): 592; Jerome B. Robertson to J. B. Hood, December 10, 1863, in Robertson, *Touched with Valor*, 53. While there were many protests for furloughs from the Texas Brigade, desire to return home was common as well among other Trans-Mississippian soldiers stationed east of the Mississippi River. For instance Aaron Estes of the Tenth Texas Infantry wrote his wife just before the Battle of Chattanooga, "that your umble servant is sick and tired of this noendable ware and I am going to git out of it just as qick as I can get a furlowe. I am going to come home if I am not captured on the way." Estes to Mrs. E. L. Estes, November 15, 1863, Aaron Estes, Tenth Texas Infantry, THM.

19. Thomas Lawrence Connelly, *Autumn of Glory: The Army of Tennessee, 1862–1865* (Baton Rouge: Louisiana State University Press, 1971), 207; Harlan to Margaret, October 19, 1863, Isaiah Harlan, Tenth Texas Infantry File, THM.

20. James M. McCaffrey, *Only a Private: A Texan Remembers the Civil War* (Houston: Halcyon Press, 2004), 46.

21. Mrs. Samuel Posey, "A Story of Terry's Texas Rangers," in *Confederate Veteran* 32 (April 1924), 138.

22. David B. Gracy III, "George Washington Littlefield: A Biography in Business," PhD diss., Texas Tech University, 1971, 59.

23. Steven E. Woodworth, *Six Armies in Tennessee: The Chickamauga and Chattanooga Campaigns* (Lincoln: University of Nebraska Press, 1988), 133; Peter Cozzens, *This Terrible Sound: The Battle of Chickamauga* (Chicago: University of Illinois Press, 1992), 91; Warren Wilkinson and Steven E. Woodworth, *A Scythe of Fire: A Civil War Story of the Eighth Georgia Infantry Regiment* (New York: William Morrow, 2002), 271–72; Steven E. Woodworth, *Decision in the Heartland: The Civil War in the West* (Santa Barbara: Praeger Press, 2008), 82–84; Baynes, *Morale*, 101; Jerome B. Robertson to J. B. Hood, December 10, 1863, in Robertson, *Touched with Valor*, 53; Steven E. Woodworth, *Jefferson Davis and His Generals: The Failure of Confederate Command in the West* (Lawrence: University Press of Kansas, 1990), 225–26; Harlan to Eliphalet, Isaiah Harlan, Tenth Texas Infantry File, THM.

24. Boothe to Wife, October 11, 1863, W. S. Boothe Papers, Peaerce Civil War Collection, Navarro College, Corsicana, Texas.

25. Young to Mom, October 10, 1863, William G. Young, Fifteenth Texas Cavalry File, THM.

26. Connelly, *Autumn of Glory*, 200, 207, 247: Wilkinson and Woodworth, *Scythe of Fire*, 272; Nathaniel Cheairs Hughes Jr., ed., *The Civil War Memoir of Philip Daingerfield Stephenson, D.D.* (Conway: University of Central Arkansas Press, 1995), 135–36.

27. Carlock and Owens, *History of the Tenth Texas Cavalry (Dismounted) Regiment*, 21; Adam Rankin Johnson, *The Partisan Rangers of the Confederate States Army* (Louisville, Ky.: George G. Fetter, 1904), 157–58; Robert Selph Henry, *Nathan Bedford Forrest: First with the Most* (New York: Konecky & Konecky, 1992), 175. "Hippo" was a common term of the time for a person experiencing depression.

28. Connelly, *Autumn of Glory*, 208; Woodworth, *Decision in the Heartland*, 86; Woodworth, *Jefferson Davis and His Generals*, 248; Hughes, *Civil War Memoir of Philip Daingerfield Stephenson, D.D.*, 138.

29. Harlan to Alpheus, January 13, 1864, Isaiah Harlan, Tenth Texas Infantry File, THM.

30. Hughes, *Civil War Memoir of Philip Daingerfield Stephenson, D.D.*, 148.

31. Floyd R. Barnhill, *The Fighting Fifth: Pat Cleburne's Cutting Edge—The Fifth Arkansas Infantry Regiment, C.S.A.* (Jonesboro, Ark.: Floyd R. Barnhill Sr., 1990), 124–25; Hughes, *Civil War Memoir of Philip Daingerfield Stephenson, D.D.*, 140–41.

32. McCaffrey, *Only a Private*, 54.

33. Hughes, *Civil War Memoir of Philip Daingerfield Stephenson, D.D.*, 141.

34. Estes to Richardson, December 11, 1863, Aaron Estes, Tenth Texas Infantry File, THM.

35. Marr to Sister, June 17, 1863, Erasmus E. Marr, Tenth Texas Infantry File, THM.

36. Smith to father and mother, October 12, 1863, Henry V. Smith, Twenty-fifth Texas Cavalry File, THM.

37. Williams to My Dear Laura, January 6, 1864, First Lt. Watson Dugat Williams, Fifth Texas Infantry File, THM.

38. Ludwell H. Johnson, *Red River Campaign: Politics and Cotton in the Civil War* (Baltimore: Johns Hopkins Press, 1958), 37, 39–40; Gary D. Joiner, *Through the Howling Wilderness: The 1864 Red River Campaign and Union Failure in the West* (Knoxville: University of Tennessee Press, 2006), 13–14; Gary Dillard Joiner, *One Damn Blunder from Beginning to End: The Red River Campaign of 1864* (Wilmington, Del.:

Scholarly Resources, 2003), 9–10; Edward T. Cotham Jr., *Sabine Pass: The Confederacy's Thermopylae* (Austin: University of Texas Press, 2004), 3; Stephen A. Townsend, *The Yankee Invasion of Texas* (College Station: Texas A&M University Press, 2006), 16–23; Stephen A. Dupree, *Planting the Union Flag in Texas: The Campaigns of Major General Nathaniel P. Banks in the West* (College Station: Texas A&M University Press, 2008), 54–61, 62–68. For the most comprehensive overview of the Union army's Texas Overland Expedition, see Richard Lowe, *Texas Overland Expedition of 1863* (Abilene: McWhiney Foundation Press, 2006).

39. Mark Christ, *Getting Used to Being Shot At: The Spence Family Civil War Letters* (Fayetteville: University of Arkansas Press, 2002), 72, 76.

40. Harlan to Ma, October 11, 1863, Isaiah Harlan, Tenth Texas Infantry File, THM.

41. Robert W. Williams and Ralph A. Wooster, eds., "A Texas War Clerk: Civil War Letters of Issac Dunbar Affleck," *Texas Military History* 7 (1962): 283.

42. Van Zandt to wife, November 22, 1863, Khleber Miller Van Zandt, Seventh Texas Infantry File, THM.

43. Van Zandt to wife, February 23, 1864, ibid.; G. L. Cutliff, note on Van Zandt's health, May 24, 1864, ibid.; Khleber Miller Van Zandt, *Force without Fanfare: The Autobiography of K. M. Van Zandt* (Fort Worth: Texas Christian University Press, 1968), 108–9. For digital copies of original records in the National Archives, Washington, D.C., see "Confederate Soldiers Service Records," http://www.footnote.com [subscription database, accessed May 2010.

44. Loughridge to George W. Brent, October 22, 1863, J. R. Loughridge Papers, Charles and Peggy Pearce Civil War Documents Collection, Navarro College, Corsicana, Texas.

45. Crain to wife, October 27, 1863, Alexander C. Crain, Second Texas Partisan Rangers File, THM.

46. James M. McPherson, *For Cause and Comrades: Why Men Fought in the Civil War* (New York: Oxford University Press, 1998), 23, 80; Felder to Mother, October 10, 1863, Rufus K. Felder, Fifth Texas Infantry File, THM.

47. Hughes, *Civil War Memoir of Philip Daingerfield Stephenson, D.D.*, 152.

48. Ibid., 153–54.

49. Hood to Cousin Jennie, February 14, 1864, A. B. Hood, Fifth Texas Infantry File, THM.

50. Caddell to Mother and Father, March 3, 1864, Jeremiah Caddell, Fourth Texas Infantry File, THM.

51. Christ, *Getting Used to Being Shot At*, 75.

52. Wilkinson and Woodworth, *Scythe of Fire*, 270, 301–3; Weitz, *Higher Duty*, 68–69; Weitz, *More Damning than Slaughter*, 245.

53. Marr to Friend, January 4, 1864, Erasmus E. Marr, Tenth Texas Infantry File, THM.

54. Weitz, *More Damning than Slaughter*, 131, 247; Harlan to Mother, January 30, 1864, Isaiah Harlan, Tenth Texas Infantry File, THM.

55. Christ, *Getting Used to Being Shot At*, 76.

56. Maury Darst, "Robert Hodges, Jr.: Confederate Soldier," *East Texas Historical Journal* 9, no. 1 (1971): 38.

57. Grear, *Why Texans Fought in the Civil War*, 131–33.

10

A CHATTANOOGA PLAN:
THE GATEWAY CITY'S CRITICAL ROLE IN
CIVIL WAR BATTLEFIELD PRESERVATION

Timothy B. Smith

It was a major occasion in Chattanooga that March 1902 day. The city had often seen notable visitors, but this one was far more exciting than most. Prince Henry of Prussia, brother of Germany's emperor Kaiser Wilhelm II, son of Emperor Frederick III, and grandson of Queen Victoria of England, was in America and toured the Chickamauga and Chattanooga National Military Park while in Chattanooga. The park commission's chairman, Henry Boynton, led the prince's tour and took him atop Lookout Mountain. Prince Henry seemed overawed. As he stood above Chattanooga, he remarked to Boynton, "This is magnificent. There is nothing in all Europe that is finer. I have never seen such a battlefield." No doubt Boynton and the thousands of Americans who read about the exchange in the newspapers were proud that one of their battlegrounds held its own in the mind of a member of royalty, right alongside the vaunted fields of Europe. Still, Americans had never been terribly impressed with European royalty. Several months later, when President Theodore Roosevelt toured the same area, Boynton told locals, "I am glad to welcome an American prince this time."[1]

Despite the obvious beauty of the area and the European recognition, the Chattanooga battlefields held other more important features. This is especially so in terms of battlefield preservation, and particularly Civil War battlefield preservation since the initial process was worked out on those fields and later implemented on other battlefields and historic sites of the Revolutionary War and War of 1812. While Gettysburg and Antietam often get more recognition for their roles in developing America's battlefield preservation theory, Chickamauga and Chattanooga were more crucially important. The park is often touted as the biggest and first preserved, but much less attention has been paid to the chopped up and separated portion at Chattanooga than to the intact Chickamauga battlefield. The engulfing of the Chattanooga battlefields by urbanization and the growth of the tourist industry atop one of the main components of those battlefields has worked to lessen the effect of Chattanooga's perceived role in battlefield preservation. But Chattanooga was extremely important in the formative years of America's battlefield preservation policy, and in fact it gave birth to one of the two major patterns of thought regarding preservation.[2]

The United States first became serious about preserving its military battlefields in 1890. The federal government offered millions of dollars in appropriations, allowing veterans and others to preserve these sites on an unprecedented scale. The federal government's participation during this era of sectional reconciliation also required representation of both antagonists in the conflict, not just the Union side. This even-handedness marked a departure from the policies of the struggling private battlefield associations and even earlier federal governmental policy regarding national cemeteries. This openness to both sides went hand-in-hand with the growing sense of reconciliation between North and South, although at the expense of turning away from Reconstruction-era gains made in race relations. The government, as well as Americans as a whole, expressed disdain for the old racial issues so prevalent in antebellum times and then ratcheted up during the war and Reconstruction. The white North and South unified at the expense of relegating blacks to another form of slavery—segregation.[3]

The federal government began preservation with a burst of activity in 1890 by establishing the Chickamauga and Chattanooga National Military Park. Congress also passed legislation to mark the Antietam battlefield that year, and later in the decade set up parks at Shiloh, Gettysburg, and Vicksburg. In the mid-1890s, the battlefield preservation effort, which was becoming nearly unmanageable with the addition of several new parks as well as numerous other pending park bills, was in need of an overall policy to guide the work. Secretary of War Daniel S. Lamont, who oversaw the battlefields, requested that Congress "early adopt and consistently pursue a fixed policy in regard to the marking of the battlefields of the Civil War." Lamont also put his own War Department staff to work on the project.[4]

By 1895, two major theories of battlefield preservation had evolved. One was espoused by Henry V. Boynton, the originator of the national military park idea. He had pushed for the Chickamauga and Chattanooga National Military Park, and once he moved the idea through Congress, he became its chief spokesman and backer. Boynton served the remainder of his life on the park's governing commission, first as historian and then as chairman. He viewed battlefield preservation in terms of totality and desired that battlefields be preserved intact, just as was done at Chickamauga, where the vast majority of that battlefield had been brought under government control. Unless there was some reason not to do so, Boynton wanted the other Civil War battlefields preserved in total as well. His ideas caught on in Congress, which established Shiloh on much the same plan as Chickamauga. Large portions of the Gettysburg and Vicksburg battlefields were also preserved along Boyntonesque principles, although urbanization played a role in precluding absolute and total preservation at each of those parks.[5]

While Boynton had the ear of the secretary of war, another War Department giant advocated a different manner of battlefield preservation. Unlike the newspaper correspondent Boynton, George B. Davis was a career army officer who had served tours on the western frontier as well as taught at West Point. Davis was more noted for his brain than his fighting ability, and as his career progressed he spent most of his service in staff duties, finally retiring at the rank of major general as the army's judge advocate general.[6]

Davis did not think that every battlefield should be preserved, or that those that were should be preserved in total. Rather, he pushed for limited preservation of fields in general, and limited work on those fields. Like Boynton at Chickamauga, Davis was able to put his ideas into practice on his own battlefield in 1894 when Secretary Lamont named him president of the Antietam Board tasked with marking that field. Antietam had garnered federal monies in 1890 when Congress put aside funds to mark the lines of battle there. The secretary of war had appointed a board to oversee the work, but they made little progress throughout the next couple of years. By 1894, Lamont had tired of their efforts and reconstituted the board, making Davis the president. Within a year, Davis had the battlefield almost completely marked.[7]

Davis's work at Antietam was limited and cost-effective; he did not buy much land. Rather, he left the vast majority of the field in farmers' hands, realizing the area would probably remain rural for decades. He marked the lines of battle as best he could on existing roadways, and built some new roads at government expense. Monuments went up along these roads, paid for by the states or units themselves. Even the land on which the monuments stood was privately owned by the group placing the memorial. Unlike Boynton at Chickamauga, Davis marked Antietam with limited land acquisition and at little cost to the government.[8]

Davis's manner of preservation caught the attention of Secretary Lamont. The secretary realized that if every battlefield were preserved in total along Boynton's ideals, with a three-man commission and other officers at each park paid by the government, the costs would be huge as more parks came into existence. For that reason, Lamont asked Congress to set up a governing policy in 1895, and asked that all future preservation be done using Davis's work at Antietam as a model. "It is earnestly recommended that Congress authorize the marking of the remaining important battlefields in the same manner adopted at Antietam, which can be completed in a few years at moderate cost," Lamont wrote. Davis's model gave rise to a new term in preservation circles—the Antietam Plan. Davis himself used the term in his frequent appearances before Congress for testimony regarding battlefields. National Park Service historian Ronald F. Lee solidified the name when he disseminated the term to national park personnel through his writings on the establishment of battlefields in the 1970s.[9]

But the term "Antietam Plan" is a misnomer. It dates back to 1895, when Lamont used it to describe Davis's work at Antietam, and the idea could conceivably even be carried back to late 1890 when Congress passed the appropriation setting up a limited form of preservation at Antietam. Predating all of that, however, was Boynton's overshadowed work at Chattanooga. Since Chickamauga gained most of the attention after that park's establishment earlier in 1890, Chattanooga did not get a lot of press. Essentially Boynton had put into effect the very same Antietam-type mentality of limited preservation at Chattanooga even while he was touting total preservation at Chickamauga. All of it was prior to any work at Antietam. Boynton obviously would have loved to preserve Chattanooga in total, but the realities of urbanization were not on his side. Thus out of necessity, Boynton envisioned and instituted the Antietam Plan long before it was ever visualized or introduced in Maryland. The idea of limited preservation should be called the Chattanooga Plan rather than the Antietam Plan.[10]

Chattanooga's battlefields, like almost all others, saw little preservation work for several years after the war. Some tourism-related tablets and markers went up during the war, primarily at Chickamauga, but there was not a major effort to preserve either Chickamauga or Chattanooga. The primary effort to honor and preserve what had happened there came when Union forces established the Chattanooga National Cemetery in 1863. On Christmas day, Major General George H. Thomas ordered that a cemetery be built "in commemoration of the Battles of Chattanooga, November 23–27, 1863."[11]

During these battles in November, Thomas had commented on the beauty of a small hill near Orchard Knob, viewing it as a possible cemetery even during the battle when "its beautiful undulating surface was made the more apparent by a line of troops which extended over its summit." In an ironic twist in which Chattanooga took precedence for a brief moment over Chickamauga, the cemetery eventually received the dead not only from Chattanooga, but also from Chickamauga as well as numerous local burial sites in the vicinity, and even the Atlanta Campaign. At the time of the cemetery's establishment, Chickamauga was far too close to enemy lines to build a cemetery there, so Chattanooga was chosen. Within a few years after the war, more than 12,000 Union soldiers were interred at the Chattanooga National Cemetery. It was here that Thomas was reported to have famously replied to a worker asking if the soldiers should be interred by state: "No, no. Mix them up; mix them up. I am tired of state-rights."[12]

As time passed, ideas emerged about preserving the battlefields near the city. One visitor remembered after the war how "At the base of Mission Ridge I was interested to find Bragg's breastworks still remaining in good preservation." By and large, however, Chickamauga received most of the attention, with several efforts in the 1880s to preserve that battlefield.[13]

Meanwhile, the city of Chattanooga was growing, and more and more of the old battlefield was being lost to urban spread. In 1860, Chattanooga had had a population of only 2,500, or perhaps even less. By 1890, however, Chattanooga's numbers had swelled to 27,805, a figure that did not include the separate communities on Missionary Ridge and Lookout Mountain. Its industries, mostly iron production, had likewise greatly expanded. By the 1890s, Chattanooga was a leader in the New South and a much different place than its antebellum counterpart.[14]

This industrialization and urbanization had a dramatic effect on battlefield preservation. By 1890, the city had almost completely covered the plain on which some of the fighting had taken place and was sweeping up onto Missionary Ridge, where the dramatic Union charge had taken place on November 25, 1863. Likewise, Lookout Mountain was becoming urbanized as tourists and the elite spent more and more time there. By the end of the 1880s when the idea of a park began to take hold, Chattanooga's battlefields were already disrupted. Chickamauga remained pristine, and thus the attention first paid to Chattanooga with the establishment of the cemetery shifted back to Chickamauga, where it would stay. Chattanooga's preservation became almost an afterthought.[15]

Such was the reality in the late 1880s when Henry Boynton began making preparations for establishing the park. He began by forming an association to lobby for the park and scheduling a huge organization party on Chickamauga's anniversary in September 1889. Boynton and other luminaries spoke to the crowd, with Boynton telling them what he had in mind. After spending the majority of his speech on Chickamauga, he mentioned, almost in passing, that part of the Chattanooga battlefields could be included as well, as they "properly attach themselves, enlarg[ing] the dimensions of our scheme." Realizing that much of the Chattanooga battlefield was already developed, he said,

"The natural features [at Chattanooga], which for all time will clearly mark the lines of battle, are such that scarcely anything is needed except tablets to mark the position of forts and headquarters, to complete the project we are here considering."[16]

When Boynton wrote the bill that Representative Charles Grosvenor (R-Ohio) offered in Congress, he continued the emphasis on Chickamauga. But by this time, Chattanooga was included as an important yet muted part of the park. Boynton was no doubt interested in the Chattanooga battlefields because he had been terribly wounded there leading the 35th Ohio Infantry up Missionary Ridge, later receiving the Congressional Medal of Honor for his actions. While Chickamauga was his main interest, he would see to it that Chattanooga was not totally left out.[17]

The bill said as much. Boynton named the entire park the "Chickamauga and Chattanooga National Military Park." In detailing the boundaries, Boynton laid out a large tract of land covering the Chickamauga battlefield in Georgia, but he also included certain roadways in Tennessee such as those around Lookout Mountain and the Crest Road atop Missionary Ridge as "approaches to and parts of the Chickamauga and Chattanooga National Military Park." He made sure that the federal government and the states could enter in and erect monuments and markers on the main park body as well as the approaches. Thus, Boynton covered Chattanooga with several roads on which the units and fighting could be explained by markers and monuments.[18]

Boynton thus made a crucial decision concerning battlefield preservation. He wanted to preserve Chickamauga in total, but would only buy certain small areas at Chattanooga, doing most of the marking and monumentalizing on existing roadways. Meanwhile, at other battlefields, taking their cue from Boynton, efforts were made to create large parks such as the one Boynton envisioned at Chickamauga. Similar large-park bills for establishing Gettysburg and Antietam moved through Congress in the same year Chickamauga was established. Neither passed in 1890, leaving Chickamauga and Chattanooga to lead the way. That same year, Antietam received only a board to mark the lines instead of a commission to build a park. Some historians argue that Congress thus made the decision for a smaller park at Antietam in 1890. In truth, it was not until Davis took control of the work there in 1894 that the real Antietam Plan came about, ironically very similar in effect to what Boynton had earlier proposed and implemented at Chattanooga. There was continual hope that Antietam's status would be raised from simply marking the battlefield to creating a park like Chickamauga, but that never materialized. Likewise, Gettysburg would not receive an Antietam-style appropriation until 1893, although unlike Antietam it was subsequently expanded to a full park with a regular commission in 1895. Thus, Boynton's decision to create a park along the lines of what would later be termed the "Antietam Plan" was made prior to 1890 when the emphasis at Antietam as well as Gettysburg was still on creating a large park at both sites. Boynton's idea of creating abbreviated parks when necessary, such as at Chattanooga, thus predated any such plan at other battlefields.[19]

For a while after the Chickamauga and Chattanooga National Military Park came into being, the Chickamauga portion continued to receive most of the attention and effort, but some work went on at Chattanooga. After the governing commission condemned most of the Chickamauga battlefield, it turned its attention to the Chattanooga battlefields and had some success in gaining key positions. As a work in progress, Boynton's idea of preserving and interpreting sites by means of signage along roadways took yet another twist when he and the commission decided to acquire a few of the most important battle sites. These the commission termed "detached reservations." By 1893, the commission had bought several of these such as Orchard Knob on the plain between Chattanooga and Missionary Ridge, Braxton Bragg's headquarters on the ridge itself, the DeLong Place also on the ridge, and part of the Tunnel Hill area on the extreme northern end of the Crest Road along Missionary Ridge. The commission was interested in acquiring other areas, but urban landowners asked such high prices that purchase proved impossible. Condemnation was an option, but the commission decided not to do that within the city.[20]

Even with the comparatively smaller amount of work in the city, Chattanooga had one advantage over Chickamauga in that most visitors to the battlefield came and went through, and often lodged in, Chattanooga. Whether for individual visitors or large veteran reunions, Chattanooga often served as the base for tourists. Such was the case with the massive dedication of the newly established park in 1895. Chattanooga became the de facto headquarters, with most events taking place there. In a move that brought Chattanooga to equality with Chickamauga, the city was given its own day of dedication.[21]

Over fifty thousand people were expected in Chattanooga for the dedication. A huge tent, described as "Barnum's big tent" which was capable of holding ten thousand people, went up near the railroad yard. Citizens decorated the city, while the local authorities, led by Mayor George W. Ochs, upgraded the road and railroad system. The city also printed an "Official Souvenir Program."[22]

Three days of events took place that September, one for dedicating monuments, one for dedicating the Chickamauga battlefield, and one for enshrining the Chattanooga battlefield. Each night, veterans gathered in the "monster tent" in the city for reunions and speeches, the different Union and Confederate armies that had fought in the various theaters holding reunions each night. Luminaries such as Vice President Adlai Stevenson and former Union general William S. Rosecrans, along with numerous other generals, senators, and congressmen, attended these events.[23]

The big day for Chattanooga came on September 20. One newspaper reported the city was "decorated with great profusion with the National colors in all conceivable design." The festivities began with a review of army as well as National Guard troops by Vice President Stevenson and army commanding general John Schofield. A forty-four gun salute from Orchard Knob began the formal proceedings at noon. The attendees listened to dedication speeches by former Confederate general and now senator William Bate and former Union general and now representative Charles Grosvenor. Many state governors also spoke to the masses. The crowds for the Chattanooga day were even larger than those at the festivities for Chickamauga. Obviously, distance played a role, as did a break in a severe heat wave on the Chattanooga dedication day.[24]

Despite the pageantry, relatively little of the Chattanooga battlefields had been preserved by the time of the dedication in 1895, just a few roads and the "reservations." Almost nothing had been done on Lookout Mountain, which was arguably the most famous of the sites even if it was not the most historic. Because of the concentration on Chickamauga, almost nothing had been done at Chattanooga as far as setting up unit markers, artillery pieces, or other monuments. The work of park building at Chattanooga thus actually began after the festivities, and the commission continually added to their Tennessee holdings, most notably on Lookout Mountain. In 1897, the commission purchased the Lookout Mountain battlefield, which sat on the comparatively flat shelf halfway up the mountain. Even better, the commission purchased land "at considerably less than half the sum originally asked by the owners." Park workers soon fashioned the new area into a park unit, clearing undergrowth and building paths and trails to reach "every difficult point of its rugged topography." They also placed historical tablets marking the positions of units during the fighting. Two years later, in 1899, sixteen acres at the top of the mountain designated "Point Park" was added to the national park. The government also bought a strip of land connecting the two parts. Boynton reported that this acquisition "completes all contemplated land purchases for the Tennessee division of the park." The commission soon erected tablets and monuments to brigades and batteries, and placed fourteen historical tablets on Lookout Mountain, where the visitor could read the narrative and view the areas at the same time. It also put up sixty-one "bronze locality tablets" in the city itself. With three major portions in the

Chattanooga wing of the park, the government hired three mounted guards to patrol and care for the three major detached components: Lookout Mountain, Orchard Knob, and Missionary Ridge.[25]

The states took advantage of the government's work at Chattanooga and began to place monuments to their units all over the city and its battlefields. Monuments sprang up on Missionary Ridge, Orchard Knob, and Lookout Mountain. Illinois, for example, placed a huge monument on Missionary Ridge, while Iowa put a couple on the site where that state's troops had attacked the Confederate line. Perhaps the most impressive was the New York monument at Point Park. Several states took advantage of Chattanooga's annual "Spring Festival" to dedicate these monuments.[26]

Relatively few controversies erupted over Chickamauga's monumentation, but several developed at Chattanooga, with the most heated being over the position where John B. Turchin's brigade charged up Missionary Ridge. Boynton had marked the area, the DeLong Reservation, as his own brigade's position, but Turchin argued that his brigade had actually taken the spot and should have the monumentation on one of the relatively few major land holdings in the Chattanooga part of the park. Boynton would not hear Turchin's arguments, saying, "I stake my reputation as the historian of the National Commission on the assertion that no claim more nearly approaching utter nonsense has been made since work on this park began." Turchin could be just as acidic. "I never heard of Boynton during the war, but I see that he is pretty well advertised on the monuments on Mission Ridge and Chickamauga Park nowadays," he fumed, and took especial exception to the monument that sat on the spot he claimed he had captured. "And upon it," Turchin seethed, "is General Boynton's name as conspicuous as the rest." Turchin never made any headway against Boynton, however, and the disagreement lasted for years, continuing after both men's deaths.[27]

Despite such controversies, the Chattanooga part of the park continued to develop, with most of the attention going into the obviously tourist-friendly Point Park region. By 1905, the government had built a stone wall across the narrow top of Lookout Mountain, with entrance gates that included "two battlemented observation towers" and a "cordeled and crenelated wall, to which is built the buttress portal, and containing an arch entrance." One observer noted that the gates, which resemble the Corps of Engineers insignia, were a "monumental entrance to the park." Inside the park grounds, the large New York monument loomed above the point of the mountain. Many distinguished visitors from presidents to princes made Point Park their place of visitation, but one was especially noteworthy to the local population in the 1930s. Babe Ruth came to Chattanooga with the New York Yankees for an exhibition baseball game. He laid a wreath at the New York monument and then, one newspaper reported, "hammered a baseball off the crest of the mountain for a distance of half a mile, thereby setting a new world's outdoor record."[28]

Over the years, new areas were added to the park lands in Chattanooga, mostly on Lookout Mountain. Local Chattanooga citizens had earlier preserved nearly three thousand acres on the slopes of the mountain, naming the area the "Chattanooga Lookout Mountain Park." Finding it too much to care for, they donated the land to the national park. Other smaller local city parks also came about, such as Boynton Park on Cameron Hill, which was dedicated to the national military park's father, Henry Boynton. In more recent years, Moccasin Bend, just across the river from the tip of Lookout Mountain, has been added to the national park. Congress passed legislation in 2003 bringing the additional acreage, with its many Native American as well as more recent historic and archeological sites, into the park. Under development in the early twenty-first century, Moccasin Bend has added nearly a thousand more acres as well as new interpretative themes to the park.[29]

Today, the Chattanooga portion of the park is ironically the best known of all the Chickamauga and Chattanooga National Military Park units. As Chickamauga is some distance from the major urban area, most people who visit that field go there specifically for that purpose. Conversely, visitors come to Chattanooga for a variety of reasons and often include the Civil War sites in their itinerary. It is not easy for tourists, however. The Crest Road atop Missionary Ridge is hard to get to, narrow, and difficult to navigate and explore, with the exception of the reservations dotting its length. Ironically, millions of people do travel over the historic battlefield each year, zooming up and over Missionary Ridge on the interstate that runs through Chattanooga. The vast majority of these travelers have no idea that they are on historic ground. Orchard Knob, which sits in a less progressive section of the city, is far off any well-traveled thoroughfare and receives only the most dedicated Civil War tourists.

In contrast, the Lookout Mountain areas, and Point Park in particular, are magnets of activity for tourists, most of whom are probably there for other than historic reasons. Fewer visitors make their way along the more historic shelf of Lookout Mountain and visit the Cravens House, unless they are on their way to tourist destinations such as Ruby Falls. They do not normally take much notice of the unit markers or monuments along the side of the road and even less often stop to read them. But the scene is different on the top of Lookout Mountain. Vacationers who are atop the mountain for a variety of tourist activities, such as the incline or Rock City, normally make their way to the Point Park portion of the mountaintop. There, a National Park Service visitor center interprets the fighting at Chattanooga, and hordes of visitors can take in the breathtaking views from the summit. While many are there for the views, they are at least introduced to the historic happenings around Chattanooga in 1863.

Few of those visitors realize, however, that they are walking on important ground. Obviously, the park was witness to fighting and death, although the very top of Lookout Mountain endured much less than other areas. In terms of the preservation movement, however, Chattanooga's relationship to Chickamauga on the park level and their illustrative combination in a larger context is significant. The way the fragmented and only partially preserved battlefields of Chattanooga came into being was an important development in the process of defining our national preservation mentality.

Henry Boynton, in dreaming the dream of a national military park and then implementing that dream, devised the two different methods of preservation. The total assumption of a battlefield was his preferred manner, and that was done at Chickamauga. The limited version of preservation, as done at Chattanooga, was not intended to be the dominant theory, and Boynton only chose that approach out of necessity because the Chattanooga battlefields were so urbanized by 1890 that it was impossible to preserve them in total.

This crucial development, coming before the more well-known action at Antietam, literally blazed the trail for future preservation efforts. The limited idea was later used more famously at Antietam, and then was used as an argument for not funding any more huge parks in the late 1890s and early 1900s. The result was a lack of any preservation effort until the 1920s, until after the coming of major urbanization. The result in the later generations of parks was a commitment to the plan first advocated at Chattanooga by Henry Boynton, now known as the Antietam Plan. Numerous parks such as Kennesaw Mountain, Petersburg, Stones River, Fort Donelson, Manassas, Fredericksburg, Spotsylvania, and Richmond are all examples of this limited preservation and thus for decades contained mere fractions of the entire battlefields they purported to preserve and interpret. Now, the preservation movement has turned back to the Boynton theory of total preservation, as evidenced at Antietam itself, where the very Antietam Plan was named. That battlefield has recently seen a major infusion of new lands purposefully left unpreserved in the original conservation effort.[30]

A coup such as that at Antietam is the exception. Such a move is impossible at Chattanooga, where the Chattanooga Plan put in motion the idea of limited preservation at Civil War battlefields. But that necessity, which later grew into choice, has had a dramatic effect on American Civil War battlefield preservation efforts.

Notes

1. "Prince Henry Surveys Civil War Battleground," *New York Times*, Mar. 3, 1902; "President's Riding Pace Too Fast for Troopers," *New York Times*, Sept. 8, 1902; "On Battle-Fields," *Washington Post*, Sept. 8, 1902.

2. For the relationship between Chattanooga and Chickamauga within the establishment of the park, see Timothy B. Smith, *A Chickamauga Memorial: The Establishment of America's First Civil War National Military Park* (Knoxville: University of Tennessee Press, 2009). For more on the history of the national parks, see Dayton Duncan and Ken Burns, *The National Parks: America's Best Idea* (New York: Knopf, 2009) and the companion PBS documentary.

3. Timothy B. Smith, *The Golden Age of Battlefield Preservation: The Decade of the 1890s and the Establishment of America's First Five Military Parks* (Knoxville: University of Tennessee Press, 2008), 31–36. For the relationship between memory and race, see David Blight, *Race and Reunion: The Civil War in American Memory* (Cambridge: Harvard University Press, 2001).

4. Smith, *Golden Age of Battlefield Preservation*, 36–42; *Annual Report of the Secretary of War—1895* (Washington, D.C.: Government Printing Office, 1895), 31–32.

5. Timothy B. Smith, "Henry Van Ness Boynton and Chickamauga: The Pillars of the Modern Military Park Movement," in *The Chickamauga Campaign*, edited by Steven E. Woodworth (Carbondale: Southern Illinois University Press, 2010).

6. Timothy B. Smith, "Biography of a Preservationist: George B. Davis, the War Department, and Early Civil War Battlefield Establishment," unpublished draft in the author's files.

7. Smith, *Golden Age of Battlefield Preservation*, 87–106. For a full history of Antietam National Battlefield, see Susan W. Trail, "Remembering Antietam: Commemoration and Preservation of a Civil War Battlefield," (Ph. D. diss., University of Maryland, 2005).

8. Smith, *Golden Age of Battlefield Preservation*, 87–114.

9. *Annual Report of the Secretary of War—1895*, 31–32; *House Reports*, 59th Congress, 1st Session, 1906, Report No. 4431, 14, 23–25; Ronald F. Lee, *The Origin and Evolution of the National Military Park Idea* (Washington, D.C.: National Park Service, 1973), 40.

10. Smith, *Chickamauga Memorial*, 23, 27.

11. U.S. Quartermaster Department, *Roll of Honor: Names of Soldiers Who Died in Defense of the American Union Interred in the National Cemeteries*, 27 vols. (Washington, D.C.: Government Printing Office, 1869), 11: 11–12.

12. Ibid., 11: 11–13; Thomas B. Van Horne, *The Life of Major-General George H. Thomas* (New York: Charles Scribner's Sons, 1882), 213.

13. "Through the South," *New York Times*, July 4, 1867. For efforts to preserve Chickamauga during the 1880s, see Smith, *Chickamauga Memorial*, 10–11.

14. *Report on Population of the United States at the Eleventh Census: 1890*, 2 Parts (Washington, D.C.: Government Printing Office, 1895), 1: 372; *Compendium of the Eleventh Census: 1890*, 3 Parts (Washington, D.C.: Government Printing Office, 1897), 3: 42. Chickamauga and Chattanooga National Military Park historian Jim Ogden's research has indicated the 1860 Chattanooga population, due to the intricacies of counting, could have actually been less than one thousand. Personal interview with author, December 21, 2009.

15. Henry V. Boynton, *The National Military Park: Chickamauga-Chattanooga. An Historical Guide, with Maps and Illustrations* (Cincinnati: Robert Clarke Co., 1895), 224, 232.

16. Boynton, *National Military Park*, 232.

17. Smith, *Chickamauga Memorial*, 15, 50. See Boynton's Compiled Service Record in the National Archives for a vivid description of his wound.

18. *Congressional Record*, 51st Cong., 1st sess., 1890, vol. 21, pt. 6: 5393.

19. Smith, *Golden Age of Battlefield Preservation*, 35–37.

20. *Annual Report of the Secretary of War—1893*, 33.

21. Henry V. Boynton, *Dedication of the Chickamauga and Chattanooga National Military Park, September 18–20, 1895: Report of the Joint Committee to Represent the Congress at the Dedication of the Chickamauga and Chattanooga National Military Park* (Washington, D.C.: Government Printing Office, 1896), 11–14.

22. Boynton, *Dedication of the Chickamauga and Chattanooga National Military Park*, 14, 21; *Official Souvenir Program*, Chattanooga Public Library Vertical Files, Chickamauga and Chattanooga National Military Park; "Filled the Monster Tent," *Washington Post*, September 20, 1895; "Chickamauga National Park," *New York Times*, September 13, 1895; "The Chickamauga Park," *New York Times*, September 12, 1895; "Where the Blue and Gray Met," *New York Times*, September 18, 1895.

23. Boynton, *Dedication of the Chickamauga and Chattanooga National Military Park*, 11–14, 200–201; "Army of the Cumberland," *New York Times*, September 19, 1895; "Army of the Tennessee, *New York Times*, September 20, 1895; "Reunion of Old Foes," *New York Times*, September 21, 1895.

24. "The Dedication Is Ended," *New York Times*, September 21, 1895; Boynton, *Dedication of the Chickamauga and Chattanooga National Military Park*, 13–14.

25. *Annual Report of the Secretary of War—1897*, 56; *Annual Report of the Secretary of War—1899*, 323–24; "The Chickamauga Park," *New York Times*, December 22, 1897; "Lookout Mountain Battlefield," *Washington Post*, December 22, 1897.

26. *Annual Report of the Secretary of War—1899*, 322; "New Jersey's Monument," *New York Times*, November 26, 1896; "Monuments Arriving Rapidly," *Washington Post*, August 29, 1897; "On the Chickamauga Field," *New York Times*, November 14, 1897; "Illinois Honors Her Troops," *New York Times*, November 24, 1899; "Chickamauga Monument Dedications," *New York Times*, February 10, 1899.

27. John B. Turchin to Absolem Baird, October 26, 1895, Box 9, Folder 8, Ezra A. Carman Papers, New York Public Library; John B. Turchin to J. P. Smartt, September 4, 1896, Box 9, Folder 8, Carman Papers; "Warm Material," undated newspaper clipping in "Reminiscences of Chickamauga," Henry Van Ness Boynton Papers, Massachusetts Historical Society, Boston.; *Annual Report of the Secretary of War—1901*, 357; *Report of the Chickamauga and Chattanooga National Military Park Commission on the Claim of Gen. John B. Turchin and Others that in the Battle of Chattanooga His Brigade Captured the Position on Missionary Ridge Known as the DeLong Place, and the Decision of the Secretary of War Thereon* (Washington, D.C.: Government Printing Office, 1896), 3, 36–37.

28. "Added to Chickamauga Park," *Washington Post*, September 19, 1899; *Annual Report of the Secretary of War—1905*, 129; *Annual Report of the Secretary of War—1908*, 161–62; "Ruth Hit Starts Yanks to Victory," *New York Times*, April 11, 1930.

29. "Lookout Mountain to Be a Public Park," *New York Times*, August 5, 1925.

30. Smith, *Golden Age of Battlefield Preservation*, 219–21.

CONTRIBUTORS

INDEX

CONTRIBUTORS

Stewart Bennett received his PhD in interdisciplinary studies (history and political science) from the University of Maine. He is the chair of the department of social and behavioral sciences and an assistant professor of history at Blue Mountain College. He has worked in higher education administration at institutions in Mississippi, Indiana, Ohio, Maryland, and Maine.

Sam Davis Elliott received his JD from the University of Tennessee and is a practicing attorney in Chattanooga, Tennessee. He is the editor of *Doctor Quintard: Chaplain C.S.A. and Second Bishop of Tennessee* (2003) and the author of *Soldier of Tennessee: General Alexander P. Stewart and the Civil War in the West* (1999) and *Isham G. Harris of Tennessee: Confederate Governor and United States Senator* (2010).

Charles D. Grear received his PhD from Texas Christian University and is currently an assistant professor of history at Prairie View A&M University. He is the author of *Why Texans Fought in the Civil War* (2010); the editor of *The Fate of Texas: The Civil War and the Lone Star State* (2008); a coauthor of *Beyond Myths and Legends: A Narrative History of Texas* (2008) and *The House Divided: America in the Era of the Civil War* (2011); and coeditor with Alex Mendoza of *Texans at War: New Interpretations on the Military History of the Lone Star State* (2012).

John R. Lundberg earned his PhD from Texas Christian University and is the author of *The Finishing Stroke: Texans in the 1864 Tennessee Campaign* (2002) and *Granbury's Texas Brigade: Diehard Western Confederates* (2012), as well as numerous articles on Texas and Civil War history. He teaches at Collin College in Plano, Texas.

Alex Mendoza received his PhD in history from Texas Tech University. He teaches at the University of North Texas and is the author of *Confederate Struggle for Command: General James Longstreet and the First Corps in the West* (2008) and coeditor (with Charles D. Grear) of *Texans at War: New Interpretations of the State's Military History* (2012).

Ethan S. Rafuse received his PhD in history and political science at the University of Missouri–Kansas City. A professor of military history at the U.S. Army Command and General Staff College, he has published more than two hundred fifty articles, essays, and reviews and is the author, editor, or coeditor of eight books, including *McClellan's War: The Failure of Moderation in the Struggle for the Union* and *Robert E. Lee and the Fall of the Confederacy, 1863–1865.*

Brooks D. Simpson is the ASU Foundation Professor of History at Arizona State University. Among his books are *America's Civil War* (1996), *The Reconstruction Presidents* (1998, 2009), and *Ulysses S. Grant: Triumph over Adversity* (2000).

Timothy B. Smith earned his PhD at Mississippi State University and teaches history at the University of Tennessee at Martin. His publications include *This Great Battlefield of Shiloh: History, Memory, and the Establishment of a Civil War National Military Park* (2004), *A Chickamauga Memorial: The Establishment of America's First Civil War National Military Park* (2009), *The Golden Age of Battlefield Preservation: The Decade of the 1890s and the Establishment of America's First Five Military Parks* (2008), and most recently, *Corinth 1862: Siege, Battle, and Occupation* (2012).

Justin S. Solonick is a PhD candidate at Texas Christian University writing his dissertation on military engineering during the siege of Vicksburg. He received his A.M. from Brown University and has published book reviews for *H-CivWar/H-Net Humanities and Social Sciences Online* and *Civil War Book Review.*

Steven E. Woodworth received his PhD from Rice University and teaches at Texas Christian University. He is the author of numerous books on the Civil War, including *Nothing but Victory: The Army of the Tennessee, 1861–1865, While God Is Marching On: The Religious World of Civil War Soldiers, Davis and Lee at War,* and *Jefferson Davis and His Generals: The Failure of Confederate Command in the West.*

INDEX

CIVIL WAR CAMPAIGNS IN THE HEARTLAND

The area west of the Appalachian Mountains, known in Civil War parlance as "the West," has always stood in the shadow of the more famous events on the other side of the mountains, the eastern theater, where even today hundreds of thousands visit the storied Virginia battlefields. Nevertheless, a growing number of Civil War historians believe that the outcome of the war was actually decided in the region east of the Mississippi River and west of the watershed between the Atlantic and the Gulf of Mexico.

Modern historians began to rediscover the decisive western theater in the 1960s through the work of the late Thomas Lawrence Connelly, particularly his 1969 book *Army of the Heartland*, in which he analyzed the early years of the Confederacy's largest army in the West. Many able scholars have subsequently contributed to a growing historiography of the war in the West. Despite recent attention to the western theater, less is understood about the truly decisive campaigns of the war than is the case with the dramatic but ultimately indecisive clashes on the east coast.

Several years ago, three of my graduate students pointed out that the western theater possessed no series of detailed multiauthor campaign studies comparable to the excellent and highly acclaimed series Gary W. Gallagher has edited on the campaigns of the eastern theater. Charles D. Grear, Jason M. Frawley, and David Slay joined together in suggesting that I ought to take the lead in filling the gap. The result is this series, its title a nod of appreciation to Professor Connelly. The series' goals are to shed more light on the western campaigns and to spark new scholarship on the western theater.

CIVIL WAR CAMPAIGNS IN THE HEARTLAND SERIES

The Shiloh Campaign

The Chickamauga Campaign

The Chattanooga Campaign

Vicksburg: Mississippi Blitzkrieg, May 1863

The Tennessee Campaign of 1864: Spring Hill, Franklin, and Nashville

The Vicksburg Assaults

Forts Henry and Donelson

Vicksburg Besieged

The Kentucky Campaign of 1862

Vicksburg: To Chickasaw Bayou

The Atlanta Campaign from Rocky Face Ridge to
the Oostenaula: The Battle of Resaca

Vicksburg: Grant's Winter Endeavors

The Atlanta Campaign from the Oostenaula to the Etowa:
Dallas, New Hope Church, and Pickett's Mill

The Atlanta Campaign from the Etowa to the
Chattahoochee: The Battle of Kennesaw Mountain

Iuka and Corinth

Peachtree Creek

The Battle of Atlanta, July 22, 1864